Humankind Facing Itself

GILLES R. CADRIN

Humankind Facing Itself

The Self-referent Animal

Translated from French by the author
and revised by Ovide Bastien

Transdisciplinary essay

Front cover:
Nicole Desaulniers: *Autoréférence*
Acrylic on canvas, 30x40 in.

Originally published in France under the title
L'ÊTRE HUMAIN FACE À LUI-MÊME
L'animal autoréférent
Copyright © L'Harmattan, 2011
Updated French Edition: © L'Harmattan, 2020
www.harmattan.fr

Copyright © 2020 Gilles Cadrin
All rights reserved
ISBN: 9798583566297

Contents

ACKNOWLEDGMENTS 9
PREFACE to the first edition 11
AUTHOR'S NOTE for the second edition 17
INTRODUCTION Origin and Presentation of the Project 19
    History 19
        The First Steps 20
            ▪ Intuitions and Personal Experiences 20
            ▪ Some Historical Trends in Psychology 22
            ▪ Epistemological Developments in Mathematics 25
        Self-Reference and Creativity 26
        A Decisive Step 32
        Human Specificity 33
        In Summary 36

CHAPTER I BASIC CONCEPTS AND METHODOLOGY 37
    Basic Concepts 37
        Autonomy and Control 38
        Operational Closure 40
        The Organization of Living Systems: Autopoiesis 42
        Closure, Openness, Isolation 42
        The Problem of Reconciling Closure and Openness 44
        Comment on Concepts Presented 45
    Methodological Issues 46
        Self-Reference as First Reference 47
        About Simplification 48
        The Notion of Paradigm 49
        A Few Characteristics of Paradigms 51
        Consistency of Discourse and Paradigm 55
        Making Explicit the Paradigm of Self-Reference as an Element of
            Methodology 57
        A Bootstrap Approach 58
        Gulliver, Fractals and the Holographic Metaphor 61

- Self-Reference and Levels of Human Reality 61
- Fractals 63
- The Holographic Paradigm 65

Philosophy, Scientific Program, or Theory? 66
Abductive Reasoning 69

The Self-Referential Matrix 70
The Attempt of J. G. Fichte 70
Self-Reference and the Advent of Totality 73
Some Founding Statements 78
Note on the Term "Self-Reference" 83
Self-Reference Explained to Aunt Josephine 86
Self-Referential Mechanics 87
- The Cat Metaphor 88
- The Metaphor of Personal Pronouns 90

Self-Reference Versus Egocentricity 100

Guidelines for a Generalization 101
The topography of the self-referential universe: a first approximation 103

CHAPTER II SELF-REFERENCE: PARADIGM AND CORE IDEA 109
About foundations 110

Summary Classification of Epistemological Schools of Thought 111
Trends Common to Internal Epistemologies 112
Trends in Derived Epistemologies 113
Constructivism 117
Experiencing and the "Self" Issue 123
Normative Implications for Theory 124

Self-Reference and "Construction" 128
The Western Paradigm 138
Construction and Hierarchy 142

To Conclude 145

CHAPTER III TEMPORALITY OF SELF-REFERENTIAL PROCESS 147

An Empirical Model of Human Development 149
Erikson's Theory 150
Criticism of Erikson's Model 152

Sketch of a Self-referential Version of Human
  Development 156
  Time Structure of Cycles... 157
  The Basic Dimensions of the Process........................... 158
  Experiencing Under Each Dimension 160
  Stages of Personal Development................................ 161
   - The First Stage: RECEPTIVITY 161
   - The Second Stage: ACTIVITY..163
   - The Third Stage: IDENTITY 163
  Specificity of Cycles at Various Levels........................ 165
  Comparison of Stages 2 for the Last Four Cycles 166
  Comparison of Stages 3 for the Last Four Cycles 167
  Comparison of Stages 1 for the Last Four Cycles 168
  Precisions on Temporal Logic of Cycles: in Search of a Heuristic
  ... 169
  Anchoring the Model 171
  Prediction Test 171
  Primary and Secondary Levels 172
  Commentary on the Phi Heuristic.............................. 175

Prospects for Generalizing to Long Cycles 177
  Preliminary Observations... 178
  Anchoring of Model and Its Deployment................... 180
  Commentary.. 184
  The Present Time... 186

CHAPTER IV COMMUNICATION 189

Communicational Zone 192
  Differentiation of an Intervening Agent in the Communicational
  Zone.. 193
  Complex Message Structure 195
  Intrapersonal Level Messages: First Approximation............... 201
  Societal Level Messages: A First Approximation 202

Internal Structure of Communicating Unities: Avenues of
  Research 204
  Internal Structure and Transactional Analysis....................... 206

Normative Dimension of the Model 208

In summary 209

CHAPTER V POWER AND SOCIAL GOVERNANCE 211

The Power Issue 212
  Ingredients of Power 213

- First-Degree Power..213
- Second-Degree Power..215
- Third-Degree Power...221

Educational Dimension of Human Existence...............222

Reference Actors at the Societal Level........................224
The Notion of Sector: A First Approximation.......................... 225
- Composition of a Sector...226
- Specific Logic of Each Sector...227
- Key Institution in a Sector..227
- Coextensiveness of the Logic of a Sector to the Totality..228

Today's Society from the Perspective of the Present Paradigm 232
Political Dimension... 233
Economic Dimension: The Creation of Underdevelopment..... 235
- A Structure of Nested Third-Worlds..................................235
- Some Side Effects..237
- Access to the Market 240

Towards a Self-Referent Society................................242
Emergence of the Social Sector in the Space Constituting the State.. 244
- Rallying Organization 244
- Powers Within Rallying Organization...............................245
- The Economy in the Development Community 249
- Generalization of the System: A Strategic Utopia 254
- Towards a Community-based Economy............................258
- Development Community's Culture 260
Neo-Keynesianism or Post-Capitalism?.................................... 260
Some Perspectives 265

CONCLUSION 267
Brief Metacognitive Feedback on the Model.......................... 268
Pragmatic Research and Development Perspectives............... 271
- Vertical Methodologies...273
- Horizontal Methodologies..277
In Summary... 278

REFERENCES 279
INDEX...285

ACKNOWLEDGMENTS

I would like to thank Jean-Louis Le Moigne, whose critical remarks for the first edition were invaluable to me. But I hope he will forgive me for not having followed all his advice and not sharing his enthusiasm concerning certain references he deemed important.

I would also like to thank Gaston Pineau from the University of Tour who agreed to comment on this project. Thanks to my reviser Ovide Bastien who patiently translated *my* English... into English. As for my colleagues from the first edition, they are still present: Germain Marsan, Jean Neuvel, Johanne Forget. A heartfelt thanks to them for their unwavering support.

I am grateful to all those whose influence, near or far, has made this project possible.

PREFACE
to the first edition

It was with great interest that I read Gilles R. Cadrin's book. Though I come from a very different intellectual background, I have been challenged by this rich and bold synthesis. The subtitle, which makes us move from *rational animal* to *self-referent animal* – a wink made to Aristotle – has what it takes to draw one's attention, and possibly to trigger controversy. To consider self-reference as a fundamental characteristic of the human being represents, to my knowledge, a recent advance that has not yet made its way in all areas of reflection on humans as individual and social beings.

What may first surprise the reader is the scope of a project that questions the very foundations of the human being and, in the extension of work on the genesis of the living, poses the radical question: what is the specifically human version of the living? Beneath the humble appearance of a sketch, one finds a great ambition, given that the author attempts to identify the basic elements of a model that would eventually extend to all areas of the social sciences, and, more fundamentally, to a self-referential praxis beyond the sciences that would one day guide the construction of a more human world, and this to the highest levels of social organization. As the author puts it, we must come up with a more lucid and coherent answer to the question: "What are we going to do with ourselves?"

A second subject of astonishment for the reader lies in the diversity of the themes addressed, which deal with various areas: human development, history, communication, governance, epistemology, etc. A first reading could leave one with the impression of a collection of articles that are not closely linked to each other. The author even suggests that they may be read in this manner. The specialist in developmental psychology will be more interested in the first part of the third chapter, the historian in the second part, the communication specialist in the fourth chapter, the specialist in sociology and political economy in the fifth chapter, and the epistemologist in the second chapter. From this point of view, the work may appear, as the author himself puts it, as a *patchwork*.

However, a reader who would limit himself to examining each theme in itself from a strictly disciplinary viewpoint risks remaining unsatisfied because he would not be embracing all of their relevant dimensions and references. The primary purpose of the work is thus not disciplinary or even multidisciplinary, but rather transdisciplinary. The author invites us to a second level of reading which alone gives the approach its full meaning: the introduction and the first chapter indeed prepare the statement of a matrix which takes the contours of the process which lodges in the heart of the living, the self-referential process. The method then consists in seeking greater internal coherence by applying this self-referential matrix to various dimensions of the human experience. Which is where the transdisciplinary dimension takes on its full meaning. Indeed, if apparently disparate themes corresponding to various levels of the human experience find their own coherence by their rooting in this same matrix, we then find ourselves in a space transcending particular disciplines. Each of the fields of experience is, so to speak, reconstructed with the same components of this self-referential matrix which is thereby itself transformed. Each theme thus revolves around a highly dense core which provides coherence to the whole. Fundamentally, it is thus not the statement of a thesis that one would first develop and then apply to various fields of experience as illustrations, but rather the progressive construction of this self-referential matrix from its interaction with the various fields of human experience. The author describes this reading as vertical.

While the first chapter focuses on methodological considerations, the second one leads the author to ask the question of foundations and to situate his approach relative to various contemporary epistemological schools of thought. He first shows how the question of foundations should be posed in a self-referential context. One knows how confusing the self-referential approach can be for the theoretician who has not become sufficiently comfortable with paradox as something that can be used in a rigorously articulated approach.

I would like to point out a few benchmarks here. The author has convinced us since chapter one that we cannot ignore the wholeness constituting a living unity. However, if this totality is essentially self-referential, it cannot find its foundation from without. So we have to look from within. But again, the author points out that no part of this totality can represent its foundation. Are we then condemned to philosophize without any foundation whatsoever as proposed by Hilary Putnam and Francisco Varela? No, points out Gilles R. Cadrin, who, not hesitating to plunge us into a real paradox, asserts that *the totality itself constitutes its own foundation*, thus leading us to oscillate between the presence and the absence of foundations, an oscillation which characterizes self-referential processes. Of course, it is only in the context of its elaboration that this reasoning becomes ever clearer and takes on its full meaning.

The author then leads us, through a classification of contemporary epistemological schools of thought, to situate his approach in the extension of the constructivist mindset and presents the statement of his conception in the section entitled "Self-reference and construction." In an approach that is both rigorous and audacious, the author goes, so to speak, beyond the framework of epistemology to propel us into the field of a pragmatics which draws a striking portrait of the situation in which we, humans, find ourselves as we come face to face with ourselves. I leave it to the reader to discover and savor this section.

This reflection leads the author to give an original interpretation of what has been coined the "Western paradigm" in which primacy is given to the cognitive over the existential. The author clearly highlights the reversal of perspective implied by moving away from this paradigm.

I would like to digress here on what evokes at this stage, in my philosophical frame of reference, the author's reflections. If we go back a century, we find in Edmund Husserl a subject viewed as pure consciousness who, withdrawing from the world, represents things to himself. In the model proposed here, however, the "subject" can no longer be reduced to a pure intentional consciousness given that he is involved in the field of his own production. What we have instead is a person building his own reality in a process that is, first and foremost, existential, pragmatic.

A similar parallel can be drawn if we consider the third chapter which deals with time. In his *Lessons for a Phenomenology of the Intimate Consciousness of Time*,[1] Husserl set forth the model of a constitutive temporality of intentional consciousness emphasizing the fact that man is, first of all, a being of knowledge whose task is to make being appear by constituting its representation. Gilles R. Cadrin proposes a model where temporality constitutes the self-generating loop which poses and maintains the living in existence. It is the unfolding of this circular process in the articulation of ternary cycles which provides the various temporal orders of magnitude experienced. The sequence of receptivity-activity-identity stages, echoing the basic ingredients of the self-referential machine, forms a cycle in which the living integrates the elements of his experience into a coherent unity, his identity. This cycle is itself integrated as the first stage of a totality of a higher level. This structure of nested cycles accounts for both the integration of the achievements of previous cycles and the progressive construction towards the projected totality. Here we have a temporal structure constituting the pragmatic experience of self-development.

The teleological dimension of this process is of a peculiar nature. In his *Institution, Passivity*,[2] Maurice Merleau-Ponty, while discussing the art of painting, asserts:

> "*How does one know what one is doing in painting? One doesn't work at random. And yet, the whole field of the painting [...] is not really given ... painters do not know what they are doing. And yet, each painter ends up finding the whole painting ... So there is a teleology of the whole, but what guides one who, while not possessing the end, is walking towards that end?*"

Indeed, the painter does not know what he will do with the white canvas before having done it, but he knows if the completed painting is successful or not.

---

1. Edmund Husserl, *Leçons pour une phénoménologie de la conscience intime du temps*, Paris, Presses Universitaires de France 1996.
2. Maurice Merleau-Ponty, *L'institution La passivité. Notes de cours au Collège de France (1954-1955)*, Paris, Belin, 2003.

In this type of example, the creator is and remains at a distance from his creation. Gilles R. Cadrin then pushes the question further: what if the creator himself is called to be the object of his own creation? This is the typical self-referential challenge of the human being, which opens the field of ethics and politics. In this context, the questions posed to the painter take on a very particular color. The teleological dimension becomes more complex. Like the painter, the human being does not know what form the result of his creation will take, but he knows that, unlike the painter, this time the creator must be carried away by his own creation and be part of the final landscape; he will also know if his work is successful or not. The fact is that the work stands as the emergence of an implicit, unthought totality, a field of experience, which operates actively throughout the work. Thus, for the human being who creates himself, the *myself* of the "I'm creating myself" would be a blank page, a cognitively empty, unobservable whole, and yet an original unity which, to be realized as such, must go through the process where he becomes both agent and product of his action. From such an approach emerges the logic of what is being created as the process unfolds. The author's challenge is to draw the contours of such a situation, identify its articulations, and point out its methodological implications.

Let us come to the fourth chapter, which deals with communication, a complex process if any, whose mystery is so hard to pierce that authors initially consider it improbable and thus a subject of amazement. And the self-referential framework adopted by Gilles R. Cadrin does little, at first sight, to reassure us here. However, the author still knows how to surprise us: far from being foreign to the self-referential process, communication is conceived as being precisely this mechanism itself. If the temporal unfolding of the self-referential loop constitutes its genesis, communication constitutes, so to speak, its mechanics. We must, of course, at the outset admit with the author that self-reference is not the prerogative of the individual level and that it applies at least potentially to all social levels, from the dyad to the whole of humanity. The interactional aspect of communication then becomes, as the author says, "the engine room" of the self-referential loop of the higher-level unit. Thus, two interacting individuals are first moved by the communication field of the dyad which they constitute, and which tends to self-construct. It is interesting to see the consistency which emerges from this daring challenge.

Finally, the author's theses would not have allowed the work to end without the proposal of the *design* of a pragmatics, which this time is developed at the societal level. When today's most pressing questions are about the very survival of the human species, presenting the matter at this level is not a luxury. It is astounding to see the gap between the awareness of the possibility of our own extinction as a species and our difficulty or helplessness in building another type of humanity. The model presented here, perfectly achievable, aims to create a network of self-building micro-societies according to principles of endogenous development specific to living beings and restoring to various societies their character of autonomy, guarantor of a healthy interaction between them and the environment. Since entities at the societal level are significantly larger than those at the individual one, some new concepts had to be introduced. It is possible that at first reading, one may not immediately see the link between these developments and the reference model. A more in-depth reading allows one to recognize, in these same developments, the same basic ingredients that make up the self-referential matrix, as was the case for the themes developed in the previous chapters. My hope is that this reflection will provide new elements that will be of help to individuals and communities in their quest for accomplishment and achievement.

Finally, a thorough reading of the book can only stimulate the reader to follow this researcher who, by exploring new paths, invites us to move ahead. There is always a risk of wanting to go beyond one's predecessors, beyond long-recognized thinkers who have established themselves in this field of fundamental research on human beings. Gilles R. Cadrin is not the first adventurer in this field, but he is now one of them and we will have to reckon with him.

Germain Marsan

AUTHOR'S NOTE
for the second edition

The purpose of this second edition is to clarify, complete, and correct various parts of the original text published in 2011. It should be recalled that the title, *Humankind Facing Itself,* [3] highlights a question from which we as a species cannot escape: what we are going to do with ourselves? The subtitle, *The self-referent animal*, echoes this as a statement on the nature of the challenge that such a situation represents. Indeed, the human being — an initially incomplete animal — is led to engage in a process of self-completion. To be, as Albert Jacquard[4] puts it, "co-creator of oneself." Or, in the terms used in our approach, "to *self*-create *in reference* to oneself."

We recognize here the challenge facing the human being, a "creative artist" summoned to become the product of his own creation, to become, so to speak, his work of art. We also intuit that if such an unusual process is possible, it is because it must respond to a precise mechanism endowed with its own coherence. This mechanism is that of *self-reference*, at the origin of life and its development. This term defines a very broad field within which we will try to circumscribe the space specific to the human being.

The self-referent animal that we are is then, by necessity, involved in the construction of his own nature. So, we cannot but invent ourselves. Thus, totally deprived of an instruction

---

3. *L'être humain face à lui-même.*
4. Albert Jacquard, *Inventer l'homme*, Brussels, Éditions Complexe, 1984. The author borrows his title from a remark by Jean-Paul Sartre in *L'existentialisme est un humanisme*, Paris, Nagel, 1970, p. 38: « L'homme, sans aucun appui et sans aucun secours, est condamné à chaque instant à inventer l'homme » (Man, without any support or help whatsoever, is condemned at every moment to invent man). Although treated here quite differently, this vision is at the heart of the present approach: man cannot rely on an external reference to invent himself. He will only be able to do so by referring to his own identity, in other words, by being self-referent.

manual[5], we are entitled to claim a privileged space in this field of self-reference where we will be both inventor and invented.

Note that this essay reflects a transdisciplinary approach: we will attempt to illustrate how the same paradigm can be fully applied to all levels of human reality, whether at the level of the individual, society or the species itself. Transdisciplinarity is thus conceived as the creative space of what can become a metadiscipline, which would be relevant to all disciplines, though not belonging to any of them. The image of the human being who emerges from this ever-ongoing construction opens up avenues of research that each discipline can then develop at the level that concerns it. And the transdisciplinary approach can also serve as a mediator between the more specifically cognitive framework of disciplines and the more pragmatic framework of human development.

Let us note, finally, that readers for whom consistency of discourse is important, would benefit from reading the whole sequentially. However, the methodological reflection presented in the first chapter would justify considering the work as a patchwork. Thus, readers who are sensitive to temporal issues could immediately consult Chapter 3, and those who are more interested in methodological issues could move on to Chapter 1, or to the question of foundations in Chapter 2. Those who are mainly interested in pragmatic issues could have a partial overview of them in Chapter 5 in the sketch of an application of the model at the societal level. This section heralds a second book in preparation, focusing specifically on the pragmatic dimension as it applies to various levels of the human reality. But first, in order to better situate ourselves, let us start out by explaining, in the introduction, the path that led to the implementation of this project.

G. R. C.

---

5. Some would claim that, given the teachings one finds in texts of great wisdom that are sometimes thousands of years old, we do have access to such an instruction manual. But that would be forgetting that such texts were written by humans. Furthermore, the diversity of these texts, sometimes their contradiction and even certain aberrations in their content clearly show that the inspiration they claim has been distorted by the human filter. In the end, whatever our beliefs about these texts, we find ourselves willy-nilly caught up with ourselves.

INTRODUCTION
Origin and Presentation of the Project

Discussing self-reference should be self-evident since it lies, according to the present analysis, at the very heart of how we function as human beings. But this is the main problem: we are so naturally immersed in self-reference that it is difficult to see it as an object of reflection or to use it as a tool of development. It's a bit like explaining to fish the principles of underwater swimming. The latter might not understand, not because they do not know how to swim, but rather because swimming comes so naturally to them that they are unable to objectify it.

The problem consists, therefore, in bringing into the field of methodical reflection that which we quite naturally are in the hope of finding additional elements to answer the question that inevitably arises concerning the fate that we reserve for ourselves as individuals, as societies, and as a species: either we allow ourselves to be swept away in a negative path and ultimately a self-destructive barbarism, or we respond to the call "to invent man," to take care of ourselves.

But why "invent man"? Hasn't nature already invented who we are? Did the lion come up with the idea of inventing the lion? At the culminating point of evolution, nature seems to have invented an animal that would not be complete unless it participates in its own making. Thus, we would not be fully human if we did not practice humanity with great care. It's the dramatic choice that nature imposes on us.

History

The question has always been raised, but our species is young. It has only had a few tens of thousands of years to reveal itself to itself as one of nature's masterpieces, a masterpiece whose authorship it should itself partially claim. We are still in the prehistory of humanity. Of course, any effort to advance to another stage can only be modest within the timeframe of a generation. But what do we have to lose by playing this exciting game which plunges us in the heart of our own identity?

The First Steps...

Let's start by situating ourselves: where are we now, from where do we start and in order to go where? We will have hypotheses on this subject regarding humanity, but more modestly, let us first situate our action. This research was born at the crossroads of two major currents of thought, one from psychology, the other from the epistemology of mathematics.

First, I will describe the circumstances which, in my personal evolution, led me to embark on this reflection, and then I will situate the path I followed in a broader historical perspective. In the following chapter, I will broaden this historical incursion to works originating from philosophy, in particular those of J. G. Fichte.

- *Intuitions and Personal Experiences*

In the late 1960s, in the department of psychology at the University of Montreal, I was haunted by a search for unity in the approach to human reality. The multiplicity and inconsistency of approaches within the same discipline, such as psychology and, a fortiori, between the social science disciplines, deprived me of any motivation to push my research further without any other form of questioning. So I issued to myself the injunction Kant issued to all researchers of his time – stop your work there! – and started formulating my modest prolegomena to any future personal research endeavor.

I suspected that it was no coincidence that psychology, nor the other social science disciplines, had ever taken *man* as an object. Psychology was at the time the science of *behavior*. Some elements were subsequently added to this definition but this effort to broaden the field of psychology failed to draw attention to the unity in question: the human being. I adhered to the so-called *humanistic* trend, but I still did not detect within the latter any integrative potential, although the synthesis proposed by Eugene T. Gendlin in his 1966 book *Experiencing and the Creation of Meaning* represented in this regard an important reflection.

A few years later and from another horizon, I was struck by the title of Edgar Morin's 1973 book *The Lost Paradigm: Human Nature.*[6] As early as 1960, Jean-Paul Sartre, for his part, had provided a sort of warning: he announced that arriving at significant developments in the life sciences required adopting as a guiding hypothesis the notion of *totality* and of *totalization*.[7] So what was the problem rendering totality so difficult to deal with? There seemed to be a limit that science did not cross: the concrete experience of a living unity forming a totality.

During a private seminar organized by a colleague, I submitted to Jean-Blaise Grize[8] a draft of the problem as it appeared to me at the time. It contained expressions such as the following:

> *One would have to accept to leave, so to speak, the sphere of knowledge.*[9]

> *Such an approach should implement a praxis reflecting the total human being, in which, among other things, the action of knowledge would be rooted.*[10]

Such expressions aroused suspicions in my interlocutor who commented:

> *The image you use – 'to accept to leave, so to speak, the sphere of knowledge' – automatically raises the question: but to go where? In other words, what is outside of knowledge?*

Unfortunately, he did not receive a satisfactory answer to his question, since the statement of my proposals derived from a still poorly differentiated intuition.

---

6. EdgarMorin, *Le paradigme perdu : la nature humaine*. Paris, Seuil, 1973.
7. Jean-Paul Sartre, *Critique de la raison dialectique*, Paris, Gallimard, 1960, p. 130, footnote 1.
8. Jean-Blaise Grize is the logician, collaborator of J. Piaget, to whom we owe the logical interpretation of the intellectual structures developed by the latter, in particular the INRC group. He was later the instigator of the main works in the field of *natural logic*.
9. *Il faudrait consentir en quelque sorte à sortir de la connaissance.*
10. *Une pareille approche devrait mettre en œuvre une praxis à l'image de l'homme total, dans laquelle s'enracinerait, entre autres, l'action de connaissance.*

I then read an article published in 1966 by Jacob Bronowski in the American Scientist: *The Logic of the Mind*. This article dealt with self-reference in science and art and led me to raise epistemological questions. Moreover, epistemological reflection was gaining ever more prominence among researchers at the time. For example, in 1967, Jean Piaget published, with specialists from all disciplines, a major work, *Logique et connaissance scientifique*. And Bronowski was then pointing out the great theorems that indicated the limits of formal systems (Gödel, Turing, Tarski, etc.), limits more or less associated with *self-reference*. On the other hand, self-reference, he hypothesized, constitutes the source of creativity in science and art.

This reflection echoed the original question that then became the following: could it be that self-reference is not limited to scientific or artistic creation but also constitutes the very foundations of human beings in the process of their own creation? The whole field of ethics was thereby opening up, more precisely, the field of responsibility that human beings have in producing who they are. Such had appeared to me, to use the expression coined by the sociologist Fernand Dumont, "the field of man."[11]

Let us step back a little in order to situate the above intuitions in the context of their historical development. First, we will examine certain trends in the development of psychology during the twentieth century. Then, we will examine certain epistemological reflections in mathematics to which Bronowski referred and that emerged over the same time period.

- *Some Historical Trends in Psychology*

The end of the 19th century gave rise to remarkable scientific development, particularly in the natural sciences. Questions about the human being then tended to migrate from philosophy to science: why not consider the human being like any other object and apply to man the scientific methods which, in other fields, have produced such remarkable results?

---

11. The original French version of this expression is *"le lieu de l'homme"*. See Fernand Dumont, *Le Lieu de l'homme – la culture comme distance et mémoire*. Montréal, Hurtubise 1968.

INTRODUCTION

It was Sigmund Freud's dream to come up with a rigorous description of the laws illustrating how human beings function. His main interest was oriented towards clinical work: how can one help people get rid of problems that prevent them from functioning normally? To this end, Freud developed an intuitive theory, based on his clinical observations, which, in turn, supported his interventions. This gave rise to psychoanalysis, whose influence throughout the twentieth century was immense.

Another school of thought, behaviorism, had the objective of limiting the study of humans to behavior that could be the object of direct observation. Behavior observed at the output of the system is seen as a response to stimuli found at the input. The links between stimuli and responses were learned through association with a reward called reinforcement. By controlling reinforcements, one can then modify links or generate new links between stimuli and responses, which can be used in normal learning situations or therapy.

It is in reaction to these two schools of thought that humanistic psychology emerged in the United States in the 1960s. The best-known representative of the humanistic school is Carl Rogers, a researcher and therapist attached first to Columbia University and then to the University of Chicago. It is this school of thought that constitutes one of the foundations of the present approach.

For Rogers and his collaborators, the individual has everything within himself to become what he or she is called to be.[12] The individual is endowed with an *actualizing tendency*, an innate tendency to actualize his potential[13]. The environment may or may not be favorable to the development of this tendency, but it does not have the primacy. Also, the individual has an internal capacity to assess what departs from or favors the

---

12. Carl Rogers, A Theory of Therapy, Personality, and Interpersonal Relationship, as Developed in the Client-Centered Framework, *in* Sigmund Kosh, *Psychology: A Study of a Science*. Study 1, Vol.3: *Formulations of the Person and the Social Context*, 1959, pp. 184-256.
13. "This is the inherent tendency of the organism to develop all its capacities in ways which serve to maintain or enhance the organism." *Ibid.* p. 196.

actualizing tendency. This is what Rogers calls the *organismic valuing process*.[14]

This concept led to the idea of non-directivity: indeed, if the dynamism and orientation of development are located within the person, one only has to let the whole develop according to its own logic, though it is acknowledged that a favorable environment may facilitate this autonomous process. This conviction was part of the spirit of the time, the *zeitgeist*, as the Germans called it. Non-directivity was applied not only to individuals but also to small groups. For example, Wilfred Bion at the Tavistock Institute would present himself in groups without really exercising leadership,[15] which could lead to random results.

It was soon realized that non-directivity as such was basically an illusion. The therapist who listens to his client by actively intervening, even with empathy, cannot honestly consider himself to be truly non-directive. Rogers himself readily recognized that, and the term non-directive therapy was thus eventually replaced by the term client-centered therapy.

Although well documented in its various practices and research concerning its therapeutic effectiveness, humanistic psychology became the object of criticism regarding the solidity of its theoretical foundations. The intuitive postulate of the actualizing tendency appears more, it was argued, as a *deus ex machina*, than as a foundation having its own meaning.[16]

Though the implicit foundations of humanistic psychology may have been expressed using mere intuitive labels, they were nevertheless strong enough to give rise to a profusion of practices constituting very precious tools for human development. We are thus left with a very rich, original approach, which, though offering something deeply foundational, resists a clear and rigorous grasp from a cognitive

---

14. "[...] the organism experiences satisfaction in those stimuli or behaviors which maintain and enhance the organism and the self, both in the immediate present and in the long range. The actualizing tendency is thus the criterion." *Ibid.* p. 210
15. See Wilfred Bion, *Experiences in groups*. London, Tavistock, 1961.
16. See the link we make in the first chapter between this aspect of humanistic psychology and the present approach, p. 70, last paragraph, and p. 71, first three paragraphs.

point of view and which, consequently, may not have all the extension it could have on a pragmatic level. But before developing this vision further, let's take a look at the second school of thought underlying the approach we are setting forth.

- *Epistemological Developments in Mathematics*

Epistemology is that realm where one questions the value of our knowledge. What does "to know" mean? What methods allow one to obtain valid knowledge? When I assert, "According to my intuition, here's what's going on in a specific domain," people may listen to me with great kindness, but such affirmations won't manage to convince anyone of the validity of my assertion. As it is based on my mere intuition, my methodology leaves to be desired in terms of arriving at a knowledge that is solid and certain. Had I arrived at the same conclusions, however, using recognized scientific methodology, chances are people would heed what I'm saying, and this, even though it would not necessarily be absolutely certain.

The question of the validity of knowledge can be raised in general terms, but it also comes up ever more frequently in the sciences themselves, which adopt their own methods in addressing the issues under study. In mathematics, for example, the 20th century was the scene of considerable epistemological questioning. At the beginning of the 20th century, the idea that science could not answer all questions was being ever more acknowledged. Scientific knowledge, it was thus believed, would never constitute a complete system.

That, however, was not the opinion of David Hilbert, for whom, at least in the field of mathematics, we could give a positive answer to the following question: "Whether it is self-evident – whether indeed it can be shown – that all mathematical assertions which make sense can necessarily be proved to be either true or false."[17] That was one of the elements of what was called Hilbert's Program.

It turns out that in 1931, Kurt Gödel proved that not all mathematical truths are demonstrable. The proof he elaborated

---

17. Jacob Bronowski, The logic of the mind, *Amer. Scientist*, 54, 1, 1966.

is a logico-mathematical version of an old paradox that prevailed among the ancient Greeks and which is attributed to Epimenides the Cretan who affirmed:

"All Cretans open their mouths only to tell a lie."

If the statement is true, the speaker, being himself a Cretan, has just told a lie. But if that is the case, it is by lying that he is telling the truth. And if he is telling the truth by lying, then the statement is false. This is the very nature of what has been called a logical paradox, that is to say, a particular type of contradiction which makes a thing true if it is false and vice versa.

This circular contradiction of paradox is one of the first manifestations of self-reference. The statement refers to itself. It's self-referent. It falls within its own scope. "I'm just saying falsehoods" is a statement that is itself part of what he's talking about. The statement is indeed a particular case of what I am saying and if it is true that I am only saying falsehoods, the latter statement must also be false and if it is false, it becomes true that I am saying a falsehood.

Gödel's genius has been to demonstrate mathematically that self-reference is not limited to a mere humorous play of words but marks the limit of formal systems based on standard logic, whose only two values are true and false.[18]

Self-Reference and Creativity

If self-reference can go as far as to thwart formal systems, it must also have unsuspected virtues. The Gödelian revolution has drawn attention to this process and given it the importance it deserves. As we have already pointed out, one of the first authors to have deepened reflection on self-reference is the

---

18. For readers interested in knowing more about the structure of Gödel's evidence, here is a brief summary of his argument. Gödel used ordinary arithmetic as a formal system. The ruse was to build a meta-level in the system that makes it able to talk about its own components. For example, he may say, "This statement is not demonstrable in this system." Let us call this statement G. If it is true that G is demonstrable, its negation becomes true. If the negation of a proposition is true, the proposition itself is false. That G is demonstrable is both true and false, which is a contradiction, therefore G is non-demonstrable. But that's what the statement says (it's not demonstrable), so it's true. It is therefore a true statement in the system, but which cannot be demonstrated. The system is therefore incomplete, because there is a true statement in this system which cannot be demonstrated by the means of this system.

mathematician Jacob Bronowski. After being invited to do some mathematical work in anthropology, he became interested in the specificity of the human being.[19]

Drawing from this author, I will approach the issue in a way that could be called impressionist, in order to trigger in the reader an intuitive grasp of the phenomenon as I myself experienced it, when I gradually appropriated this notion at the beginning of my intellectual journey. I will present more detailed, explicit, and rigorous descriptions and definitions of this phenomenon in the following chapter.

According to Bronowski, the creative capacity of the human mind, both in art and science, is related to its ability to operate in a self-referential way, whereas in a logical system, self-reference, as was illustrated in the paradox of the lying Cretan, rather appears as a limit and leads the mind to oscillate between the true and the false. Thus leaving it unable, within the framework of this system, to determine the truth of the statement.

But while self-reference leads standard logical systems into an impasse, the latter also constitutes the exit door that brings us precisely into this creative space that leads to the development of other systems. This space of creation does not operate according to the principles of standard logic. Indeed, several elements can coexist in experiencing without necessarily forming a logical system. These elements provide fertile ground for the exploration of ambiguity and the discovery of hidden connections that are expressed at the level of language in metaphors and analogies. Such elements are associated more with creative imagination than with rigorous processes of knowledge.

In this context, imagination, which is a free agent compared to the constraints of logical necessities, allows experiencing to generate a represented version of itself. One does not wonder whether this version is true or false, but rather whether or not it is consistent with the experience as lived. For example, referring to my experience of the night before, I can assert, "I had a wonderful evening." This expression adds to my experience and

---

19. Jacob Bronowski, *The Identity of man*, New York, The Natural History Press, 1965. The logic of the mind, *Amer. Scientist*, 54, 1, 1966.

is now part of it, but I, at the same time, realize that it doesn't say everything, that it's not quite adequate to the original experience because of a few elements that do not correspond to that assessment. For this reason, I may qualify my initial assertion by adding, "... if I leave out the little event X that I found less pleasant."

In short, any lived experience, intellectual or not, can be compared to itself in an expression that becomes an example of itself, a process that somehow mediates the relationship of this experience to itself. It is, one might say, the experience that makes its self-portrait.

In this regard, Gendlin quotes the philosopher Susanne Langer, who basically states that any experience is never just *that* experience, but that it is at the same time a *symbol* for the conception of *such an* experience. And Gendlin formulates this same idea in a principle he calls "iofi", this latter expression representing the acronym for "instance of itself." All experiencing, any felt meaning, argues Gendlin, is simultaneously an instance of itself.[20]

It is, therefore, a way for experiencing to refer to itself, in other words, to be self-referent. Thus, the oscillation between the true and false, which thwarts formal systems and leads to an impasse, gives way to the creative oscillation between an experience and its double under the aegis of an agent not subject to the prescriptions of binary logic.

Let us take the example of an emotional experience. I'm very sad, I'm feeling overwhelmed by this sadness, and I'm, so to speak, imprisoned in this emotional framework. Let's now assume that I express this emotion by saying, "I'm overwhelmed by sadness." This statement is distinct from my raw emotion as such, but it nevertheless expresses this emotion. It is an image of it, a version translated into a virtual framework. Through my statement, it is my emotion that is referring to itself. Thus, it is a self-referent expression of my emotion. To the extent that this expression, when confronted with its source, is felt as adequate, it confirms my emotion, but at the same time, helps free me from this same emotion. As a matter of fact, my lived experience is no

---

20. Eugene T. Gendlin. *Experiencing and the creation of meaning.* New York, Free Press 1962, p. 185.

longer reducible to this emotion or its expression, because a third party was added as a witness to the match between the two. It was first necessary to observe the emotion, then translate it into an expression, this time verbal, and finally to assess the congruence between the expression and the raw emotion.

My experience, therefore, is no longer only my raw sadness or my expressed sadness: it is also the emergence of a new space from which to evaluate this experience. So, I have a fresh start for a new expression. Thus, the more I am faithful to my emotion by expressing it, the more I free myself from it, because, thanks to the third party that has been added, my experience can expand beyond the initial dichotomy and enrich itself with new elements until eventually finding a space of serenity that takes precedence over the sadness that is then not avoided, but rather assumed.

Here again, we see that the oscillation which, in the logical paradox, creates a vicious circle now becomes a creative oscillation that forms a virtuous circle of new experiences.

However, should the expression diverge from the original experience, this divergent expression will re-enter into the original experience, thus weakening it. And the following expression will diverge even more. In other words, one gradually disconnects ever more from one's experience to the point, eventually, of being totally cut from it. The art of psychotherapy consists in helping the person to stay focused on the heart of her or his experience.

Let us now take the example of artistic creation. For a painter, the urgency of painting has an implicit content that has not yet received a definite expression. An explicit version is then inaccessible to everyone, including to the painter himself.

The implicit content that motivates the painting project is then the initial frame of reference. The first brushstrokes represent explicit expressions of this initial frame. It is as if the implicit content forming the initial frame of reference was giving itself an explicit version of itself; explicit, but still nevertheless partial. And that is why the painter must refer again to the frame of reference both to compare this expression with this initial reference and to continue to go on painting. However, after a few brushstrokes, the implicit content of the frame of reference is no longer in its original state, as the partial expression that has been made is now part of it. If this partial expression is in harmony with the initial impulse, a new expression will then be added, and so on.

Let us pause for a moment and focus on this very important point. If the explicit content of the expression is not consistent with the implicit content that is used as its frame of reference, then the self-referential link is weakened. It is as if the expression of the reference content is partly foreign to that content. It refers to something other than itself. There is a divergence, and the creative process gradually peters out, because if the expression is re-entered into the original frame of reference and it reflects something foreign to that frame, the following expression will diverge even more. It happens that a painter destroys his painting in the middle of the process. An outside observer might have wondered why a painter would destroy what appeared to him, the observer, so promising. What happened in this case is that the more the painter advanced in his work, the less the initial frame of reference could be recognized. In other words, the self-referential link between the content of the initial pulse and its expression was compromised. On the other hand, when Vincent Van Gogh, in a letter to his brother about one of his paintings, asserts that he considered it a great success, this does not at all mean that it would have been considered of greater objective value to an outside observer, but rather that it perfectly actualized, for Van Gogh, the implicit content that gave birth to it The painting is, so to speak, a way for this implicit initial content to express itself. It is the self-referent expression of it.

Let's take one more step. Suppose that the creation process develops properly and that the creator recognizes his initial intention. There comes a time, during the process, where it is no longer the initial inspiration that is used as a reference, but the work itself. A reversal takes place, and it is now the product – the painting itself – that takes over and triggers the inspiration of the painter. In other words, the initial creative agent then switches to a receptive mode in relation to his own product, which then presents itself as a self-contained, self-referencing version of the inspiration that gave birth to it.

Let us keep in mind this pattern: *a process generates a product that becomes necessary to maintain and develop the same process.* This is a fundamental and unavoidable mechanism of self-reference, which takes on a particular color when the creator is called to

INTRODUCTION

become himself the product of his own creation, as is the case with the human condition.

Turning now to a creative experience in science, let's take Newton's classical physics as an initial frame of reference. The laws concerning, for example, mass, time, and space constitute a coherent system, except for this anomaly that was discovered at the end of the 19th century: the behavior of light. Speed additivity does not apply to light: its speed is constant.[21] Einstein finds himself struggling with the axioms of classical physics, with a certain number of consequences on mass, time, and space ... but also on this delinquent item, light!

He then places himself in a receptive mode, outside of any logical system, leaving aside all previous certainties. It turns out that the idea that emerges and that he is about to develop is to no longer consider the speed of light as an exception, but rather as the reference of the system. In other words, a product of classical physics, through a singular reversal, takes over and becomes the reference for a complete reorganization of the system. The speed of light then passes from the field of consequences to the field of axioms.

Referring to this intuition of a new, though still implicit, coherence based on this choice, Einstein then made explicit the consequences on other dimensions such as time and space which lost their status as constants and then became relative. The new system thus integrated the old one into a broader coherence.

Let us note in passing this very important principle which we will revisit: in order to truly go beyond the system in which we find ourselves, we must identify the real impasse of this system and make it the reference of the new one. The impasse of the system of classical physics being the speed of light, Einstein thus made it the first reference of his system. In the case we are

---

21. In classical physics, speeds add up. If a train is moving at 50 km/h and you are inside the train and walking in the same direction at 5 km/h, you are advancing, relative to the train tracks, at 55 km/h. But in a similar circumstance, light misbehaves, its speed remaining constant: it will never exceed 300,000 kilometers per second. Assume, using another scale, that the train is traveling at 50 km per second. If the train turns on its headlights, the light thus produced will still advance, after one second, at 300,000 km and not at 300,000 km + 50 km. It is then time that becomes relative. The faster one moves, the more time slows down.

considering, self-reference being the impasse of standard formal systems, it becomes the key to human creativity.

It is worth returning to the notion of paradox. Within the framework of a binary logic whose only values are true and false, self-reference locks us into the paradox where the statement is true if we first consider that it is false and vice versa. In the case of creation, we also have two complementary poles, but a third is added and places us once again before a paradox, but of a different nature this time: if the first imprisons us, the latter liberates us, though still remaining paradoxical.

To illustrate this process, let's revisit the example of the experience of sadness mentioned earlier. The first reflex is to try to escape sadness so as not to be reduced to this experience. However, the self-referent expression leads us instead to try to express this sadness as clearly and accurately as possible. We thereby have the impression that we are trapped in a sadness that then covers the whole field, that of raw emotion and that of its expression. But it turns out that the *third agent* that emerges and measures how well the resulting expression corresponds to, or is congruent with, the original sadness, actually stands apart from both sadness and its expression, though its existence emerges from this very dichotomy. Paradoxically, the more we fully enter, in this way, into the world of emotion, the more we get out of it. In other words, this *third party or agent* is part of the system to the extent that it is outside the system. But this paradox, now, is a liberating one.

A Decisive Step...

At the same time, in the late 1960s, two Chilean biologists, Humberto Maturana and Francisco Varela, were making self-reference the fundamental characteristic of the living. According to these authors, all life is a form of self-production, self-creation. To designate this particular case of self-reference, the authors formed a neologism: autopoiesis.[22]

Such were the research advances of these two authors that self-reference became a new paradigm. It is, therefore, now

---

22. The Greek verb *poiein* (ποιειν) means to make, produce, create, invent and the Greek prefix auto (αυτός) means self. The term autopoiesis thus refers to self-production, self-creation, self-invention.

possible to see life from this particular angle. This extension of the application of self-reference, then called *autopoiesis*, to all the living would make it possible to describe more accurately the main mechanisms of the process, and this advance would benefit all the researchers engaged in this path.[23] But then, what about human specificity?

Human Specificity

It should be noted at the outset that the human individual, as a living biological being, is no different from other living beings. He is also autopoietic: he maintains himself in existence by developing an internal organization that allows him to maintain his own identity and to adapt effectively to his environment. Other animals, however, once they have reached maturity, only have to exercise, to maintain themselves in existence, the ability they then possess. Bees, for example, know how to make honey, and they know how to live in society: there will be a queen, various specialties, etc. A bee knows how to be a bee and it need not ask itself this question.

However, when we humans reach maturity, we are not endowed with biological determinisms that would tell us how to operate in order to be in conformity with our own nature. Part of what we call "own nature" has yet to be invented. We cannot, like our fellow animals, simply rely on the creative functioning of a ready-made machine: we must complete the construction of the machine that we are, and this deprived of a clear guide or an instruction manual.[24] We are thus faced with what appears to us as a void.

A painter has before him his canvas which stands apart from him. But when we are dealing with an artist who must himself become the work to be produced, there is absolutely nothing standing in front of him when he fully adopts the position of the creator. Should he instead adopt the position of the work to be created, there is no longer any artist to create it. The void is then even greater.

---

23. For a summary of the basic concepts of this approach, refer to Chapter 1.
24. See footnote 5.

It is in this paradoxical context that we have the choice, either to try to invent ourselves by becoming more and more human or to allow ourselves to become inhuman. Indeed, we cannot do just anything, because nature has already made us specific beings that cannot be confused with other species. However, though we humans have our own identity as a species, we must, in order to fully actualize this identity, complete its creation. And as in all creation, what we bring as a new expression of ourselves must be an extension which is consistent with the initial frame of reference provided by nature, that is, consistent with what we already are, but, at the same time, it must lead us to something new and original, and that differs from the original framework and makes it evolve.

So we therefore have the choice to build ourselves and to develop systems fostering our humanity or to do the opposite. And it turns out that, historically, we have not hesitated to push in both directions. What would then be the strategy to make sure we don't just end up behaving erratically? Our challenge, let us remember, is to achieve a creation of which we will be the product. This is the most complete and dramatic case of self-reference, which, as we have seen, makes us lose our bearings and places us in front of a void. What, in the end, are we going to do with ourselves?

Generally, in such a case, clearly acknowledging wherein lies the problem brings us straight to the solution. This, you will recall, is exactly what Einstein did with the speed of light, which had its own behavior and did not fit into the Newtonian reference system. Einstein the scientist then took this peculiar behavior of light seriously and made it the reference of a new system.

Let's follow the master. Self-reference places us in front of a void and does not fit with our binary, continuous, and linear mode of operation. However, therein precisely, in this process itself, lies the answer. We have seen that this process of self-reference has an autonomous meaning, that it has its own coherence, that it speaks of itself (in a double sense: **about** itself as an object, and **from** itself) and that in so doing it carries on in such a delinquent manner as to challenge the most established orthodoxies, namely that of the formal systems at the base of classical science. Thus, we need but make self-reference our primary reference, and this process will ultimately reward us by referring us to ourselves, by making us our own reference!

The intuition we have of this process is already rendered partially explicit. Let's revisit the example mentioned earlier of the painter: from an implicit frame of reference that represents the inspiration for the painting project, the artist starts painting until he reaches a point where, by a reversal of perspective, the painting itself becomes the source of his inspiration. As previously noted, but in more abstract terms, "a process generates a product that becomes necessary to maintain and develop that same process." If now the creator himself is part of the whole in whose creation he is involved, the resulting product must be able to take over the action and come back to include him, the creator, in the final product. For this to happen, a new agent will then have to emerge from the product itself to allow the creator to let go and integrate into the final product, thus indirectly becoming the object of his own action. This emerging agent will be called a *paradoxical agent* and will be the keystone of a creation this time completely self-referent.

Such a pattern can be applied to all levels of the organization of human reality: individuals, groups, societies, and the world. Whatever level is considered, it is "the artist himself" who is called to become his own work of art. As Giambattista Vico puts it: "Humanity is its own work of art."[25] That is what our reflection has been about from the very beginning: man inventing himself. Hence the question, "What am I going to do with myself, what are we going to do with ourselves?"

This creative process is complex and will have to be explored on two fronts at the same time. Indeed, from self-reference as an implicit frame of reference, we must create, by successive approximations, a prototype of this self-referential machine, both on the purely cognitive level and in pragmatic terms. In the first case, the machine will be made of an assembly of notions and concepts forming an abstract fabric, which is the object of this first volume. In the second case, the object of a forthcoming second volume, it will be made of an assembly of people and groups, forming a human fabric. The autonomous development of self-reference on these two parallel levels, cognitive and pragmatic, will enrich each other and, on occasion, will serve as an evaluative benchmark for each other. This is a way of coming

---

25. "L'humanité est son œuvre à elle-même." Quoted by Jules Michelet, *Cours professé au collège de France*, 1847-1848, Paris, Chamerot, 1848, p. 214.

together with ourselves. As the Quebecois poet Gilles Vigneault once put it: "It takes a lot of time, a lot of steps, a lot of words, and a lot of choices, to discover that, in the end, one is simply going home."[26]

In Summary

In psychology, we have identified a school of thought, behaviorism, according to which the reference for human development comes from without: human behavior is the result of conditioning obtained in one's milieu. On the other hand, for the humanistic school of thought, the reference for development comes from within: the dynamic force lies within persons and unfolds in reference to their own identity.

Moreover, in mathematics, the reference to oneself, already identified as problematic by the ancient Greeks, appeared as the impasse of formal standard systems. However, this same impasse turns out as an opening into a place where what appeared as an insoluble paradox in the previous system becomes the central ingredient of creativity, more precisely, of the process of creation in which the creator is called to become himself the object of his own creation.

Thus, overcoming formal systems and broadening the field of humanistic psychology leads us to explore self-reference as a paradigm at the heart of human reality. This is the subject of the following chapters. The following chapter will deal more specifically with methodological issues and will allow us to further define this concept.

---

26. « On met beaucoup de temps, on fait beaucoup de pas, on dit beaucoup de mots, on fait beaucoup de choix, pour revenir apprendre qu'on s'en allait chez soi. »

Chapter I

Basic Concepts and Methodology

In the introduction, we raised questions arising from the adoption of this new self-reference paradigm. The very adoption of the latter paradigm highlights a realm that is indeed radically different from more traditional approaches. What makes this realm unique and differentiates it from others? What are the basic concepts without which one could not distinguish this realm from those surrounding it?

Discussing the above questions and setting forth, as an introduction, a few basic concepts is the object of the first section.

The following one deals with methodological issues, thus laying the groundwork for the statement of the author's methodological choice, which is explained in the third section entitled "The self-referential matrix." This methodological choice includes founding statements, which constitute, so to speak, the postulates on which the whole approach is based.

Basic Concepts

Several authors have already explored this realm whose contours nevertheless still remain unclear. In addition to those mentioned above, let us note the work of researchers who have made complexity both their method and object of study, such as Morin, Le Moigne, as well as those participating in the research program *European Complexity Modeling (MCX)* and the *Association for Complex Thinking (APC)*. The latter researchers analyze the issue of complexity and do so using a complex thought process.

However, my main source will be the works of Varela, whose orientation is more compatible with my approach. I will have the opportunity along the way to point out how my ideas diverge from those of Morin and his colleagues, but it goes without saying that despite such divergences, their school of thought remains an unavoidable source of inspiration.

The basic concepts set forth in what follows are mainly based on the reflections proposed by Varela in his book *Principles of biological autonomy*.[27] They will be applied to various levels of reality while undergoing the necessary adaptations. Thus, they will reappear throughout this book.

Autonomy and Control

The first distinction between the realm defined by self-reference and the other realms can be represented by the notions of *autonomy* and *control*. To the first concept are associated the ideas of internal regulation, generation, and affirmation of one's own identity. To the second notion are associated the ideas of definition from without, input/output systems, and external control. The idea of control is familiar to us, and it has gained considerable popularity, while that of autonomy is more suspect. Varela summarizes below the description that is generally made of them.

First, he explains control:

> [...] *something in/process/something out. We stand on both sides of in and out, whether an economic system, a compiler, or a person's mind. The fundamental paradigm of our interactions with a control system is* **instruction,** *and the unsatisfactory results are* **errors**.

Then autonomy:

---

27. Unless otherwise indicated, all quotations in this section are from Francisco J. Varela's book, *Principles of biological autonomy*. New York Elsevier North Holland, 1979. Although Varela's viewpoint is presented here in part and with some personal additions, I have tried to be faithful to his viewpoint and to stick to those aspects in it that I find useful and consistent with my approach. Generally, one will find in this book, even apart from direct quotes, Varela's own expressions. A more critical point of view, concerning certain methodological or theoretical stances taken by the author, will be introduced in the second section of this chapter and in the following chapter.

BASIC CONCEPTS AND METHOLOLOGY

> *Autonomy is less fashionable. It is usually taken as a more vague and somewhat moralistic term, and waved off as a question of indeterminacy. There is little understanding of its generic import, let alone its representation in formal terms. The fundamental paradigm of our interaction with an autonomous system is a* **conversation**, *and its unsatisfactory results breaches of* **understanding**.[28]

It is interesting to note in passing that in the first case, we are in the exclusive realm of knowledge, while in the second case, we enter the world of communication. We'll revisit this issue.

Let us return to autonomy, literally the self-law of a system: it is based on recursive, self-referential mechanisms that refer to the unitary character of that system. In intuitive and intentionally redundant terms, autonomy, at its root, is "being oneself by oneself." Even when interacting with the outside world, primacy has shifted to within. Through the disturbances resulting from such interacting, the unit in question does not, basically, transpose within itself information representing the outside world but rather ensures its own internal coherence in the continual maintenance of its identity. One's own identity becomes the reference, because there is no architect who designed this system and to whom one could relate its operation.

Because of the circularity that characterizes it, the concept of autonomy has an odor of paradox and recalls certain circles that we have become accustomed to seeing as vicious. That is why *autonomy* is not seen as an exact concept, contrary to *control*, which is its conceptual counterpart. But we will have to convince ourselves that this circle is not essentially vicious and that it even has creative virtues that it would be wrong to neglect. Indeed, were we but to retain the perspective of *control*, we would probably get part of the picture but would be missing what is essential, given that such an approach cannot but lead us to a false understanding of natural systems, as well as to important epistemological, ethical, and political difficulties. It is, therefore, vital to make every effort to introduce maximum rigor into our approach to *autonomy*, while meanwhile remaining tolerant relative to what at first sight may appear strange.

---

28. Op. cit. p. xii. (Emphasis added).

It is not the least of oddities to note that in autonomous units, components generate elements that become themselves necessary for the production of such components. Most authors, following Douglas Hofstadter,[29] use the term *entangled hierarchy* to evoke this phenomenon. Indeed, the hierarchy of operators and operands is not fixed: that which, at a given moment, acts as an operator finds itself at another time in the field of operands. In other words, products play an operational role in the processes that produce them. Maturana and Varela (1980) provide the example of the emergence of a cell:

> *A cell emerges from molecular soup by defining and specifying the boundary that distinguishes it from what it is not. However, this specification of frontiers takes place through the production of molecules, which require the very presence of these boundaries. So, there is a mutual specification of chemical transformations and physical boundaries. The cell itself emerges from the homogeneous background; if the self-production process stops, the cellular components cease to form a unit and return to homogeneous molecular soup.*[30]

Operational Closure[31]

Varela introduces here the concept of *operational closure*:

> *The chain of operations closes, producing an operational closure, where the results of production find themselves at the same level as the agents of production. With such an organization, the usual distinctions between producer and product, beginning and end, or input and output, cease to have meaning.*[32]

The thesis of operational closure would be enunciated as follows:

Every autonomous system is operationally closed (1979. p. 58)

---

29. Douglas Hofstadter, *Gödel, Escher, Bach : an Eternal Golden Braid*, New York, Vintage Books, 1980.
30. Author's translation of Varela, F. *Autonomie et connaissance. Essai sur le vivant.* Paris, Seuil, 1989.
31. Originally, the term "organizational closure" was used but presently the term "operational closure" is more commonly used.
32. Author's translation of Varela, F. (1989), p. 21.

Consequently:

> *[...] closure and the system's identity are interlocked in such a way that it is a necessary consequence for an operationally closed system to subordinate all changes to the maintenance of its identity. (Ibid. p. 58).*

This mechanism of identity preservation can thus be found in a social organization if it can be legitimately said that it is operationally closed. This reversal of perspective, which makes it possible to place autonomy at the center of human and social functioning through a process of operational closure, cannot but have major ethical and political implications.

Let us recall here a crucial point made by Varela:

> *But it should be noted that closure is not isolation: the term closure refers to the fact that the result of an operation is located within the borders of the system itself; it does not mean that the system has no interaction with what's outside, which would be isolation. My study is not about isolated systems.* [33]

In a unit endowed with operational closure, consistent and quite distinct behavior appears as an operation of the unit, although it is impossible to see within that unit the starting point of the operation. Knowledge is not localized but distributed through this constantly repeated circle.

This leads to a particular epistemological conception. There is not, on the one hand, a predefined external world with its characteristics, the images of which would be printed in our brain to be decoded by a subject with a greater or lesser margin of error. Nor is there, on the other hand, a subject who would be the starting point of our knowledge and who would project his subjectivity onto the world. Subject and object, from the present perspective, simultaneously emerge and build themselves through our common history as living and social beings.

Note that this conception of Varela is altogether consistent with the epistemology of Piaget. For the latter, it's not a matter of searching for an absolute foundation for knowledge, either on the side of the subject or on that of the object. Instead, it's about entering into the history of a process from which simultaneously emerge, both subject and object.

---

33. Author's translation of Varela, F. (1989), p. 217.

It is thus from within this circle that we must always operate. No external foundations to which we could cling exist. We are, argues Varela, part of

> ... *a world where no one can claim to have an understanding of a universal nature. The world of the living, the logic of self-reference, and the whole natural history of circularity should teach us that tolerance and pluralism, a detachment from our own perceptions and values that leaves room for those of others are, at once the true foundation of knowledge and its fulfillment. Here, actions speak louder than words. (Ibid. p. 31).*

The Organization of Living Systems: Autopoiesis

As already indicated, Maturana and Varela coined the term *autopoiesis* to refer to the process of self-production in living beings.[34] It is a subclass of autonomous phenomena that the authors are reluctant to generalize and apply, for example, to social phenomena. They prefer for the moment to limit its application to systems which are based on chemical networks, as are the organisms that we are and that we observe around us. They would accept extending *autopoiesis* to other classes of phenomena were it possible to give a precise meaning to the processes of **production of components** and of **generation of a border**. We'll revisit this point.

The living being thus distinguishes itself from its environment and constitutes a concrete unity in the space where it exists, and it maintains its identity by a network of production processes of components which, through their interactions, constantly regenerate this same network. Like all autonomous systems, autopoietic systems are operationally closed.

Closure, Openness, Isolation

Before going further, let's come back to the question of the links between the concepts of closure, opening, and isolation. Asserting the primacy of operational closure can give the impression that one is neglecting, or almost denying, the importance of openness and interaction with the environment

---

34. See footnote 22.

Basic Concepts and Methodology

that are both deemed fundamental in so-called systemic or ecological approaches.

Such a concern appears in comments made at the 1981[35] Cérisy conference on self-organization, including that of J. Robert, who asked Varela whether operational closure did not represent a new form of solipsism that ends up calling into question the very possibility for humans to building a shared world.

And Morin also sets forth a similar concern (2008, p. 295)[36] when, after acknowledging

> "the extraordinary insight of von Foerster, Maturana, Varela (von Foerster, 1976; Maturana and Varela, 1972; Varela, 1975, 1976) in identifying the idea of self-reference, of "autopoiesis," of closed logic with regard to living beings,"

adds that this insight "is not legitimized to reject the notion of openness." An astonishing statement after the positions taken by Varela, who claimed from the start that his proposal did not exclude the notion of openness.

Morin nevertheless persists:

> "The idea of autopoiesis is still too localized in a school of thought. One that has isolated itself by insisting on the idea of closure, at a time when, on the contrary, the idea of openness of living systems was taking on ever greater prominence." (Ibid. p. 675).

Indeed, at that time, the work of Ludwig von Bertalanffy aimed at giving the notion of system its letters of nobility, which foreshadowed the idea of closure. But curiously, these developments led to consider as characteristic of living systems the fact that these systems are open and, therefore, in constant interaction with their environment. Already in 1967, Piaget spoke out against such an erroneous interpretation:

> The central ambiguity is that of "open system"; for if there is a system, something happens that looks like closure and needs to be reconciled with opening. [...] closure meant as a cyclical, not linear kind [...][37]

---

35. Paul Dumouchel, Jean-Pierre Dupuy, *L'auto-organisation. De la physique au politique*, Paris, Seuil, 1983.
36. Unless otherwise specified, references to Edgar Morin's *La Méthode* refer to this 2008 edition, which includes all six volumes.
37. J. Piaget, *Biologie et connaissance*, Paris, Gallimard, 1967, p. 220.

In such a context, the following remark by Morin is surprising, to say the least:

> *The principle of ecological relationship definitively opens up the closed concept of identity which isolates objects in self-sufficiency, excluding from its principle both otherness and the environment. (Ibid. p. 289).*

As just mentioned, Varela has always been quite clear in emphasizing that closure does not mean isolation. The fact that Morin, after acknowledging the value of Varela's insight, would consider the notion of closure linked to identity as a solipsistic closure seems to me as a big blunder. This problem must hide a particular difficulty, which would explain the extent of such a misunderstanding.

The Problem of Reconciling Closure and Openness

For Morin, opening up to what is outside implies that the environment introduces itself into "the recursive loop of self-production." (*Ibid.* p. 287). Such an intrusion breaks the operational closure and threatens the very life of the unit concerned. What characterizes this unit as a living being is precisely the fact that it distinguishes itself from its environment through a closed system of operations whose raison d'être consists in preserving the system's identity. Breaking this closure would be tantamount to bringing about its death. Moreover, though Morin's metaphor – "the hemorrhagic breach" – is very accurate it does not serve his purpose particularly well. For if the dependence of the living being on its environment takes the form of a hemorrhage, then the living would be in danger.

Living beings, of course, draw from the environment what they need to stay alive. Our organism, for example, must continuously draw from the environment the quantity of oxygen needed for its functioning. It must also feed itself. But it must be clearly understood that food in no way breaks the operational closure of the organism. It is not the apple I eat that decides what will happen to it. All transformations are subject to the coherence of the internal processes that operate according to the system's identity.

Thus, operational closure is a *prerequisite* for a unit's opening to the environment, not the opposite. Moreover, the richer this structure and the greater its capacity in keeping its operational closure intact, and this despite a wide variety of environmental disturbances, the greater the openness of the system to its environment. The reciprocal is also true: the more fragile the operational closure, the less open it is. We are far from solipsistic closure.

Comment on Concepts Presented

This brief presentation of a few Varelian notions allows us to arrive at a first approximation of the self-referential circle underlying autonomous entities. However, one should avoid transposing in a servile manner biological concepts at the individual and social levels as this may lead to rather short-sighted views, which, in the end, would obscure the essence of the self-reference process specific to these levels. For example, no sooner would an organism show any rigidity in its evolution than one would fall back on a supposedly self-referential explanation of the phenomenon. One will assert, for example, that the organism is acting in reference to its own identity and that it cannot, therefore, be open to changes that would affect the expression of this identity. Reasoning in this manner, however, obscures the whole creative richness that generates novelty in the evolution of life. And when one is dealing with the specifically human realm of self-construction, which implies development and therefore plasticity in the very structure relating to one's own identity, such obscuring is even more significant.

Self-reference takes on an altogether new dimension when it unfolds in the sphere of the person and the human community. As mentioned in the foreword and introduction, the living from other species that we know have a more complete nature at the start, and they do not feel responsible for being the co-creators of their specific identity. They are content with simply manifesting and maintaining their identity in their environment. The dog does not worry about its nature as a dog, and when it finds himself in a pack, it does not question the type of social organization in which it finds itself. Bees know how to build a hive. They don't question whether there will now be a queen, or whether or not they will function democratically. Human beings, on the other hand, must participate in the construction of their own identity, whether it be as individuals, as societies, or as an entire species. Merely maintaining their nature-bestowed identity would basically cut them off from the more advanced and specifically human expression of self-reference.

In short, while the processes described above remain fundamental, the form they take when applied at higher levels of complexity will need to be explored. Thus, the central objective of this book is to embark into the self-referential circle, to examine its essential articulations, to provide a general transdisciplinary expression of it, and finally, to draw the methodological consequences on both theoretical and practical levels.

Methodological Issues

Obviously, the scope of the task discussed so far is well beyond that of this essay. However, one can expect this essay to set forth what could form the basis of a model leading to the development of a research agenda and, ultimately, a theory as such.

Contributing to giving more coherence and extension to the self-referential approach: such is the main purpose of this reflection. To this end, avenues of research will be specified, and this with as much depth and rigor as possible so that anyone wishing to explore such avenues will have a sufficiently good understanding to do so.

We will thus constantly refer to processes, paths that bring us closer to that... path that we are searching for. In other words, we will discuss "meta" "odos,"[38] – "method" – and our project can thus be described as methodological.

This ambition has nothing to reassure anyone about the magnitude of the task and thus calls for a few introductory comments, the subject of this section. These will allow the reader to better identify the orientation of our approach and situate it in relation to other approaches concerned about methodological issues.

---

38. From the Greek words μετα: beyond, and οδος : path.

Self-Reference as First Reference

In the present approach, all the emphasis is placed on the self-referential process, and this not only in terms of the idea to be developed but also in terms of how it will be developed. Self-referentiality constitutes, in a way, the great invariant of the system, such as the speed of light, metaphorically speaking, in the theory of relativity. In other words, we will try to place all issues, as far as possible, within the framework of self-reference.

First of all, such a choice is not entirely naive. We know what risk we are exposing ourselves to when establishing a beginning, a foundation, to something: that of requiring, to lay this foundation, the very foundation we set out to establish! Yet such a circle is no more vicious than that of the autonomous entities themselves, where components generate products that are themselves necessary for the production of such components.

Secondly, persisting in this choice is also not entirely innocent. At this point, we will take the time to point out that what would serve as a "foundation" here is precisely this "apostle of sedition in the kingdom of the orthodox",[39] this generator of paradoxes, that only allows itself to be apprehended by promising to let you set your foot firmly somewhere on a carpet that he is about to pull out from under your feet at your following step. Undoubtedly, the autonomous character of such a process throws a wet blanket on the over-ambitious researcher, yet does it not justify in return the choice of making it a primary point of reference? Let us thus not back away from this challenge: not only will self-reference be the *core idea* to be developed, but, also and equally important, it will represent the *paradigm* underlying its own development.

The orientation taken in this approach is likely to be of concern to those who profess the paradigm of complexity and who would view with suspicion the effort to anchor a model at a point that is both as simple and as comprehensive as possible. May emerge here the specter of the *paradigm of simplification*. This point thus calls for a comment.

---

39. Richard Howe, Heinz Von Foerster, "Introductory Comments to Francisco J. Varela's Calculus for Self-Reference", *Int. J. of General Systems*, 1975, Vol. 2, p. 1-3.

About Simplification

There is some confusion about simplification, as if it were a shortcoming to be avoided or, at best, a necessary evil to be compensated for by other operations. Any approach to reality cannot but be simpler than reality itself. The matter is, therefore, not whether or not one simplifies, but rather what kind of simplification may be acceptable according to the objective one is pursuing.

One way of simplifying consists in reducing a complex unit to one or more of its elements. This is the reductionist approach always taken by classical science. Alternatively, one can simplify, but adopting instead the path of complexity. To stimulate the imagination, we will draw inspiration from the way nature proceeds, either following the path of reductionism or that of complexity.

Nature sometimes "simplifies" by reducing complex forms to simpler ones as in the process of entropy. There is then disorganization, a juxtaposition of isolated elements, up to the most degraded form of energy, which is heat, where the particles randomly collide. This reductionist process, at the limit, can be productive in specific contexts. Place a log in the hearth and you obtain heat and light, something that would be impossible were the wood fibre to remain intact.

And nature sometimes adopts the path of complexity as can be observed in natural evolution. The process of complexification that leads to the development of life is so to speak a stratagem to create units that, as such, are simple. Each living being constitutes a single unit, and yet this unit emanates from the complex interaction of a very large number of processes. From another point of view, that of origin, a complex organism composed of billions of cells comes from a single cell that contains the information necessary for the development of that organism. The great art of complex evolution is to always maintain a simple unit in its entirety, from the origin to the end of the process, despite the very great multiplicity of elements and operations put in place to achieve this.

Methodologically, we can proceed in a way that recalls this possible dual orientation concerning complexity. Indeed, a single and simple conceptual framework can ensure that complexity is taken into account or, conversely, lead to reducing complexity to elementary constituents. This second reductionist tendency, Cartesian in its inspiration, metonymic in its orientation, is the most common in classical science and has produced convincing results in the fields where it is applied. However, in order to develop those aspects of reality that are more difficult to access by classical methods, the opposite non-reductionist trend is increasingly asserting itself. As we shall see, the notion of *totality* then becomes central.

We would, therefore, be entitled to be wary of elementarism when dealing with a complex universe. In this sense, it would be the *reductionist paradigm* that should be avoided and not that of simplification. We will thus seek to simplify as much as possible in order to come up with a single frame of reference which, while encompassing and taking into account the richness of human reality, nevertheless avoids falling into reductionist simplifications that seek the truth of the whole in one or other of its parts. In order to end up with what is simplest but avoids reductionism, a principle of economy and parsimony will be applied, a principle which, in my view, remains an imperative for any rigorous approach to reality, however complex.

The Notion of Paradigm

The avatars of the notion of paradigm are the subject of both considerable suspicion and great enthusiasm. One would be tempted to use another term to avoid all the ambiguities attached to it. This is, moreover, what led Thomas Khun[40] himself to abandon the term. I nevertheless prefer to keep it, first because of its increasingly widespread use, and second because it has given rise to reflections, some of them referred to as "paradigmatology" (Maruyama, 1974, Morin 1991).

The Greek origin of the word paradigm (παραδειγμα) refers to the idea of example, or model. Using it in the sense of example aims at highlighting an implicit dimension, making it more easily accessible in order to be able to apply it to other cases. An example is thus used to evoke and help one understand the underlying schema which guided its concrete explicit realization.

---

40. Kuhn, Thomas S. *The Structure of Scientific Revolutions.* 3rd ed. Chicago, IL: University of Chicago Press, 1996.

Let's say I give as an example a certain type of argumentation; I would like the person listening to be able to decipher the structure of this type of argumentation, so that he or she could subsequently produce, using this structure, similar argumentations.

The term has kept the same meaning in certain linguistic uses. For example, when it comes to designating the inflectional forms of words declensions or conjugations. The paradigm for English verbs has three main tenses: the Infinitive, the Past Simple, and the Past Participle. There are four different types of paradigm, one for regular verbs and three for irregular verbs. For all Regular verbs, the Past Participle is the same as the Past Simple. Just add ED to the base form of the verb. (Base form = Infinitive without to.) For example: Live, Lived, Lived, etc.

An attempt has been made, again in linguistics, to give a more fundamental meaning to the term paradigm. One finds, in most authors, two main lines of thought. The first, horizontal, evokes the sequencing of linguistic units in relation to each other: this is the syntagmatic axis. The other, vertical in relation to the preceding one, is where the speaker draws each unit of discourse from a virtual reservoir where the elements are associated on the basis of common characteristics: this is the paradigmatic axis.

After analyzing the strengths and weaknesses of various meanings, including those of Ferdinand de Saussure, Louis Hjelmslev, Roman Jacobson, and Noam Chomsky, Christian Vandendorpe[41] takes a detour through cognitive psychology and relates the notion of paradigm to that of pattern or *schema*. Schema is a structure of action and representation. Experiencing and learning do not store in memory the various elements that make them up as isolated units next to each other. Instead, they form organized units that function with a certain degree of coherence and autonomy, and that can adapt to the circumstances that called for them. For example, if I know how to drive a car, I don't have to reinvent and rebuild each gesture as I had to do when I first learned to drive. My actions are spontaneously carried out in a way that is adapted to the

---

41. Christian Vandendorpe, « Paradigme et syntagme. De quelques idées vertes qui ont dormi furieusement », *Revue québécoise de linguistique théorique et appliquée*, 9, 3, 1990, p. 169-193.

circumstances. I can even become totally distracted at times, and everything continues to function normally. The same is true of various contexts that are familiar to me; I spontaneously know how to behave in them. Both the notion of schema and the notion of paradigm are "theoretical constructs accounting for the structuring effects observed in the cognitive as well as the linguistic realm."[42]

Thanks to Kuhn's historico-critical reflections on science, the concept of paradigm associated with these "structuring effects" has gone beyond linguistics and found its way into the social sciences. The multiple meanings that T. Kuhn (1983) has given to the term paradigm all refer essentially to the same idea, that of a matrix, or, in the words of Denis de Béchillon (1997), to "the structuring background of scientific activity." And as its use expanded, this concept spilled over into all aspects of human behavior.

Historically, therefore, the meaning of the word paradigm has shifted from the idea of example to that of underlying pattern. It has come to designate what is at the origin of all our cognitive productions. The latter can be those of an individual, a group, a society, a civilization, an era...

A similar inward shift occurred with the term *persona*. Initially, it meant mask, in other words, the most apparent and external reality, but it ended up designating the founding reality of this exterior appearance, the character, and finally, the person himself or herself.

But what is the precise nature of this reality that presides over the emergence of the universe that we inhabit and to whose construction we contribute? How can we speak of this original state of our experience, of "our mute contact with things when the latter are not yet expressed in words?"[43]

A Few Characteristics of Paradigms

The first, and not the least, characteristic of the paradigm is that it places the speaker in a paradoxical position to talk about

---

42. *Ibid.*
43. Maurice Merleau-Ponty, *Le visible et l'invisible*, Paris, Gallimard, 1961, p. 61. "[...] notre contact muet avec les choses quand elles ne sont pas encore des choses dites."

it. Indeed, one must decide what comes before the word and presides over its emergence. To define what a paradigm is one must have recourse to a paradigm. In other words, one is in a situation of self-reference even before deciding anything about self-reference!

Moreover, the process is blind to itself. Just as the vision of an object does not allow the eye to see itself seeing, the paradigm that presides over making a content explicit cannot, through this same making-explicit-process, make itself explicit. One can thus only make an assessment after the fact, by the effects.

Of course, nothing prevents us from considering the paradigm like any other object. It will suffice to remember that the eye itself as "object" sees nothing, that it is merely the construct of an observer who sees. In the same way, nothing emerges from the paradigm itself as "object," as the latter is itself only the product of an active paradigm that remains in the shadows. But, just as good knowledge of the eye and the visual system can lead to interventions that can help the eye to see better, so good knowledge of paradigmatic reality can help us to improve our activity of knowledge.

Let us begin with an intuitive approach to this reality by referring to what was already pointed out in the introduction. In a situation where I am creating – a text, a work of art, a craft object, a new way of proceeding in this or that field, etc. – the impulse to create, it was asserted, does not emanate from a void. I am trying to let emerge something that is still implicit. I cannot consider this "something" directly as an object until it is created. And yet, when I'm in the act of creating, I am nevertheless "referring to it." Moreover, once the object is created, I can evaluate whether or not it adequately expresses the implicit reality that is at the origin of its creation. I can, therefore, compare the created object to the "non-object" that presided over its creation. Furthermore, if the creation is successful, the result is experienced as going further, as being more than the mere expression of something that was already implicitly there. The expression makes the experience move forward by confirming it.

To deepen this intuition and bring out more clearly what characterizes the present conception, we can draw from the reflections of Georges Spencer Brown (1969) and his notion of *distinction*.

BASIC CONCEPTS AND METHOLOLOGY

When a paradigm is at work, a distinction is actually being made, positing a reality as "being" relative to everything else that this reality is not. It is the very basis of any *form* to distinguish between what is that form and what is something else. The whole calculus of indications of Spencer Brown[44] is based on this property, and the author elaborates an arithmetic and an algebra from a single operator, which is a boundary operator indicating by its very existence the reality that circumscribes this boundary. Even when something very simple is expressed, the statement only makes sense if it establishes a distinction, generating a sort of figure on a background. Asserting to someone "It's a nice day today" only makes sense in a geographical context where the possibility of bad weather exists. The beautiful weather is then distinguished against an implicit background of possible bad weather. For people in some cultures furthermore, the preceding statement would not make sense even if they were able to understand the meaning of the words and phrases expressed, given the fact that in their culture, no such paradigm for distinguishing beautiful from bad weather exists. For these people, there is no such thing as "beautiful" or "bad" weather. Rain is as beautiful as sunshine, and sunshine can be as bad as rain.

This leads us to see that this distinction implies another, implicit distinction, which is the overall reality from which this distinction derives. It is, in fact, a whole field of experience that is called upon, in this case the weather, and which is distinguished from other fields, such as education or fishing, for example. It can, therefore, be seen that the first explicit distinction (good vs. bad weather) is internal to a particular field of experience. This field constitutes an implicit totality that is posed, at that precise moment, as *reality* – weather – versus any other field of experience. This implicit *reality* comes with numerous possible distinctions that give rise to a first explicit distinction and a hierarchy of sub-distinctions, allowing as many elements to emerge as figures on a background. This same *reality* that is the weather would be made explicit in a very different way in another culture because of the difference in paradigm.

---

44. George Spencer Brown, *Laws of Form*, London, Allen & Unwin, 1969.

This description of paradigm in terms of an *implicit distinction of a particular field of experiencing from which a first explicit distinction emerges* can be applied, as in the present example, to what could be called a surface paradigm that gives meaning to this sentence in particular and allows us to understand it. But the paradigm can be applied to more complex units of a larger order of magnitude. It can be a text, an entire work, or even the manifestations of an entire culture or civilization.

We sometimes wonder what a particular author might have meant in a particular text or in his entire work. In so doing we are basically asking ourselves what is the first explicit distinction that gives meaning to the whole text and to the entire work, and that at the same time delineates an implicit realm.

Henri Bergson's famous assertion reminds us of this: "A philosopher worthy of the name has never said but one thing. And even then, it's more that he tried to say it than he really said it."

The philosopher did say this "thing"; his work does make an explicit distinction. But what is at the origin of this distinction remains in the shadows, so in a sense, the "thing," as points out Bergson, is not "really said."

There is, therefore, basically a "thing," a universe or background, which is at the origin of all production but remains implicit. It's what I would call *the first implicit distinction*. The first *explicit* distinction and all those that follow represent both that which reveals and that which masks this first implicit distinction.

It is, of course, possible to name this implicit distinction and thus render it explicit for itself. That is what Gilles Deleuze[45] does, for example, when he tries to compare the phenomenological approach to Bergson's approach :

> *... if one accepts that the secret of phenomenology is contained in the well-known stereotypical formula 'all consciousness is consciousness of something,' by which they thought they would overcome the duality of consciousness and body, of consciousness and things, the Bergsonian approach is completely different and its stereotypical*

---

45. Gilles Deleuze, « Image mouvement, image temps ». Cours Vincennes-St-Denis : Bergson, *Matière et mémoire* – 05/01/1981. In *Les cours de Gilles Deleuze*, http://www.webdeleuze.com. Retrieved January 3, 2006.

BASIC CONCEPTS AND METHOLOLOGY

> *formula, were we to invent it, would be 'all consciousness is something.'*

The content of what Deleuze is rendering explicit above evokes the structuring background that gives rise to the work of Bergson. But this content is not itself this background. Knowledge of the formula – *all consciousness is something* – does not allow us to reinvent the work of Bergson. The paradigm that actively operates is not of the order of things said. But the fact of saying it, of objectifying it, can, on rereading, help us to better understand Bergson's thought.

As for the first *explicit* distinction, it highlights what Morin (1991)[46] would call the "key category of intelligibility," which we have hitherto referred to as the *core idea*. This category indicates what the reality that we are trying to circumscribe is made of, and which gives meaning to everything that follows. Morin gives as an example Order in deterministic philosophies, Matter in materialistic philosophies, and Spirit in spiritualistic philosophies. This distinction attempts to make explicit the implicit universe which one then seeks to circumscribe, and which basically represents the "totality of the real". Here we see the paradox emerging in the effort to circumscribe the totality of the reality of which we are a part. We will revisit this issue in the next section.

In another order of example, we can even try to name the first implicit and explicit distinctions that characterize the productions of an entire civilization. Morin[47] speaks, for instance, of the Western Paradigm. Whether or not one agrees with his interpretation of the nature of the matrix underlying Western civilization's historical achievements, one accepts that the question makes sense.

Consistency of Discourse and Paradigm

Paradigmatic reality sometimes gives rise to strange phenomena. It happens, for example, that in the development of a thought, the first explicit distinction and all those that follow

---

46. Edgar Morin, *La méthode. T. 4 : Les idées*, Paris, Seuil, 1991.
47. *Ibid.*

do not correspond to the fundamental distinction or cleavage of the implicit field of experience that one seeks to circumscribe and make explicit. The result is a cognitive dissonance that makes reading the work uncomfortable and prevents the paradigm from unfolding in all its strength. There is thus, in this case, a conflict of paradigms, because the modes of expression derive from a paradigm foreign to the one meant to be revealed. It thus becomes necessary to continually correct the discourse to regain its coherence.

The following example that I will use to illustrate this phenomenon of coherence is drawn from a work that, surprisingly enough, Varela himself wrote in collaboration with Evan Thompson and Eleanor Rosch (1993): *The embodied mind.* It is not a question here of discussing the value of the theses exposed in the book, which, one rapidly notices, are essentially the same as those developed by Varela in his other works. Rather, it is about seeing how the patterns used to express ideas are often at odds with what one perceives as the purported purpose of the work. The result is an amalgam that many readers consider to be the most bizarre and puzzling work co-produced by Varela.

The book discusses *human experience.* Curiously, the first distinction, even suggested in the book's title itself, is that of *body* and *mind.* Clearly, the book purports to show that mind and body are not separate entities but rather constitute an integrated whole, in an effort, one might think, to avoid dualism. Yet the result is precisely the opposite: the very Cartesian dualism the book is trying to avoid reappears. Indeed, for the experience of expression to have any meaning, body and mind must be distinguished. The latter distinction, which seems to be given from the outset and which does not result from the differentiation of the unity that one seeks to reveal, will never recover from having tried to indicate this unity which would be a prerequisite for it.

A few examples to see what difficulty this poses. In the book's chapter 2, it is asserted, when discussing the link between body and mind:

> "In fact, body and mind are seldom closely coordinated. [...] the results of mindfulness/awareness practice are to bring one closer to one's ordinary experience...".

Thus, there are two independent, uncoordinated entities that a hypothetical subject, separated from his experience, would have the choice of coordinating through specific practices. But on page 26 of the same book, we are told that "there is no abstract knower of an experience that is separate from the experience itself." In the context of learning a practice, one can easily understand the meaning of these words. Our intention here is simply to show that this dualistic schema does not do justice to the underlying thesis of self-reference.

Other similar examples can be drawn from Varela's book *Ethical know-how*[48] where one finds rather surrealistic formulations. The author speaks of a *selfless self*, (or virtual self) of "a nonsubstantial self that acts as if it were present [...]" Even in this case, it does not seem that its action manages to confer to it the least bit of existence. Varela also refers to *the selfless nature of our selves*. First of all, *our* selves: we see the subject resurface; it is indeed our own selves. This *"we"*, which we have learned to see as non-existent, is equipped with a self without reality that acts, and whose nature is to be itself without *a self.*[49]

The author must constantly correct his affirmations by their negation to avoid the trap of the paradigm that presides over their elaboration. Here we recognize the contours of theories of common sense that are used to convey a thought that is in various respects at the opposite extreme.

Once the foundations of our present approach have been provided, we will draw other examples from the same works to indicate the difference in treatment that the self-reference paradigm would require, particularly concerning the question of foundations.

Making Explicit the Paradigm of Self-Reference as an Element of Methodology

As noted earlier, coherence requires that the paradigm of self-reference underlies the formulation of self-reference as a *core idea*. Noteworthy here is the fact that a paradigm can be objectified as

---

48. Varela F. J. (1999) *Ethical know-how. Action, wisdom, and cognition.* Stanford University Press, Stanford CA.
49. We will come back to this in the Self-Referential Mechanics section as well as in the second chapter.

long as one remains aware that the *paradigm as object* is not really the active paradigm giving rise to the various achievements flowing from it. The wager we are making is to generate a "template", one might say, which would take the contours of the self-referential process and serve as a sort of matrix for the schematization of various fields of human experience. The description of this matrix is the subject of the following section entitled "The self-referential matrix."

We will then ask ourselves what form a specific field of experience, for example that of communication, could take if it were schematized using this self-referential matrix. Developing this latter and other fields of experience will give rise to descriptions that will gain in autonomy, and that will themselves enrich the initial matrix that gave birth to them, in all coherence with the self-referential circle evoked from the beginning. Our way of proceeding will therefore be, as far as possible, a replica of the process we wish to describe.

Here we find this idea of *meta odos (μετα οδος)*, of "superposed path", which will never replace the path of reference, but which will be able to help us, in an ever-renewed effort, to find our way in the self-creating circle of our human identity, both in terms of its theoretical expression and its practical realization.

A Bootstrap Approach

One of the characteristics of the process presented in the previous paragraph is that the initial description of the process that serves as a matrix cannot be used as a set of axioms from which one would sequentially derive all theorems by simple deduction. The break involved in the process of self-reference makes such an approach illusory. History shows that endeavors to proceed in this manner are doomed to failure, as well illustrated from the attempts of Hilbert to the decisive theorems of Gödel at the beginning of the 20th century.

The approach we will thus use is more of a *bootstrap* type.[50] The bootstrap approach was developed in physics in the 1960s

---

50. The term owes its origin to Eric Raspe's book, "The Adventures of Baron Munchausen". It is said that the baron had fallen into a deep hole. At the moment when everything seemed lost, he thought of lifting himself up by pulling his bootstraps. This adventure became the humorous symbol of all that

BASIC CONCEPTS AND METHOLOLOGY

by Geoffrey Chew, professor in the Department of Physics at the University of California at Berkeley. His approach is diametrically opposed to a more classical vision in which one looks for a fundamental particle, a bit like a "fundamental block of matter". "The bootstrapper, asserts Chew, seeks to understand nature not in terms of fundamentals, but self-consistency, believing that all physics flows uniquely from the requirement that components be consistent with one another and with themselves."[51] It is, in fact, the physical version of a self-referential model. Indeed, a bootstrap approach necessarily has some characteristics of a self-referential approach and vice versa. When describing the implicit postulate of any bootstrap philosophy Chew asserts: "Nature is as it is because this is the only possible nature consistent with itself."[52]

While the classical approach starts from the idea of fundamental constituents from which one would try to reconstruct the whole, the bootstrap approach adopts the opposite idea that it is the consistency of the whole as such that represents the fundamental reality. This whole is differentiated into sub-totalities, which themselves have their own consistency. At this global level, as Chew points out, one cannot really speak of a scientific approach. To obtain a perfect bootstrap, it would be necessary to include the totality of reality, which, of course, takes us out of the scientific project.

The scientific part of Chew's model was developed in the field of hadron physics. Unfortunately, this current of thought did not prevail in physics. As explained by physicist Jess Brewer of the University of British Columbia:

> *Chew's models represented a genuinely new paradigm that gained a good deal of purchase on the problem when suddenly the attention of the particle physics community was diverted by a revival of perturbation theory in the form of a quark model, [...]; since then Chew's approach has been sadly neglected, which I suspect is a great*

---

something does, so to speak, by itself and with its own means. The term is used in computer science and physics, as well as in other fields, for example in statistics.

51. Geoffrey Chew, "Hadron Bootstrap : Triumph or Frustration ?" *Physics Today*, octobre, 1970, p. 23.
52. Geoffrey Chew, "« Bootstrap » : A Scientific Idea ? ", *Science*, 1968, vol. 161, p. 762.

loss to physics. Still, if we can get answers more easily by 'recycling an old paradigm,' the outcome is inevitable.[53]

Physics may not be the ideal place to start developing bootstrap models, and the tools built there are unlikely to be suitable for an approach to human reality. The method proposed here, inspired by the bootstrap model, will rather consist in building small, initially approximate islands of coherence from a matrix itself approximate,[54] islands with some internal coherence and but also a certain degree of arbitrariness. Proceeding thus by successive approximations, some of these islands of coherence will be able to give rise more quickly than others to scientific development. On the surface, therefore, these islands, though emerging from the same source, may appear discontinuous.

One may find this way of proceeding disconcerting, given how accustomed one is to horizontal sequential linkages in the development of thought. One may sometimes feel a lack of continuity between various parts of the book and thus lose sight of the link between the thesis initially presented and its application to particular fields of experience. For example, one may wonder how Chapter 3, which deals with the development of the temporal dimension, is connected to Chapter 4, which examines the realm of communication.

One must read the book searching for unity and linkages from a *vertical* rather than horizontal perspective. One will then notice that all topics are treated using the same very few concepts which constitute the components of the basic matrix. This matrix nevertheless takes on particular colors according to the field of experience – communication, time or social functioning – to which it is applied. Instead of ideas being connected in a sequential manner as in a straight line or spiral sequence, they are vertically linked, thus manifesting a bootstrap type

---

53. Jess Brewer, "The Perturbation Paradigm Stumbles", *High Energy Physics*, http://musr.physics.ubc.ca/~jess/p200/hep/node5.html. Retrieved on December 30, 2005.
54. Needless to say, the term "matrix" used here is a simple metaphor whose meaning is borrowed from everyday language and therefore has nothing to do with the mathematical idea of matrix used by G. Chew, in particular the S-Matrix.

BASIC CONCEPTS AND METHOLOLOGY

methodology in which the same matrix is applied to different topics.

The challenge, in short, consists in imagining how a field of experience can, on the basis of the matrix of self-reference, generate itself. This is, of course, a construction of the observer, but one flowing from this intention.

Our hope is that gradually a richer, purer, more encompassing and coherent model will emerge from this set of initially isolated islands.

One will notice that the matrix used for one topic benefits from the enrichment of this same matrix flowing from its use in the previous topic. Furthermore, all these "islands" will have to be integrated into a larger domain forming a continent whose coherence will also have to be discovered and built, which leads us to the following methodological remark.

Gulliver, Fractals and the Holographic Metaphor

Gulliver's Travels introduces us to a character who moves back and forth from an infinitely small universe and to an infinitely large one. This metaphor evokes the situation of the observer who finds himself in the dual position of being, on the one hand, himself made up of an inner society, as Marvin Minsky's work[55] suggests, and therefore having to grapple with the ultra-small units of which he is made, and on the other hand, being a member of an inordinately large unit, society, which he helps to build. We will talk here about levels: the personal level, the societal level, etc.

- *Self-Reference and Levels of Human Reality*

Since self-reference is the invariant of the present approach, each of the levels should be schematized by the same self-referential matrix. We thus find ourselves with a self-referential or potentially self-referential totality, made up of subtotalities which are themselves self-referential or potentially self-referential.

---

55. Marvin Minsky, *The Society of Mind*. New York, Simon & Schuster.

Some might see this as an opposition: the identity of the totality would compete with the identity of the sub-totalities. But this is not so. The levels of the *whole* and the *part* must be relativized to the self-referential invariant. To stimulate the imagination, self-reference could be seen as a single field in which the various levels participate. It follows that the best tool of self-reference of the whole is the self-reference of the parts, and conversely, the best tool of self-reference of the parts is the self-reference of the whole. Any appearance of inter-level conflict is only the projection of conflicts between the parts. From this perspective, the personal level version of self-referentiality and the societal level version will constitute the milestones of a transdisciplinary approach that will not replace the disciplines, but which will make it possible to ask original questions that these disciplines can answer.

Addressing as we do the various levels of human reality – from the individual to the human species – by attributing to them a common founding principle contradicts certain aspects of the modern sociological approach known as *methodological individualism* (Jean-Pierre Dupuy, 1992).[56] In such an approach, it is the individual who is the agent of reference. The individual is the one who, through his actions, creates social phenomena. On the other hand, the latter phenomena, so to speak, escape their authors and operate according to their own laws. The autonomy of the social is thus affirmed, which makes it possible to avoid psychologism. What precedes appears logical, but the problem arises, however, when all responsibility is deemed to be that of individuals, thus emptying the social of its substance.

The perspective proposed here leads us to dissociate ourselves from this position, without, of course, prejudging of its value. When viewed through the postulates of the present approach, methodological individualism seems to be subject to the effects of an idiocentric[57] perspective, one that, in our opinion, is unwarranted. We will resume the discussion on this crucial point in the section "Guidelines for a generalization."

---

56. Jean-Pierre Dupuy, *Introduction aux sciences sociales*, Paris, Édition Marketing, 1992.
57. In the broadest sense of centering on the individual level.

Suffice it say, for the time being, that in our approach, no one human level is granted a privileged status. Every autonomous or potentially autonomous human totality in the full sense of the word is faced with the challenge of the integral self-referential process. This challenge is not just that of humans as individual entities, but also as social entities and even as an entire species.

As we shall see, our model is not of the "Russian doll" type in which units would be complete in themselves at all levels without including, as an integral part, units of lower levels. Such a model would be solipsistic. Indeed, the Russian doll of a given level is enclosed in the doll of the upper level but is not an integral part of it. Each doll is complete in itself. The hierarchy of human levels referred to in our approach is not at all of this type. Units of a given level are the constituents of the higher level while generating at that level a specific behavior that is not reducible to the lower levels. See "Construction and Hierarchy" in the next chapter.

From the strict perspective of epistemological empiricism, our approach could, of course, be questionable, given that when one observes humans at the level of society and that of a species, one does not find an accomplished self-referential process. Indeed, the human species does not constitute in itself a unit from which one could identify, at this stage of its evolution, the recursive processes that would make it an operationally closed entity. Yet from a constructivist perspective and insofar as these levels are called to manifest self-reference, one can search for an isomorphy between these levels, in the double sense of detecting signs thereof, but above all of making it real. This last aspect will be developed theoretically in the second chapter, more specifically in the paragraph entitled "Self-reference and construction."

- *Fractals*

The structure of a process, here self-reference, which manifests itself integrally at various levels, evokes the notion of fractals that we find in chaos theory. We speak of a fractal if a whole, at a given level, has a structure that we find in the elements that make up this structure, and in the same way, in the sub-elements that make up these elements, etc. (figure 1)

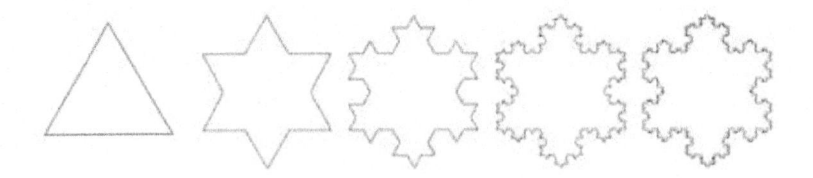

Figure 1. Koch snowflake.

We use fractal here as a metaphor, not as a mathematical object to describe such realities. More precisely, it will serve the following methodological purpose: to illustrate our postulate that globally there exists an isomorphism between the manifestations of self-reference at all levels. The chapter on time gives rise to a development that clearly manifests this principle.

An observer looking at the same process, but at a higher level of organization, will be able to see certain elements more clearly, as if he or she were looking at these elements under a microscope. Observing the same process in a broader universe has, so to speak, a magnifying effect that will allow one to check whether such elements could be significant at lower levels. On the other hand, some of the better-controlled realizations at lower levels may inspire possible constructions at higher levels.

In all probability, it will be realized that some relevant, visible, or even essential elements at a higher level are neither visible nor relevant at lower levels. This is why one will be wary of a form of reductionism consisting in restrictively projecting descriptions adapted to lower levels – at the biological level, for example – onto realities of higher levels, something our method allows one to avoid. In short, even if it is basically the same self-referential process, it will be seen from different perspectives, each perspective revealing aspects that are invisible from other perspectives.

- *The Holographic Paradigm*

This leads us to the holographic metaphor. Holography consists in taking a photo of an object without a lens, so that the light reflected by each point of the object is printed everywhere on the photographic plate. The result is an interference pattern in which the object cannot be distinguished. But if the image is restored from the plate by a suitable process, the virtual object is reproduced in three dimensions.

From the above experience, one usually retains the following characteristic: if one restores the object using only part of the plate, one finds the whole object, regardless of the part of the plate used. Here, though, we will only retain a complementary aspect, namely that any restoration of the image which uses only a part of the plate gives only limited and more blurred angles on the object. To restore the object from all angles and with full precision, one needs the whole plate.

Let's take a simple example. You take the holographic photo of a microscope so that you can see not only the microscope as an object but also what you can see in the microscope, for example, a bacteria magnified X times. The restoration of the three-dimensional image will show us a virtual three-dimensional microscope which we can approach to observe the bacteria, which will then be visible as in the real microscope. If, on the other hand, we restore the image from one of the corners of the plate furthest from the center, we will indeed see the whole microscope, but it will be impossible to see the bacteria in the microscope. In short, even if each part of the plate makes it possible to restore the whole object, none of the parts restores the object from all angles and with all the precision obtained when using the whole plate.

This is analogously the case with the present approach. All the partial observations of human reality will always provide a picture of the whole self-referential process, but none of the particular descriptions will be able to give all aspects of the process, and with all the expected precision. Thus, all the islands of coherence will be approximations that will have to be enriched and coordinated to gradually provide a more complete image of the matrix, which corresponds, in our analogy, to the totality of the photographic plate.

Philosophy, Scientific Program, or Theory?

The question that F. Capra[58] asked in an interview he was conducting with physicist Chew is entirely relevant to our subject:

> *Now, what would you say about the nature of the bootstrap idea? Is it a scientific hypothesis which has perhaps now turned into a theory? Is it a philosophy? How would you characterize it?*

Chew's response is interesting:

> *Well, it is certainly a philosophy, and I think operationally it has turned into a scientific program. I suppose this science program has now enough substance to call it a theory. It's very hard to say when you make those transitions from one category to another.*

This answer applies *mutatis mutandis* to the present approach. The intention is certainly to provide sufficient research avenues to offer an outline of a scientific and pragmatic program for human development. More locally, one may see in it elements whose greater rigor heralds the development of a theory in the strict sense. Here again, several questions arise: what kind of theory will it be? In the social sciences and humanities, there are all sorts of montages that present themselves as theories and which some of the loosest criteria would forbid us from classifying in this category. For convenience, I propose a minimal provisional classification of theories, the sole intention of which is to situate the level of rigor that is aimed at in the theoretical developments that can be found in this book, or that one would hope to eventually attain in its less developed sections.

Let's start with the theory's level zero: experiencing. There is nothing theoretical about one's here and now experiencing. It can, of course, be theorized, but it is not experienced as theory in the here and now. From it emerge patterns, as in language, for example, which spontaneously manifest certain fundamental mechanisms of our reality. But using language, even in its most primitive conception, is not in any way theorizing.

---

58. Fritjof Capra, "Bootstrap Physics : a Conversation with Geoffrey Chew", in Carleton DeTar, J. Finkelstein, Chung-I Tan (eds.), *A Passion for Physics. Essays in Honor of Geoffrey Chew*, Singapore, World scientific publishing, 1985, p. 249.

Basic Concepts and Metholology

The first level of theory is that of *common sense*. Not, however, according to the specific meaning given to this expression by Hannah Arendt (1972, p. 283), for example, or other philosophical currents. But rather in the meaning it has for people in simple everyday life. In other words, common sense here refers to the popular wisdom – of a community, a society, a civilization, an epoch – which seeks to give simple cognitive support to complex experiences that cannot be rigorously accounted for. The existence of the support is more important here than the rigor of its content.

An example to illustrate: common sense may determine that certain things always happen in a particular way. When something happens that does not fit this pattern, one will then say: "The exception confirms the rule!" However, from a strictly logical perspective, an exception in no way confirms a rule but rather clearly invalidates it. But then the whole theory expressed in common sense would have to be revised, which would be very complicated. So one prefers to settle the issue by saying that the rule is confirmed by that very thing that contradicts it! Consistency is not the prerogative of common sense. Obviously, a more coherent interpretation of this aphorism can be found by considering that the exception confirms the existence of the rule and its application in all other cases.

The second level of theory is what I would describe as *empirical-intuitive*. The first part of the term refers to elements of observation involving intelligence. The second part refers to functions relating more to perception than to specifically intellectual processes. We know that perception and intelligence are two complementary but distinct functions. Perception is global, immediate, syncretic, and lacks the rigor of intellectual processes, in the field in particular of objective verification. Intelligence, on the contrary, gives rise to reasoning more accessible to criticism, to the evaluation of coherence, to the objective verification of facts. I will call intuition the mode of thinking based on perception.[59]

---

59. Perception tends to produce certainties that give rise to beliefs, often perceived as self-evident, that are not likely to be questioned. Intelligence, on the other hand, generates questions and gives rise to uncertainty and hypotheses whose truth or falsity will have to be verified. For example, let us ask a car driver how he perceives, in his rear-view mirror, the movement of a car that is passing him.

In these theories, halfway between intelligence and perception, which I qualify as *empirical-intuitive*, everything happens as if the principles of construction of the descriptive or explanatory schema were not sufficiently autonomous to develop and make themselves explicit according to their own coherence, freeing themselves from observation and perception. The descriptive or explanatory schema does not have the autonomy found, for example, in the models of the physical sciences. In physics, in particular, it is the theory that decides what is to be observed. Neutrinos have not been discovered by mere observation. They were theoretical necessities before being facts of observation. The theoretical model provides sufficient precision to allow observations to be made, which empirically confirm the discovery initially made on the strictly formal plane. This is not the case with the vast majority of theories in the humanities and social sciences, which are more of the *empirical-intuitive* type. We shall give an example of this in the third chapter with the theory of Erikson.

The third level of theory I would describe as *pre-formal*. Theories of this level develop in the same way as *empirical-intuitive* theories do. As the latter, they are based on observation and appeal to intuition. However, they go one step further in their development. They free themselves from their point of origin to develop from an internal coherence. The principle of construction acquires sufficient autonomy to allow the theory to determine what one will be entitled to observe. However, all this is expressed through ordinary language and not through any kind of formalism. It is this third level which is referred to in the more specifically theoretical parts of the present book or in the later developments where the self-reference matrix is applied to various aspects of human reality, something as yet barely elaborated.

More precisely, let us ask him in which direction he sees the car moving and on which side he sees the driver of that car. He will spontaneously answer that the car is coming in the same direction as he is and that its driver is on the right side. An intellectual evaluation will start from the known principles of mirrors and will make the hypothesis that the passing car, as seen in the mirror, is moving in the opposite direction and that its driver is on the wrong side. Perceptual verification in a real-life situation will reinforce the evidence on which the first belief is based. Intellectual verification, however, will confirm the second belief.

Finally, *formal* level theories have the same characteristics as those of the previous level, but they are expressed through a logico-mathematical formalism. Pre-formal theories should tend to express themselves so that they can eventually be formalized.

It should be recalled, however, that at this stage the present exercise as a whole represents more of a heuristic arrangement than an attempt to establish once and for all a general transdisciplinary theory. From this perspective, one should not be surprised to note the predominance given in this book to a special kind of reasoning, abduction, whose meaning is explained below.

Abductive Reasoning

The reasoning we are most familiar with is deduction and induction. In deduction, if we hold *a* to be true and also hold true the fact that *a* implies *b*, then *b* is also true. In induction, we look for a general law based on the observation of particular facts: each time we observe *a*, we also observe *b*. We conclude that *a* implies *b*, until we observe a case where that is not true.

Abduction, a term "coined by Charles Sanders Peirce in his work on the logic of science,"[60] represents a very different type of reasoning. In what follows, I will illustrate its meaning using an example taken from this book.

Let us suppose that someone finds himself in a situation that triggers both astonishment and questioning. Someone like N. Luhmann (1990) who was deeply puzzled by the fact that communication, though improbable, was nevertheless a fact of observation. Or P. Valéry,[61] who considered that communication was "the strangest of problems" and that "everything happens as if it were impossible." Moreover, attempting to solve such a mysterious yet observable phenomenon by using a self-referential framework, as we do in chapter 4, obviously does little to eliminate the sense of bewilderment and strangeness.

Let's call C this strange fact of observation *communication*. Chapter 4 develops a self-referential model of communication

---

60. *Peirce on Abduction*, Stanford Encyclopedia of Philosophy. Retrieved May 21, 2020.
61. Quoted by Jean-Louis Le Moigne on page 217 of his book *Le constructivisme. Tome 2. Épistémologie de l'interdisciplinarité*, published by L'Harmattan in 2002.

that we will call "Model A." If A is an adequate model, C (communication) should be taken for granted and stop appearing as a curious phenomenon. It is the absence of communication that would then become strange and inexplicable.

If Chapter 4 manages to illustrate that this is indeed what happens, it is because Model A presents the C phenomenon more consistently, and it no longer appears to be an oddity. And if this is so, it would make sense to take this model seriously and to search for ways of making it more explicit, of going about developing and testing it. Such is the process known as abduction or abductive reasoning, a process that will be used throughout the book, notably in chapter 3 concerning the temporality of the self-referential process.

Let us now return to the strategy described above, whereby a template with the contours of the self-referential process is produced as a tool for mapping various fields of human experience. Explaining such a tool, called "self-referential matrix," is the subject of the following section.

The Self-Referential Matrix

The famous statement of Epimenides the Cretan reminds us that self-reference has haunted people ever since the time of the Greeks. Historically, two trends have emerged: one which aims to dismiss self-reference as an undesirable actor in the field of thought because of the paradoxes it triggers; the other which gives prominence to self-reference and takes it as a paradigm.

As mentioned earlier, N. Whitehead and B. Russell, with the Theory of Types, are the most illustrious representatives of the first of these tendencies in contemporary thought. One might think that the second trend is new and that it derives primarily from the epistemology of science, but it also has its history in philosophy. It is worth mentioning in passing the reflections of a German philosopher who, at the turn of the 19th century, attempted to describe self-reference: Johann Gottlieb Fichte.

The Attempt of J. G. Fichte

Fichte's ambition was to construct a general epistemology (which he then referred to as theory or doctrine of science) that would constitute a perfectly encompassing system, revealing the

BASIC CONCEPTS AND METHOLOLOGY

ultimate structure of all knowledge. As Isabelle Thomas-Fogiel[62] points out, someone objected to Fichte, arguing that his endeavor represented "an exorbitant pretension, a senseless quest for an ultimate and primary foundation that is forever unattainable by the incredibly finite beings that we are." Fichte reacted by referring the objector, who claimed to be telling the truth, to the truth of his own assertion. Either you show me how you can demonstrate the truth of that assertion, Fichte retorted, or you simply remain silent! In so doing, the latter was inviting his objector to make the theory of his own assertion, thus embarking into epistemology, what he then called, as noted above, the theory of science.

Fichte accused Kant of not making the theory of his own assertions, which, in his view, made him "dogmatic" and invalidated the content of his assertions. For Fichte, one must be able to answer the question of "how" one arrives at objectively valid representations. A philosopher, he insisted, should always be able to clearly set forth the methods he uses to make any statement.

Only using this method could the Kantian categories lose their *a priori* status, indecomposable data that are given, inaccessible, and that one would simply attempt to relate to experience. The question then becomes: "what is the operation that presides over their development?" The validity of a notion no longer depends on the fact that one can have an intuition of it, but rather on one's understanding of its genesis.[63] It is this same point of view that Piaget would take up again a century and a half later, using means other than abstract and discursive thought alone. His genetic epistemology would then reveal to scientific observation the construction of such categories.

Fichte is thus engaged in a self-referential process which he claims to be able to complete. It is probably because of what P. Heath and J. Lachs[64] call "his heavy and unnecessarily complex style" and also because sometimes "his theoretical syntheses

---

62. Isabelle Thomas-Fogiel, « Les principales caractéristiques de la doctrine de la science » in Johann G. Fichte, *Doctrine de la science nova methodo*, Paris, Librairie Générale Française, 2000, p. 8.
63. *Ibid.* p. 14, 16, 20
64. Peter Heath, John Lachs, "Preface" in Johann G. Fichte, *The Science of Knowledge*, Cambridge University Press, 1982, p. vii.

appear to be ... obscure linguistic sleight of hand" that Fichte felt he had achieved his goal. That said, the latter's endeavor remains fascinating as it obliges the author to trace the contours of the self-referential process. That is undoubtedly what brings D. Julia to say that "one cannot understand this work, in the philosophical truth that it contains, from something other than itself."[65]

Even if we accept with some reservations this other statement of Julia according to which "the abstract character of the W. L. [the doctrine of science] is indeed that of the great discoveries which have not yet found particular historical resonance in human consciousness ", it is quite appropriate to make a brief reference to it. Of course, we will have to, later, take care to express in a more current language Fichte's abstract mode of thought, which remains dependent on a purely idealistic approach.

Fichte is directly confronted with the paradox of a self that poses itself as existing. In the 1794 version of his theory of science (Fichte, 1982, p. 97), he refers to the self with the following words:

"It is at once the agent and the product of action."

To illustrate the above paradox, we can draw inspiration from the summary given to this phenomenon by W. Rasch[66] when discussing the same work (Fichte 1982, pp. 106–108). How can the self refer to itself without making of itself something other than itself, asks Rasch, something that can be referred to, as if it were not this thing itself that operates the reference? For pure consciousness to be conscious of itself, it must be conscious of itself as other; it must split itself in two, he pursues. It must posit itself both as a self-positing subject and as an object posited or reflected upon. Thus, the self-positing of the self must also posit its own negation, the not-self (Rasch, 2002, p. 4).

Fichte plays with these two contradictory poles linked to each other in an organic way as in all paradoxes: if one of the poles is

---

65. Didier Julia, « Préface du traducteur » in Johann G. Fichte, *La théorie de la science. Exposé de 1804*, Paris, Aubier Montaigne, 1999, p. 13.
66. William Rash, "Introduction," in Niklas Luhmann, *Theories of Distinction. Redescribing the Descriptions of Modernity*, Stanford University Press, 2002, p. 4–7.

true, it necessarily implies that its opposite is true, and vice versa, as in the paradox of the Cretan who asserts that all Cretans only tell lies: if what he says is true, then of necessity it is false; and if what he says is false, then of necessity it is true.

How does one pole not cancel out the other? Fichte solves the question by affirming that the two poles do not really cancel each other out, but only "limit each other." (*Ibid.* p. 108). There thus appears a finite space shared by the parts of a divided self.

But another problem arises from this situation: this relative self which is limited by the not-self is no longer the original self from which this operation arises. This original self, absolute, must remain as the foundation of the unity and the difference of the self and the not-self.

> "*The absolute self is not something (it has and can have no predicate); it is what it is [...] it is posited as indivisible whereas the self to which the not-self is opposed is posited as divisible. Hence, insofar as there is a not-self opposed to it, the self is itself in opposition to the absolute self. [...] I would wish to express the outcome in the following formula: In the self, I oppose a divisible not-self to the divisible self* "(Fichte 1982, pp. 109–110).

The self-referential position of the self thus brings into play two distinctions that operate simultaneously: one severing self and not-self in a space of mutual determination, and the other, implicit, separating the absolute self from this limited space of the empirical self and its indispensable partner, the not-self (Rasch, 2002, p. 6).

Self-Reference and the Advent of Totality

Our present endeavor does not have the same claim as that of Fichte for whom "everything that is to emerge hereafter in the system of the human mind must be derivable from what we have established here" (*Ibid.* p. 110). It will reduce to more modest proportions the absolute character of both concepts and ambitions. Yet it is noteworthy that one will constantly find Fichte's structure of the self-referential circle in our description of every living totality.

So, rather than talking about the absolute self, we are going to discuss any complex *totality* that constitutes a unity: be it a cell, an organism, a person, a society, or even for that matter the entire universe! It is at this last level that Spencer Brown (1969), the author of the highly acclaimed *Laws of Form*, places the discussion in his note to Chapter 12, reported again quite pertinently by Rash (2002, pp. 8–10) and summarized here.

As Spencer Brown points out, "we may take it that the world undoubtedly is itself." The observation we make of it is a phenomenon that emerges from that same universe and is therefore included in it. It is, in a way, the universe that observes itself through our activities and our observation tools. In doing so, the universe makes a distinction between the observer which is "itself" and the object of observation which is "other." It alienates itself so to speak, being distinct from itself. It sees itself only partially. Thus, the observation cannot but be incomplete, for it does not include from the outset the observer whose description should be part of this universe. A new observation that includes the previous one suffers the same evil, and so on in a regression to infinity. The universe is enriched each time and each of its "expansions" always precedes the observation or description that can be made of it.

But Spencer Brown's assertion *that any description or observation of the world is partial* itself appears as a non-partial, or total observation. It is paradoxical, because in order to make sense, it implies that there is a totality that differentiates itself in such a way as to generate observations that will only be partial. Something partial can only express itself in relation to something that is total. Thus, the affirmation encompasses everything, the initial state, and the split state, and, by the same token, it refutes itself. Yet the initial state of the undifferentiated totality remains an inconceivable and inaccessible horizon, and any attempt to recover it or to see it in its original unity pushes this horizon back even further. One seems therefore condemned to limit oneself to creating forms in a world already formed, to creating distinctions in a world already divided.

This bias leads us to Luhmann's view that society can only be described from the inside and, therefore, only partially observed. This condition is one of the inescapable "facts" of society. Thus, Luhmann does not aspire to a vision of the "whole," nor does he deplore its absence.

Again, the observation that society can only be seen from within, and only partially, is itself *a fully total observation about the impossibility of making a total observation.* One is thus plunged into the same paradox, but a paradox not seen as a path leading to a dead end, but rather as the point of origin of all paths.

The theory must, therefore, take into account this paradox and the limits it highlights, not to get out of it, but to include it as one of the constituent elements of the universe described by the theory. Thus, for Luhmann, the original totality is evacuated in favor of the operations of its differentiated subsystems, and each of these subsystems seeks to negotiate its existence with all the others, which then constitute its environment. It is interesting to note that Luhmann's reference work on society published in 1995 is entitled: *Social Systems*. It is, therefore, about social *systems* and not about *the* social system.

From what has just been said, we must distinguish two elements: first, the fundamental problem flowing from a situation of self-referentiality with its resulting paradoxes, and secondly, the stance to be taken in the face of such a situation. The problematic, in a word, is that of differentiated subsets of a totality that can only partially access this "totality," which leads to the conclusion that any approach to this totality of which one is a part can only be partial. As for strategies, the position of the authors discussed consists in saying, let's make do with the situation. Let's forget this inaccessible totality and limit our approach to what happens inside, in the interaction of the subsets of this totality of which we are part.

Thus, though the title of this section announced the advent of totality, we now find ourselves, strangely enough, with authors who, as seen above, try by all means to evacuate totality, regardless of the level of totality being considered. A paradigm supposedly allowing us, in our approach, to move towards the inclusion of totality brings us instead back to the starting point.

We find this same reflex in discussions involving the totality that constitutes a person. Such is the reflex, for example, of Varela, who, as we have seen, put a lot of energy convincing us that there is no longer anyone, that any impression of identity linked to the fact of being oneself is just an illusion. A point of view which, we argued, is inconsistent with Varela's main theses.

In short, the strategies just examined only partially develop this new paradigm, fundamentally dedicated to the restoration of totality. If, on the other hand, we claim to be able to take up the challenge, one should not expect that we will manage to avoid dealing with paradox. On the contrary, we will plunge ever deeper into it. Undoubtedly a riskier endeavor, but perhaps also a more coherent one.

The present approach attempts to see what would happen if the response to the problem consisted in simply following its contours, and this without eliminating any of its parts, and then attempting to draw all the resulting consequences.

The above-mentioned authors attempt to base the self-reference approach on a total observation. They assert that any observation cannot but be partial. In our opinion, such a way of proceeding does not constitute a masterpiece of coherence! It appears more like a voluntarist decision taken by someone feeling powerless in the face of an insoluble problem. As already pointed out, totality is present, like it or not, even in this strategy.

It is interesting to note that historically, in the face of this type of impasse, the greatest breakthroughs have come from an attitude of letting go, an attitude that led one to a literal acceptance of the data of the situation. Let us recall again the most famous example, that of Einstein, when he did something truly scandalous in the light of previous theories: he interpreted the results of Michelson-Morley's observations literally by making the speed of light a constant, which then led to the relativization of mass and time.

Should one not, regarding the issue being considered, simply take into account this inescapable fact of the presence of totality to build, around the affirmation of this totality, the total observation that will form the basis of subsequent developments? That total observation has *totality* at its center resonates quite well with the idea of self-reference. But the paradox emerges as a monster, because, as we have seen, totality in the context of self-reference is inaccessible as such to the subsets of this totality, it is a *non-object* for these subsets. In a self-referential context, total observation will thus consist in placing at the heart of the approach this unobservable, this *non-object*, which one will have to acknowledge instead of seeking to ignore it. This "ghost" will preside over the second stage of the paradox, which will force us to conclude that any observation, in this context, is partial, because the non-object is unobservable.

BASIC CONCEPTS AND METHOLOLOGY

Though always the same paradox, it has now been put back on its feet, with totality at its center. The challenge is to draw all the consequences flowing from this choice.

One might think that we are moving towards a form of transcendentalism that presents as inaccessible the origin of everything we can conceive. We will discuss this problem in Chapter 2. Let us reassure ourselves, for the moment, by affirming that totality is completely accessible as an object to an outside observer. Totalities at all levels, whether of the individual, the group, or society, are observable realities.

So, we have not left, after all, the planet earth for a transcendental world. What we have done, instead, is assert that the viewpoint of an external observer always represents a second, so to speak subordinate viewpoint, and one that, though useful, actually veils the richness of an internal approach, however strewn with paradoxical pitfalls the latter may be.

Nevertheless, here we are once again confronted with the *non-object*, the "void", which is at the heart of what constitutes the essence of our approach. Such a void may trigger reticence in us, one evoking those historically triggered when the zero was introduced in mathematics.

Mathematical thought developed from the need to count. Yet counting the observable, as we all know, does not require the zero.[67] It is not very useful indeed to take into account zero sheep. It never occurred to anyone to invent a number to represent the absence of an object. Even after learning about the Babylonian system that contained the zero, the Greeks were reluctant to use it. The zero was linked to the idea of void, to nothing, which caused fear and anxiety. It threatened systems of thought with its bizarre behavior. The zero ignores the known properties of number operations, it changes nothing when added to itself or to other numbers, and it manages to undermine the simplest calculations, such as multiplication and division.

The zero was finally welcomed in India. Indian civilization had never been afraid of infinity or emptiness, which held – and still holds – an important place in all oriental thought. It is this

---

67. Charles Seife. *Zero: The Biography of a Dangerous Idea..* New York, London: Penguin, 2000.

same emptiness or void that we find, but following other paths, at the heart of the paradigm of self-reference. These reflections lead us to make explicit the founding statements of the present approach.

Some Founding Statements

The following statements form the basis of this approach. The first is as follows:

1. **The emergence of a living unity brings into play two distinctions: the first, founding one, by which this unity relates to itself, thus posing itself in existence as an autonomous unity, and the second, by way of consequence, which distinguishes this unity from its environment.**

We thus have, from the start, the outline of the distinction at the basis of Spencer Brown's calculation. But there's more. It is by first distinguishing itself from itself that a unity arises and maintains itself in existence. The expression "distinguishes itself from itself," calls for an explanation. From the outset, this operation of distinction has two components that unfold simultaneously, on the one hand, making a totality pass from an undifferentiated (undistinguished) state to a differentiated state, thereby posing, in this second state, a sub-totality as an operator that is distinguished from the complementary sub-totality that becomes the operand. This scheme echoes that of Fichte.

Simplifying, we could say that within a totality, a sub-totality differentiates itself as an operator from the rest, which becomes the operand. We thus have a distinction between the undifferentiated state of the totality and the differentiated state, which manifests itself in the distinction of two subsets, the operator and the operand.

But for this totality to be maintained as a unity, the operations in the differentiated state must bring the totality back to a new state of integration, a state from which a new differentiation can be made, in a cycle that is always restarted. It is this self-generating loop that will be explored, and which constitutes what is called here *the first distinction*.

Yet by appropriating the processes of its own existence in this way, such a unity, by the very fact, operates a second distinction, which distinguishes it from its environment. Indeed, the environment loses its primacy in the operations of this unity. It is, therefore, impossible to make the first distinction without at the same time making the second. Conversely, the second cannot take place without the advent of the first. Thus, it is important never to consider as separate the processes that derive from each of these distinctions, which does not prevent these processes from being considered fundamentally distinct. The latter processes will thus constantly interact and enrich each other.

For the moment, let us insist on the importance, in the present approach, of giving primacy to the internal relationship (first distinction) over the external relationship (second distinction). This primacy is not temporal but rather existential, in the sense that internal operations are oriented primarily towards maintaining the identity of the unity in question.

2. The first distinction will be called *existential*; the second will be called *adaptive* (in the Piagetian sense).

The first distinction is called *existential* since it is at the origin of the very existence of the self-referent unity. The second is said to be *adaptive* because it is at the origin of the relationship of this unity with its environment. The unity must indeed find an equilibrium with its environment to maintain its ability to maintain itself in existence.

3. Existential and adaptive relationships both have an implicit and explicit dimension.

The initial undifferentiated state of the totality is inaccessible to this totality and its subsets and thus remains implicit. As we have already mentioned, the transcendence of the totality relative to its constituent parts does not originate from the fact that the totality is part of a transcendental world, but simply from the fact that the part which accesses must distinguish itself from that to which it accesses, which gives rise to the differentiated state where the totality is split into two complementary unities that interact with each other, thus opening the universe of the *explicit*.

Similarly, the adaptive relationship is rooted in the *implicit*, for it is the disturbances coming from the environment that activate this adaptive process, which in this case brings out *the [explicit] world of objects*, emerging from the relationship of the unity in question with its environment, which is then posed as distinct.

4. **The existential relationship is the basis of the communication process. The adaptive relationship is the basis of cognitive processes.**

We have seen that the existential relationship and the adaptive relationship are two inseparable sides of the same process of life. They are nevertheless distinct. This is the case with communication processes and cognitive processes. Communication is full of cognitive processes, and the latter would be inconceivable outside of a context of communication. Despite this, they are presented here as distinct processes. Communicational processes are rooted in the *first distinction*, the cognitive processes in the *second*, these two distinctions being always concomitant.

In the chapter on communication, we will explain the amazing reversal of perspective implied in the present approach. People normally see communication as the relationship that one unity establishes with another unity that is external to it, as opposed to a strictly internal relationship. The vision developed here reverses things. It argues that it is precisely the development of this internal, existential, relationship that constitutes the very substance of communication. This relationship of the unity with itself gives rise to an interaction of the sub-unities which compose it. At this level of the sub-unities, we find, therefore, the explicit, interactional aspect of communication to which we are used to. But communication primarily encompasses the implicit part of the process.

What exactly goes on, for example, when two persons are communicating? According to our analysis, these two persons represent sub-unities of the dyad they form, and communication is the process by which this unity, the dyad, attempts to develop and maintain its identity and which tends, like all human entities, to become self-referent. Communication is, therefore, in this case, a process peculiar to the dyad, and the interaction of the two individuals is but the engine room of the self-referential relationship through which this dyad comes into existence. Communication is thus the very fabric of the self-generating loop of a unity, whatever the level of this unity. Chapter 4 will be entirely devoted to this statement.

As for cognitive processes, they derive, inversely from the relationship of the unity with the outside, with *what is not it*. Piaget has shown that cognitive processes are processes of adaptation to the environment that lead to the creation, in the subject, of increasingly complex structures of action.

Communication relationships are thus internal relationships within a unity and constitute the fabric of the existential process of that unity. Cognitive relationships, however, are external relationships of this same unity with its environment and constitute the fabric of its adaptive processes.

Although these issues are discussed further in Chapter 4, it is important to clarify one thing at this point. Given that the two individuals in the previous example are external to each other, even though they are parts of the self-referential loop of the dyad, are they not then of necessity involved in a cognitive relationship? The answer is that there will always be a cognitive dimension to any communication. As more generally mentioned in statements 1 and 2, any existential relationship always carries with it its adaptive double, which does not prevent the two relationships from being radically distinct.

One of the two individuals referred to above in the example may decide not to actualize the communicational potential of the situation. Instead, he may content himself with taking the other individual as a simple object of study, view him as something external and just as far removed from him as the moon or the stars. Such an attitude would obviously disturb the communication initiated by the simple presence of the two actors, given that for communication to happen, it must be mutually agreed upon. One may be satisfied to simply carry out an observation on someone unbeknownst to him or her; but that would not be communication!

Beyond this particular example and in a more general way, we will see that communicational relationships contribute to enriching cognitive structures and conversely, that cognitive adaptation can foster communication. This leads us to the next statement.

5. **Considered in itself, the existential relationship is cognitively empty. Considered in itself, the adaptive relationship is foreign to the communication process.**

What I am, I don't know.
What I know, I am not.

Angelus Silesius

In its very foundation, communication, defined as an existential relationship (or if you like, as the first distinction), is inaccessible to cognition. This is what makes Angelus Silesius say, "What I am, I don't know." This "cognitive void" is not existentially empty because it is the source of all the recursive processes which pose and maintain the living into existence, and which constitute the fabric of the communication process.

Conversely, the adaptive relationship, which gives rise to cognition and thus to the emergence of the object, does not bring us back to the existential relationship, because the adaptive relationship is in a way centrifugal, being oriented towards the external relationship, towards what is not self, which makes Angelus Silesius say: "What I know, I am not". From this point of view, contrary to that of Piaget, the internal structures that are built in the person in the course of his construction of the world are not the structures that define the person in his being, but rather only in his adaptive relationship. In other words, the structures of intelligence are distinct from the structures of the person.

6. **Totality, as such, is not in the realm of action. Action is characteristic of the sub-sets resulting from distinctions.**

The totality, as such, does not act. It is through the differentiation of active sub-sets that the totality can access the realm of action. The explicit dimension of communication is only the tip of the iceberg of a more complex, implicit process that takes root and is resolved in the totality.

This point of view differs from that of Morin, for whom the totality acts on the parts. Let us take as an example the following statement:

> *Thus, the phenomenal whole can remain on the surface, ignoring the organization and the parts, although it can control them globally and retroact on their actions or movements. (Ibid. p. 183).*

In such a statement, the whole is considered to be an agent on the same level as the parts: it can control them, act on them, or ignore them, etc. If we refer to our direct experience through the prism of a common-sense theory, we can easily adhere to this statement. For example, "I can, as a person, stay on the surface, ignore the parts I am made of, or act on them…"

However, this way of seeing things overlooks the fact, previously noted in our analysis, that if I act on myself, it can only be through the differentiation of an agent (which is a part of me) that exerts this action on another part. The totality as such cannot act on itself or one of its parts without the necessary coming forth (differentiation) of a part that exerts the action. This is, moreover, an aspect of the paradox of self-reference by which a living unity maintains itself in existence autonomously. We will often revisit this important point.

Such are, therefore, the statements at the heart of our approach and whose meaning and implications will be explained throughout the book.

At this point, we will attempt to get inside the self-referential circle, examine its essential junctions, and set forth its general expression. This birds-eye-view of the workings of the self-referential process will lay the basis for future developments, both theoretical and practical.

Note on the Term "Self-Reference"

Let's analyze the term itself: self-reference. First of all, the prefix *self*, when preceding a term involving action, means that the latter's object is the very subject from which the action originates. *Community self-development* indicates that the community is both the origin and the object of this development operation. It develops itself. In *self-criticism*, the person who is the object of criticism is precisely the one making the criticism.

One criticizes oneself. In short, in any *self-operation*, actor and acted upon constitute the same unity: a person, a group...

As for the term *reference*, we will see that it has a double meaning. A first meaning of referent: that to which one refers, the indication of a referent. In Saussurian linguistics, the *referent* is the object I am talking about, the object of my discourse: "My worktable is functional." The referent, the object I'm talking about, is my table. If we go beyond linguistics and generalize to actions other than discourse, we can say that the referent of a given action is the object to which that action relates. If I move a table, the referent of this action of displacement is the table. If I create a table, the referent of my creation is the table. If I create myself, then the referent becomes me, the object of my own creation. I am then *self-referent*. In this sense, then, it is a self-referential activity of creation: it is *me* who is the object of my creation. In this first sense, then, the reference refers *to what my action is about*, in other words, the *object of my action*.

A second meaning reinforces the first one: reference can mean the benchmark or standard used to carry out an operation. Should I create myself, for example, referring to mere external instructions that I have not assimilated and made mine, then I am alienating myself; my self-creation distances me from myself and will have destructive effects. Instead of such exterior criteria, I should use my own identity – who I really am – as the benchmark of my self-creation. So, to the primary meaning of reference mentioned above, *the object of my action*, is added another one, *that on which I must base my action*. Applied to an operation of creation, self-reference is, therefore, the creation of oneself, *in reference* to oneself.

It should be noted that this is a reinterpretation of the two principles of humanistic psychology mentioned in the introduction: the *actualizing tendency* and the *organismic valuing process*.[68] Actualizing one's potential means developing oneself in such a way as to become what one is called to be. I am thus the object of my own action. I am my own *referent*. But what I do must be *evaluated* according to internal criteria reflecting who I really am, in my actualizing process. My own identity is my

---

68. See notes 12 and 13.

reference. Here we have the basic ingredients of self-creation, in other words, of self-reference in the making.

One may then wonder what the term self-reference adds to those of humanistic psychology. As mentioned earlier, the advantage of the notion of self-reference is that it corresponds to a process that has its own coherence and can be developed autonomously, both on a purely cognitive [69] and pragmatic level. Moreover, as noted in the fifth founding statement of our approach, the existential relation to the "totality that I am" is for me cognitively empty, inaccessible as an object. It is the blind fixed point of the totality.

In Rogers' analysis, one does not detect this "original lack" or cognitive emptiness, an omission which led humanist psychology, especially in its early days, to consider the person as spontaneously having all that is necessary to acquire total mastery of what he or she is, the need for accompaniment by others being limited to eliminating the obstacles to freedom of action that come from the environment. According to Rogers, asserts Georges Lerbet,

> the idea of optimal functioning that operates "when the structure of the self is such as to allow the symbolic integration of the totality of the experience," does not leave an explicit place for that which self-reference structures, namely the inherence of incompleteness.[70]

Moreover, self-reference as a general process offers a second advantage. It provides an approach that, freed from the individual perspective of humanistic psychology, can thus encompass other dimensions. Such is, indeed, the challenge of the approach that we are setting forth.

But before addressing this challenge more directly, let us try to take one more step in the intuitive perception of the process of self-reference. More precisely, let us imagine that we are

---

69. As examples, we can refer to formalized expressions of the self-reference process: see Francisco Varela's article "A calculus for self-reference" in *International Journal of General System*, 1975 and Allan Goff's article "Nonlinear Logic (NLL) – Making sense out of Logical Self-Reference," in *AIAA Paper 2006*. This opens up a whole field of research that would consist in developing a formalized version of the present approach.
70. Georges Lerbet, *Carl Rogers et la pensée constructiviste complexe*. https://docplayer.fr/29065408-Carl-rogers-et-la-pensee-constructiviste-complexe.html. Retrieved on February 22, 2020.

trying to explain this process to a person we know in our environment and who, though not at all keen about theoretical developments, does show an interest in such a topic.

Self-Reference Explained to Aunt Josephine

Let's go back to real-life situations. Suppose we take a few moments to look back on our life. As the film of our past goes through our mind, it triggers in us a feeling of greater or lesser satisfaction, and we are led to wonder how much time we have left to live. There may be ideals that are close to our hearts but that we have not managed to attain as much as we would have liked to. There may also be mistakes that we would like to repair... etc.!

That we are asking ourselves such questions or doing everything to avoid them indicates that our human condition puts us before our responsibility: who am I, who am I becoming, what am I making of myself? Such questioning reflects self-reference experienced at the highest level by the human being that we are: we are confronted with the choice of making something of ourselves. The choice of becoming, one could say, "totally us." In other words, of actualizing our potential, both individually and collectively.

But there's more: if I want to fully actualize the being I am, I cannot do so by behaving erratically. I have to do it with reference to my own identity, with reference to myself, in self-reference. We have all experienced situations where we did not listen to ourselves and let ourselves be led by others to do what did not really suit us. We have been hetero-referent; in other words, we referred to others for something that concerned us first. We felt a kind of self-betrayal or alienation. The word alienation comes from the Latin *alienus*, which means other, foreign. The other became our first reference. We became strangers to ourselves.

Such is the case, for example, with one's sense of self-esteem. Throughout our education, we may have met people who convinced us of our worthlessness. Having integrated this value judgment, we thus came to see ourselves through other people's eyes. But if we succeed in repatriating this judgment, in becoming our own locus of evaluation, in other words, in evaluating who we are in terms of our own identity, there is no reason why we should not regain our sense of self-esteem. If we succeed, then we will have gone from being hetero-referential to self-referential.

But then, how does one go about making such a change? And how does one go about distinguishing between changes fostering growth and changes that are detrimental? These same questions inevitably come up not only for individuals, but also for societies and, indeed, for humanity as a whole. Societies and the whole of humanity are also called upon to become self-referential.

As presented here, self-reference represents a goal, an arrival point. Yet there unfortunately does not exist an instruction manual[71] showing us how to reach it. Our challenge in this project is thus to make self-reference not only a point of arrival but also a vehicle that can be used at the start to reach this point. So, we would not only have self-reference as the arrival point, but also as the process to get there.

We will see that self-reference is a device that has its own coherence and that before putting it to use, it would be wise to start by examining its nature. Thus, we will follow in the footsteps of a child who, very fascinated by the toy he is playing with, suddenly stops and starts taking it apart to see how it is made. To do this, we will use the simplest gestures of everyday life, which, at their level, illustrate the underlying mechanics of self-reference. It is, therefore, necessary to accept to enter into a methodological reflection and not to be scandalized by the great simplicity of the examples. What interests us here are the nuts and bolts of self-reference.

Self-Referential Mechanics

Self-reference, in its simplest expression, occurs in ordinary actions of everyday life whenever a person's action concerns the whole person as such and not just a part of him or herself or an external object. This is the domain of reflexive pronouns and verbs: "I'm moving myself." Were I to move an object on the table, there would be no problem, because only a part of myself would be involved, my arm and the object being moved, which is

---

71. See note 5.

outside of me. But when I'm moving myself, it's all of myself that I'm moving. The operation is then more complex: I have to lean on one leg so the other is free to move forward one step; the latter leg then takes its turn in becoming my second point of support, thus allowing the first one to perform the same movement, make another step forward. I thus moved all of myself forward, but to do so I had to resort to a transfer of responsibility between several parts of myself that had to operate in a coordinated and relatively independent manner.

We have already noted the caricature depicting a person who tries to move himself but without realizing that the parts must enjoy a relative autonomy for this to happen. Baron Münchhausen wanted to lift himself out of the well, and he tried to do so by pulling on his bootstraps. He had not fully grasped the problem of self-referentiality: as the one who was pulling (the agent) had no autonomy in relation to the one who was being pulled (the object), the whole could not move itself. One of the parts must have a minimum of autonomy in relation to the other; otherwise, the *whole* (the baron) remains trapped where it is. A whole cannot act upon itself without involving parts of itself whose autonomy is sufficient to interact productively with each other. Self-reference has its reasons.

We are going to develop another example that will allow us to identify all the elements that come into play when acting on ourselves involves all of who we are. Let's take inspiration from our feline friends and take a closer look at a cat's grooming operation.

- *The Cat Metaphor*

Suppose that one day the cat's wanderings have been particularly intense and laborious and finds itself at the end of the day all covered with dust. The cat then begins to groom, but the operation will have to cover the *entire* coat. We know that it can only rely on itself and that the part responsible for washing is also covered with fur and is, therefore, part of the totality we are talking about. It is therefore self-referential grooming, a self-grooming that meets the feline's criteria and affects the *entire* coat.

BASIC CONCEPTS AND METHOLOLOGY

The cat then gets to work. It distinguishes an active part – globally the head, the neck, the tongue – that we will call the *agent*. We will call this distinction a differentiation of a part within a totality. The agent thus differentiated is acting on the rest of the coat, which constitutes the receptive part, which we will call to simplify *the receptive*. The *receptive* is the part of the coat that is directly accessible to the agent and which receives its action. The operation continues until the receptive is completely groomed. But the cat is not at the end of its efforts, because a part of the coat has not yet been groomed: the part that covers the *agent* and that is inaccessible to this agent.

A strategic reversal is then carried out and follows the following sequence: first, the *agent* invests part of the *receptive* – in this case, the right front paw (our hero being right-handed) – of a mission that will allow the action to loop on the totality. The agent thus properly moistens its paw, lets go of its grip on action, and places itself in a receptive posture. Reciprocally, the initially receptive paw puts itself in an active posture and starts grooming the part of the coat linked to the agent, i.e., the coat covering the head. This operation can be repeated as many times as necessary.

There is thus a reversal in the hierarchy of functions, the washing agent becoming the washed object, and the washed receptive becoming the washing agent. We will then speak of a *hierarchical reversal* of functions (of washing in this case). This operation reintegrates the *agent* into the field of washed things and restores the entire coat to its original purity. We could speak here of the process of *integration* of the agent into the totality (washed), a process that is the counterpart of the initial process of *differentiation*.

Note that the paw is not strictly speaking a washing agent, and yet it acts as an extension of the action of the initial agent. It is thus sometimes in a receptive mode, sometimes in an active one. This special agent – which is not an agent at the outset and which can fulfill the two poles of the function, sometimes the active and sometimes the receptive – will be called a *paradoxical agent*.

Noteworthy here is the fact that this example gives an impoverished version of the function of paradoxical agent; it only reflects one meaning of reference: a totality which is the *object of its own action*. It leaves aside the other meaning, which makes of the paradoxical agent the *locus of evaluation* of the operation, its benchmark (in this case, *correctly groomed or not*). Thus, the cat's paw alone can hardly claim the title of the function. However, the example makes it possible to identify the general outline of the process and to specify the terms used to describe it.

Let us now give yet another example, this time from the field of language: personal pronouns.

▪ The Metaphor of Personal Pronouns

Languages generally provide clues, most of the time partial but significant, illustrating how the self-referential process works. Personal pronouns have been used, for example, to this end.

Unfortunately, this metaphor has been very badly abused, especially in French. One of the most important deviations has appeared in psychoanalysis. In German, Freud proposed the following terms: Das Es, das Ich, and das Über-Ich. These terms have been translated into French by *le Ça, le Moi,* and *le Surmoi*. However, the form *Ich* corresponds in French to *Je* and not to *Moi*. In its reified form, *le moi* becomes a part of "moi". This misunderstanding is a source of confusion and gives rise to many discussions about the illusion that this *moi* within me would make me who I am. It is more than an illusion; it is an equivocation and confusion in terms.

In psychoanalysis, there is no confusion in English to designate the various agencies, because the Latin forms are used: Id, Ego, Super-ego. However, in psychology, there is such confusion with the term "self". Rogers, for example, indicates that "self" refers "to the organized consistent conceptual gestalt composed of perceptions on the characteristics of the "I" or "me" and the perceptions of the relationships of the "I" or "me" to others and to various aspects of life [...]"[72] One may ask Rogers:

---

[72]. Carl Rogers, A Theory of Therapy, Personality, and Interpersonal Relationship, as Developed in the Client-Centered Framework, in Sigmund Kosh, *Psychology: A Study of a Science*. Study 1, vol. 3:*Formulations of the Person and the Social Context*, 1959, p. 200.

BASIC CONCEPTS AND METHOLOLOGY

if the "self" is made up of perceptions relative to the "I" or "me," who is the perceiver? If it is the "self" that perceives, what is the status of the "I"? Why shouldn't it be the "I" that is the agency that perceives, as in German *das Ich*, or in Latin the *Ego*? The *self*, as defined by Rogers, thus seems to suffer from the same confusion as the French "*le moi.*"

We will try to use the metaphorical richness of personal pronouns, respecting as far as possible the way they are used in everyday language. We will try to be cautious about the widespread habit of substantiating or, if you like, nominalizing the various forms of personal pronouns, although it is advisable to do so in certain cases. Moreover, each use of the pronoun will be matched to the objective designation of the reality indicated.

Personal pronouns generally take three forms in English and French. One of these forms refers to the totality, that is, the person as a unity. In French, it is *moi, toi, lui, elle, soi* depending on whether it is the first, second, or third person, or a person in general. All these terms can be followed by the word *même* which gives more strength to the reflexive aspect: moi-même, toi-même, lui-même, elle-même, soi-même. In English, one finds the same forms: myself, yourself, himself, herself, oneself, but the form "me" can also design the totality, which is not the case in French.

From this totality is differentiated an agent, a subject, who initiates action. In French: *je, tu, il, elle, on*. In English: *I, you, he, she*. For a person in general – "*on*" in French – the agent often takes the form of the first-person plural, *we*, or the term *one*: "*one does this and that...*"

An important side note here. Let us recall Varela's discussion of "a selfless self [...] a nonsubstantial self that acts as if it were present [...]" As we have already pointed out, the problem does not lie in the author's thinking as such, but rather in the way he expresses it. The form of the pronoun that designates the totality (myself) is frequently confused with the subject form (I), and then "the self" as part of me must become virtual, and somehow "without self"...

From the present point of view, the *agent* of which we speak as a part that differentiates itself in the totality is not in contradiction with the substance of Varela's thought. When he explains what happens at the biological level, he readily speaks of a " cooperation and competition between distinct agents activated by the current situation, vying with each other for differing modes of interpretation for a coherent cognitive framework and readiness for action... [One of them] finally prevails to become the behavioral mode for the next

91

cognitive moment, a microworld" (1999: 19). The agent that prevails and induces behavior is precisely the one we are talking about and referring to when we say "I." Biologically, it is a very concrete neural network and not the illusion of a selfless self, acting without being present. On the other hand, "me," the totality, is an emerging reality to which "I" cannot have access, like all the internal agents that will never be able to access the totality either. It is the totality that constitutes the cognitive emptiness, the void, that all internal agents face (see the fifth founding statement).

By the very fact of differentiating a subject within the totality, a complementary part is created, the receptive part. In French: *me, te, lui, elle, se*. In English: *me, you, him, her, us*.

The French language allows us to have all these forms in the same sentence, including the initial state of the totality:

" Moi, je me développe moi-même "

The English language is more elliptical, and some forms are implied:

"Me, I develop myself."

Who am I developing? Me... and I do it myself. The illustration is a little less clear in English, because the form "me" can designate either the object of the action within the totality or the totality itself to which this action is ultimately attributed.

Unfortunately, in neither language do we have a form of pronouns to designate what we called in the previous example "the paradoxical agent." It is this agent that completes the operation of the initial agent by allowing the latter to be included as receptive to its own action. It is a hierarchical reversal of the functions by which the initial operator is brought back in the field of the operands.

Of course, these three instances, *totality, agent, receptive*, are not independent of each other. If the self-indicating totality "me or myself" differentiates within it the agent "I," it is clear that this agent is a subset, which is, in a way, an "active version," of the totality, although it is not and never will be this totality.

We have said that the totality, as such, is not in the realm of action. But then, how can we attribute an action to the totality? If I am moving, it is indeed me as a whole who is moving and not only the part of me that is the agent. We will then see that the action of the agent will have to set in motion the cycle of the self-

Basic Concepts and Metholology

referential process so that we can finally attribute the action initiated by the agent to the unity in its totality. To reach this result, the agent alone cannot complete the process and will have to let go and rely on the paradoxical agent.

The totality is the lieu of two internal processes: differentiation and integration. Although these processes are dynamic, they do not constitute actions as such of the totality. It is a bit like when a sculpture is disintegrating; the latter is not an action of the sculpture as such, but rather a process that affects it in its being. Similarly, differentiation is a form of temporary disintegration of the totality, the latter being recovered at the end of the operation by the complementary process of integration. Thus, the totality, through the interplay of its active components, is restored but to a state distinct from the initial state. We will then say that the unity, even as a totality, has acted, thus downplaying, for convenience, all these internal processes. At its level, therefore, the unity is deemed to act in an aggregated way without one having to take into account lower-level interactions.

From these examples, let's extract the elements that constitute the major pivots of self-referential mechanics:

The totality. We use the term totality, but we could have used other similar terms, such as the *whole* or the *whole unity*. *Totality* designates any unity considered as a whole, such as a person, a group, or a society. It allows one to distinguish between what is at the level of the *whole* or its *parts*. Does a given action involve the whole unity or only one of its parts? If I move my arm, only a part of me is involved. If I move myself, it is all of me, the whole, that is involved. In the superficial case of grooming, *totality* refers to the cat's entire coat.

Of course, totality refers to actions that are more complex than merely moving one's arm or a cat grooming itself. If someone wants to realize himself or herself as a person, it is the totality of what that person is that is involved in all its dimensions and not just a part of himself or herself.

To stimulate the imagination, we will represent the totality using an ellipse:

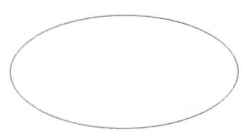

Figure 2. Representation of the totality in the non-split state before differentiation.

Differentiation. We have seen that for an action to occur, a totality must first allow that a distinction be made within itself, more precisely that stands out a part capable of initiating an action. We call this operation of distinction *differentiation*. The latter can be seen from the point of view of the totality: *the totality is differentiated*, we would then say. It can also be seen from the point of view of its parts: *a part is differentiated in the totality*, we would say. Or in other words, one part stands out from the rest. Differentiation is thus the introduction of a difference that concerns a part in relation to the others, in this case, the *agent*, about a particular operation, the grooming in the case of our feline hero. In short, it is the passage of the totality from the non-split state to the split state.

The agent. This part of the totality that differentiates and initiates the action will be called the generic name of *agent*. It is the subject of the action. In grammatical terms, it represents the subject of the verb. For example, for the person speaking, it is "I." In Latin, the person speaking is "Ego," in German it is "Ich," and in French, it is "je." The same goes for the person we talk to (you) or the person we are talking about (he, she); all of latter can also be the subject of a verb.

Let's go back to the first person. When we say "*I*," we feel that this pronoun immediately implies all of who we are. Yet that is not the case: "*I*" is the *agent* setting into motion and leading the action, but it is only at the end of the process that the totality (that we are) will be involved. We will come back to the harmful effect of this confusion between *agent* and *totality*, which will bring us to make the fundamental distinction between egocentrism and self-reference. A distinction that will allow us to situate our thinking in this respect relative to certain conceptions of *subject-agent* that have developed in Western philosophy.

Figure 3 shows a differentiated totality.

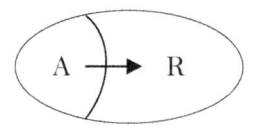

Figure 3: Representation of the totality in the split state resulting from the differentiation of an agent A which acts on the receptive R.

The receptive.[73] The receptive (R) is the part of the totality remaining outside the agent once differentiation has been made. It is the part that is the object of the agent's action, that can, so to speak *receive* the action. In the case of our cat, it is the part of its coat that is directly accessible to the tongue. It is the "me" form of the pronoun in pronominal verbs. If we asked the cat what it is washing, the answer would be "*me.*"

Another example. If I want to get rid of my habit of smoking, I have to decide to quit smoking. This decision by the "*I*" agent affects everything else I am. It upsets my habits, my behavioral pattern… in other words, it changes something in my life. The *receptive* is everything that is affected by the agent's decision; in other words, everything in my life that is affected by the decision *I've* made.

The hierarchical reversal. Let's revisit our cat. If we analyze this reversal process in detail, we have as a starting point an action (grooming) taken by the *agent* (neck-head-tongue) that is exerted on the *receptive* (the rest of the cat's coat). Secondly, the

---

73. As we do in French, we use this adjective as a noun, meaning: the complementary **receptive** part of the agent in the totality.

agent invests part of the receptive (the paw) with a mission that is in continuity of its action. Thirdly, this part will differentiate itself from the receptive and become an agent, whereas the initial agent lets go of its active role and moves into a receptive mode. This reversal allows this new *paradoxical agent* to exert its action on the initial agent who has newly become receptive.

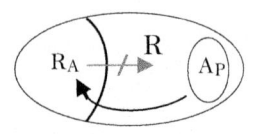

Figure 4: Hierarchical reversal of the action going from the paradoxical agent A_P to the initial agent then placed in receptive mode R_A.

The paradoxical agent. The paradoxical agent (the paw in the case of the cat) has the characteristic of not being at the origin of the action nor of being its specialist. But without this paradoxical agent, the action of the initial agent cannot be complete. The paradoxical agent is differentiated from the *receptive*, but it is no longer identifiable with this specific mode. It thus escapes the rigidity of the initial *agent-receptive* dichotomy, and it allows to go beyond its limits by reversing the functions to restore the totality in its entirety.

Integration. The paradoxical agent thus integrates the initial agent in the field of the objects targeted by its own action and thus completes the picture of the totality. The paradoxical agent constitutes the key to the relationship that totality can have with itself, that is to say, to be self-referent. *Integration* is the passage from the level of the parts to the level of the totality. It is the counterpart of the initial *differentiation* that allows the passage from the totality to the parts.

In the example of the cat, everything is clear and biologically programmed. However, when these notions are applied to human behavior, it is not always easy to pinpoint the paradoxical agent. In the example of the smoker who wants to quit smoking, we have identified an agent "*I*" who decides to make the totality, *me*, become a non-smoker. If *my* operation is carried out in a superficial manner, in other words, if *I*, in deciding to quit smoking, failed to solidly embed such a decision in the rest of my life (the receptive), no elements of my experience will emerge to play the role of *paradoxical agent*, to give continuity to and support the initial decision and reinforce the decision-maker that I am. Thus, the decision may be overturned since the decision-making agent is not in a position to include himself in giving continuity to his action. In such a situation, I will probably go back to smoking.

That is why changing things in one's life is so challenging. The agent "*I*," who is busy triggering the change, is not immediately included as an object in his or her field of operation. He or she must thus take care to embody the change in the *receptive* with enough effectiveness so that a *paradoxical agent* emerges, and one whose autonomy is such as to allow the initial agent to let go and become himself the object of the action.

Let's go back to one of the first examples given above concerning one's sense of self-esteem. Essentially, the problem comes down to the following assertion: "I have very little self-esteem." To restore one's self-esteem, it is not enough to merely declare, "Okay, now I have a healthy self-esteem." Whatever methodology is used to obtain a result, one can imagine that the operation will generally take the form of the process just described.

Table 1 provides a schematic version of the process.

Table 1. Example of the self-referential cycle.

The totality	First of all, from "*myself*" as a totality emerges a feeling of low self-esteem.	"Low self-esteem"
The agent	I (A) decide to apply a methodology X represented by the arrow: ⟶	A ⟶
The receptive	... a methodology that leads me to gradually modify *my inner world* (R)	A ⟶ R
The paradoxical agent	Once this operation is completed, I let go (⟶) of my action and put myself in receptive mode (R_A) relative to what I feel as a change, not a change I am doing, but rather that is being done and that I am welcoming. This is the hierarchical reversal: the agent I switches to the receptive mode in favor of another agent, the *paradoxical agent* (A_P) originating from the *receptive*. The paradoxical agent is thus this vital force, coming from my inner universe, the *receptive*. This force, first activated and fostered by the agent, has acquired enough autonomy to invest the space of the agent and free it from its roots that generate low-self-esteem.	R_A ⟶ R (A_P)
The totality restored	It is then all of *me* who is invested with a sense of self-esteem linked to my own identity.	"Healthy self-esteem"

These are real-life experiences. One undergoes therapy to free oneself from personal problems. One works hard until, having let go, one finds oneself in a new space, freed, so to speak, from oneself. One feels as if a profound change has taken place, but one not resulting from one's own doing. One happily finds oneself with a result that seems to have happened by itself.

This being acknowledged, one must bear in mind that without the client's initial work, it is likely that this change would never have taken place. To let go, there must be something one was clinging to.

We immediately see that this paradoxical agent that takes over the action is rather mysterious and that we have trouble clearly pinpointing it. It is an active force that can be associated with the complex function of witness-mediator-facilitator-catalyst. It facilitates the process of change, but it is not engaged in the content of the operation it facilitates. In the previous example, the paradoxical agent acts outside of value judgments. It only applies to the initial agent the change initiated by this agent, which, this time, allows itself to be modified, which makes the operation of the change coextensive to the totality.

This paradoxical agent function can be more easily identified at the social level because it can be fulfilled by one or more distinct persons. One finds a natural version in the family, where grandparents fulfill the function of paradoxical agent concerning parent-child relationships. As they do not have, as grandparents, the educational responsibility of the children, this gives them the possibility of adopting the points of view corresponding to the two poles of the function alternately, sometimes that of the parents and sometimes that of the child.

As noted above, there is no specific linguistic personal pronoun to identify the paradoxical agent. This is, of course, normal because the explicit awareness that we have of things is related to the functioning of the agent, the *I*, the *Ego*. And as the agent, when in a receptive mode, is not acting, it thus does not have access to the processes occurring outside of itself and is limited to observing their effects.

The basic thrust of this book will therefore consist in identifying the paradoxical agent, better understanding it theoretically, and above all, making it an effective pragmatic tool.

The paradoxical agent should not be seen as a function that does not regularly appear in people's everyday life and in personal and community development methodologies presently being implemented. Such a function does exist, but, more often than not, it is applied randomly, when it is not totally absent, which brings us to the topic discussed in the following paragraph.

Self-Reference Versus Egocentricity

We often see, for example, in Buddhist writings altruism being opposed to self-centeredness or egocentricity. In such a mindset, altruism represents the ideal one should seek to follow. Though one can intuitively understand the good intention underlying such thinking, there is nevertheless a risk of confusion. If the center of reference becomes the other, we find ourselves faced with the possibility of a double perversion: that of alienating ourselves to the benefit of the other, or that of turning to the other without really having the least bit altered our attitude of self-centeredness, in other words, alienating the other by reducing him or her to ourselves. The mere fact of going out of oneself to reach the other does not guarantee that this desired goal will be achieved.

Self-reference is fundamentally different from self-centeredness or egocentricity. While the latter means focusing on the Ego, in other words, on the differentiated agent of the totality, self-reference means focusing on the totality.

We have seen that the totality is inaccessible directly to the agent, in this case, the Ego. To reach the totality, the Ego must let go and allow himself to be carried away by the action that he has initiated, and that comes back to him from the *receptive*. The totality as such thus transcends the direct action of the parts.

Yet the presence of the differentiated agent, the Ego, is very important in the process. Without the Ego the totality cannot maintain itself or progress. It is worth insisting on this point. Various writings present the Ego as if it were a defect or even an illusion. However, the Ego in itself is an essential cog in the process of self-reference. Were we to remove the personal pronoun "*I*" from our functioning, and thus all the actions that it triggers, there would be little left for us in terms of resources to survive, and even less to become self-referent.

This being said, it is quite easy for the Ego to take itself as the reference for the totality and to refuse to let go. Doing so would be egocentricity. When this happens, the operation fails to reach the totality, because the *agent* tries to maintain its power over the *receptive*. According to the views set forth in this book, this would be the main difficulty of human development: the agent, in this case, the Ego, the first tool responsible for triggering action in the totality, believes itself invested with the mission of maintaining its hold on the action until the end. Thus, instead of fostering the advent of totality, egocentricity, by thwarting self-reference, actually blocks it. And when self-reference is similarly thwarted at the societal level, it produces totalitarianism.

According to the model, we are setting forth, self-reference alone leads to authentic altruism. Self-reference represents, let us recall, a relationship to oneself as a totality, *not* a relationship to the Ego. Whether relating to oneself or relating to the other, the Ego must let go in favor of a totality that transcends it. There is a striking similarity between the way one relates to oneself and others. Very revealing in this regard is the title of Paul Ricoeur's previously quoted book *Soi-même comme un autre* (Oneself as Other).[74]

Guidelines for a Generalization

This section is made up of preliminary reflections that could constitute avenues for further research. More precisely, we will evoke the possibility of generalizing the self-reference model at all hierarchical levels, from the individual to the whole of humanity.

One will recall that the premise at the origin of the present approach is that the self-referential process is called to manifest itself at all different levels of the human reality, even though, in the present state of affairs, one does not observe the blossoming of self-reference at all levels. This implies that potentially the structure of the self-referential process is isomorphic from one level to another.

Such a postulate is not compatible with the point of view developed by Dupuy (1992), which he describes as methodological individualism:

> *Collective beings have a particular mode of existence, they can be the cause of events or phenomena, the support of decisions, but in no case can we attribute to them the attributes of a **subject**: will, intention, consciousness, etc. This is the golden rule of individualistic methodology in the social sciences.*

---

74. Paris, Éditions du Seuil, 1990.

The notion of *subject*, as developed since the Greeks, is perhaps one of the most ambiguous in Western philosophy. Let us repeat that in the present model, to say that a person is a subject appears limiting and imprecise. We prefer describing the person as a self-referential totality that generates in itself a subject capable of initiating action, the totality as such not being primarily in the domain of action. And to avoid confusion, we use the term *agent* instead of subject. It is only through the autogenerative loop that the subject's action can be (or not) attributed to the totality, but the subject (the agent) will never be this totality.

The term "subject," in the above quote, seems to have particular connotations. According to Dupuy, *"will"* would be one of the exclusive attributes of a "subject." An individual could want something, but not a collective being. It is not clear why that would be the case. When France decided not to take part in the war in Iraq in which the United States wanted to drag it, this conveyed an intent, a particular will. Of course, one could always argue that it was not France that was acting but only a few individuals who, at the time, happened to represent the government within the French state. They, and not a collective being, were the ones who made the decision.

But France, as is the case with all totalities, never acts as a totality, the latter not being in the realm of action. The totality that is France can only act indirectly by differentiating within itself an active instance, or agent, which brings it into a distinct state. The French government is that instance. As far as we know, the French government can make decisions which constitute France's decisions.

The same goes for persons. *I* make a decision that commits *me*. The active instance is not the totality. One could object that "the decision *I* make commits the whole person involved in the decision, whereas the decision made by a government does not have the support of everyone." Here, again, the apparent difference between the societal level and the personal level is the result of idiocentric illusion. As a matter of fact, the decision I make is perfectly analogous to the decision that the government of a nation makes.

When *I* make a decision, there are parts of *me* that may not agree with the decision. Who has not had the experience of making a personal decision without due regard to the antagonistic forces within oneself, only to see the latter forces finally succeed in overturning the decision? The obese who go on weight-loss diets or smokers who decide to stop smoking, for example: they know perfectly well what we are referring to here. Powerful internal lobbies often succeed in keeping control and overturning decisions that are made by the highest-level authority, *"I,"* who should be able to relate these decisions to the totality, *myself*, but in this case fails to do so.

Besides, it is ironic that one spontaneously accepts theoretical essays where the person is seen as a society, such as Minsky's essay already quoted, but is scandalized when it is suggested that a society can be seen as a social person. That there are specificities at each level, individual and societal, is something we can all agree on. But the general problem of self-reference remains the same.

While the above-mentioned examples do not indicate any fundamental difference in the various levels of human reality, they do indicate shortcomings in the self-referential process related to the type of governance found both within society and the individual. Some decisions taken seem to be in tune with the totality, while others seem so alien to it that they end up being overturned. How does one go about things so that the interaction of internal agents is such that the latter represent emergences of the totality that activate all dimensions of this same totality? How can this interaction organize diversity around coherence rather than around conflict?

So many of the questions to which this book will gradually attempt to provide some elements of an answer.

Now let us examine the equivalence of the terms that, from level to level, define the space where the self-referential process is played out.

The topography of the self-referential universe: a first approximation

We have identified in general terms the elements of the self-referential cycle that we can see as various spaces within the unity under consideration. The unity most often used as an example was that constituted by the person. Now we will try to develop intuitively a slightly more accurate description of these spaces or agencies depending on whether we apply it to the person as a unity or to social unities.

For each of the levels, we must first specify the general term common to all these levels, then as much as possible the objective reality in question at each level, and finally, the correspondences from level to level. To specify the various agencies, it is also possible to refer to the linguistic metaphors in the section *The metaphor of personal pronouns*. Let's start with the *totality*.

The totality. It is rather peculiar to note that, in general, theories do not have a word for the *totality*. In psychoanalysis, for example, the designated spaces or agencies – id, ego, superego – represent but a deconstruction made by a person responding to Cartesian criteria of analysis. For all intents and purposes, there's no one. In other words, the person as a totality is nowhere to be seen in this theory.

On the other hand, in the present approach, totality becomes the primary reference, because it is, or tends to be, precisely self-referential, and this is the main issue. It must, therefore, have its place in our theory.

The individual. At the individual level, the objective reality designating *totality* is the *person*. The title of one of Rogers' books is precisely *On Becoming a Person* (1961).

The group. At the social level, the objective reality designating the totality that tends towards self-reference can be called *community*.

Society. At the societal level, the objective reality is precisely *society* or, if you like, *the social system*. Since the totality is inaccessible from within, i.e., as a direct object of the action of its parts, one usually chooses to ignore it. This is an excellent way of missing the heart of the matter since self-reference is precisely the reference of a totality to itself!

The agent. Let's now turn to the agent that differentiates itself from the totality. Let's see what form it takes at each level of organization.

The individual. One could use the term *subject* to designate the reality in question, but this term is so polysemic that it would create more confusion than clarification. We will, therefore, use the Latin term *Ego*.

The *Ego* (the "I") is not an illusion, contrary to what is asserted, for example, in some Buddhist writings. The *Ego* is, within the totality, the agent of the highest level that is responsible for action and is present both to the internal universe and the internal and external environment. This presence gives rise to what can be called *explicit consciousness*, which transforms disturbances coming from within and without (the totality) into treatable data. The function of the Ego is essential to the self-referential cycle because, without this agent that triggers action, no modification can be made in the totality, which, as we have seen, is not in the realm of action but of being.

The group. Within groups, the agent function is represented by the leader(s) who exercise their leadership in various ways depending on the type of group.

Society. At the societal level, the agent is the state apparatus with the *government* at its center. In our modern societies, we can broadly say that this is the public sector, which, by the way, should be called civic rather than public.

The receptive. As far as the *receptive* is concerned, it is, in relation to the action of the agent, an unorganized space where one still finds the richness of the totality, except for the space occupied by the agent.

The individual. This very rich space is not organized as a single unity, but it does not lack organization. It would be the place of an *implicit consciousness* that is only indirectly accessible. This is what is erroneously referred to as "the unconscious". For the moment, we will use the expression *receptive inner universe* for lack of a better term.

The group. For the group, the *receptive* corresponds to all *participants* who do not have the leadership of the operation in which the group is involved.

Society. As for the societal level, the receptive corresponds to all space lying outside the public sector. One could call this the private sector though in reality it represents the universe occupied by citizens. We sometimes use the expression *"civil society"* or "the people", terms used in opposition to their counterparts, the world of leaders.

The paradoxical agent. The function of *paradoxical agent*, as mentioned above, is linked to a synthesis of the notions of witness, mediator, facilitator, and catalyst. Let us try to see what it can correspond to at each level.

The individual. At the intra-individual level, it is difficult to find an objective description for it. It is a function that is little controlled and exercised randomly. One perceives its effects in certain creative emergences as if the creation came from elsewhere as if it were a kind of revelation, an insight. As in oriental meditations, one can associate the notion of witness to the function of paradoxical agent. It is always possible to witness what is going on inside oneself by taking into account of its reality without, however, interfering at the first level with what is going on. I can, for example, observe – witness – an ongoing conflict within myself without intervening at this first level.

In short, any internal symbolization of my experience at a given moment (an idea, an image that comes to me…) constitutes an intervention that is made within this field of experience and this process can always be taken into account by a *receptive/active witness* who then plays the role of a paradoxical agent. Any experience can be at the same time the experience of this experience. The paradoxical agent is the agent that experiences my experience.

The group. In a group, this is a function that is sometimes called *facilitation*, a term that differs from animation, which would instead refer to the agent. Any form of mediation is also of this type.

Society. At the societal level, this would be the *associative social sector*, whose redefinition would make it possible to arrive at a mediation involving the various transactions of the public and private sectors with citizens to arrive at an increasingly endogenous development of society. This social sector would, so to speak, escape the public / private dichotomy.

We will see that we must first redefine the concept of *sector* and then show how the social sector must be transformed to become a real sector and how this sector could play in society the role of paradoxical agent. Table 2 below summarizes all of this.

Table 2. Topography of the self-referential universe at different levels.

	Individual	Group	Society	World
Totality	Person	Community	Society	Humanity
Agent	Ego	Leaders	Government/public sector	...
Receptive	Receptive inner universe	Participating Members	Citizens/private sector	...
Paradoxical agent	Witness	Facilitator-mediator	Social associative sector	...

Summing up...

It must be understood that the adaptation of this general topic to the levels of the individual, the group, and society is a first approximation that should at least provide a grounding for methodologies aiming to make the various systems evolve towards a self-referential functioning characteristic of the living. Varela hesitated to attribute to social entities the characteristic of the living, which he called *autopoiesis*, and he was quite right, given the current state of human development. As we see it, although modern societies have everything to become living entities – thus self-referent in the creation of themselves – they have not yet achieved this. Their development is still largely exogenous and egocentric.

The present template is a kind of matrix that serves as a *methodological agent* allowing one to outline various fields of experience. However, it will have to itself undergo the repercussions of its excursions in these multiple fields, both cognitive and pragmatic. From the latter will occasionally arise as *many paradoxical agents* that will transform the matrix itself with additions, revisions, and salutary corrections.

The following chapter deals with the philosophy of the approach we are setting forth, a reflection that is basically epistemological. It will provide us with the opportunity to address the problem of foundations as it arises in general, but especially relative to this approach.

Chapter II

Self-reference: Paradigm and Core Idea

The self-referential matrix we have outlined was developed in reference to concrete realities such as a person, a group, a society, etc. However, it is possible to take a metacognitive step back on the nature of the model that is taking shape and to use the same scheme, applying it this time to the theoretical notions that are at the basis of the approach. In short, the model applies to itself. This would be the first self-referential application of the model.

We might wonder, for example, what serves as the *totality* in this theoretical development. We can immediately answer that it is self-reference as a *paradigm*. Indeed, the paradigm has characteristics in common with the totality. It is blind to the developments to which it gives rise, even though it is these developments that feed it and keep it alive. Likewise, the totality is inaccessible to the parts that make it up, even though it is their interaction that ensures its maintenance and development.

In the unfolding of the paradigm, we might also wonder what now serves as the *agent* that differentiates itself to schematize its complement, the *receptive*, and to ensure the life and development of the paradigm. The answer is, once again, self-reference, but this time as the *core idea*; it is the one that will guide the development of the process. This core idea has taken the form of this scheme that we have called the self-referential matrix. In other words, the *self-referential core idea* is the differentiated agent within the *self-referential paradigm*.

Let us first note that there is a certain coherence in the fact that the very idea of self-reference is the agent that presides over the development of the self-reference paradigm. One can hardly be more self-referential! But this beautiful coherence has a surprise in store for us. We have seen that the *agent* that differentiates itself in the *totality* does not cover the totality. It in fact distinguishes itself from *that*, in the totality, *which it is not*, the latter then being placed in *receptive* mode. Thus, the core idea of self-reference distinguishes itself from that which it is not, thus from what is not self-referential in the paradigm of self-reference. In other words, at this differentiated level, hetero-reference becomes the obligatory complement of self-reference, as a subset of the self-reference paradigm, a subset which then constitutes the receptive element.

The self-referential *agent* will then have the task of schematizing what appears before it as a hetero-referential universe – "apostle of sedition" this time in the world of self-reference – so that this universe becomes one of the components of the paradigm of self-reference. But the *agent* will do so at its own risk, because from the hetero-referential field of experience thus schematized may emerge a *paradoxical agent* that will, in turn, schematize the initial agent and make it more consistent with the totality that it claims to represent and that gave birth to it. The fact of thus taking self-referentiality as the invariant of the system, to the point of including in it hetero-referentiality, leads us to the question of foundations.

About foundations

The sole purpose of the following discussion consists in highlighting the constraints imposed by the chosen paradigm on how certain questions should be asked, namely those pertaining to foundations, used here as an example.

The idea of foundations has its origin in everyday life experiences. If the foundations of a building are deficient, the building collapses. The foundation on which a building rests is thus that which allows it, so to speak, to "hold together."

This metaphor has been applied to various fields, such as knowledge, human conduct, belief systems, etc. "Foundation" thus came to represent the basis on which each of these realms is built, or, in other words, the origin, that which gives meaning and coherence to the whole construction and without which everything collapses. It is thus at this point of origin that takes root and unfolds the articulation of the various elements that make up the essence of the construction.

Foundations are always the foundations of something: foundations of mathematics, foundations of ethics, etc. There is, therefore, a necessary distinction between "what founds" and "what is founded."

We may be searching for foundations because we want to avoid finding ourselves without reference points, in a world whose meaning we cannot make out, at the mercy of a chaotic disorganization that would threaten us in our own being. The foundations of exactly what would we then be looking for? Of the reality from which we originate; of ourselves, and what we are going to do with ourselves in this world; of the knowledge that we can have of reality; and finally, of all that we have undertaken in our lives and to which we have given some importance.

One such endeavor is precisely the arsenal of knowledge that the West has worked hard to develop, and to which we have turned in an attempt to replace ancient traditional landmarks, in the hope of ensuring for ourselves a more solid grounding in reality. We have thus wondered throughout history about knowledge and the foundations that would justify the methods used to ensure its validity. This is the field of epistemology, some of whose schools of thought will be evoked to deepen this reflection on foundations. This will be followed by a presentation of the epistemological position adopted in the present book.

Summary Classification of Epistemological Schools of Thought

The epistemological framework presented here is intended to provide context for the epistemological position characterizing our approach, which is set forth in the following section. This introductory epistemological reflection, not being developed for its own sake, will thus be of limited scope.

The general framework for the discussion is borrowed directly from the final presentation of Piaget (1967), drawn from the book *Logique et connaissance scientifique* (Logic and Scientific Knowledge) that he edited and in which he sets forth the common trends in the internal epistemologies of the various sciences as well as the trends specific to epistemologies that he describes as "derived."

The internal epistemologies are an integral part of each science; they represent the search for foundations using the methods of these sciences. However, some of the major currents of thought that run through each of these sciences can be abstracted.

As for the derived epistemologies, they attempt to specify the nature of the relationship between subject and object that makes knowledge possible. In a nominalist perspective, for example, mathematics is reduced to a mere language, whereas in a platonic perspective, it is the reflection of pre-existing ideal objects. By adopting either of these positions, one says something about the object, linguistic or ideal; but, if one adopts a constructivist point of view, one considers that in the two previous cases, and in a different way, one minimizes the activity of the subject in the construction of the object. So here we have, for example, three different points of view on the relation of the subject and the object in the framework of derived epistemologies. Let us first look at the common tendencies of the internal epistemologies and then of the derived epistemologies.

Trends Common to Internal Epistemologies

In all sciences there is a conception according to which "explaining consists in identifying the existence of irreducible structures, in other words, that one cannot reduce to simpler elements: it would then be the properties of these irreducible structures that would account for the elementary properties" (p. 1226).[75] The Gestalt Psychology School is of this type. The overall structure or "gestalt" is a primary fact that can only be explained by itself. The common characteristic of this type of conception is anti-reductionism, namely the use of the most general structural features, which would be immediately grasped by a sort of "primitive" intuition. In such a conception, the idea of genesis is absent from the debate. It is thus a matter of structures devoid of genesis.

---

75. For this section, unless otherwise specified, the pages refer to the above-mentioned reference work: Jean Piaget, dir. *Logique et connaissance scientifique*, Paris, Gallimard, 1967.

Another trend, opposite to the first, which is also found in all sciences, is the reductionist vision, which consists in reducing the superior to the inferior or the complex to the elementary. This trend is certainly the most widespread and is strongly embedded in the West since Descartes. Thus, the living is reduced to physics and chemistry, and society to the combination of basic individual characters. One attempts to apprehend complex realities using methods of atomic composition. Though the idea of genesis – of construction over time – indeed appears here, the resulting edifice does not have the character of a structure endowed with its own properties that would not be reducible to the combination of elements. So here we do have the idea of genesis, but without structure.

A third explanatory tendency consists "in seeking the key to intelligibility neither in structures that are all given, nor in a reduction of the complex to the simple, but in a progressive construction of structures" (p. 1228). This is the specifically constructivist view. Every structure is conceived as the product of genesis and every genesis as proceeding from previous structures. There are thus a certain number of relational interactions that generate a process of totalization that can only take place over time. This is a general version of a dialectical model, within which the elements brought into interaction can be complementary opposites without necessarily being contradictions, as in the strict form of the Hegelian dialectic (thesis, antithesis, synthesis) which is only a particular case of the general dialectical circle. Thus, structure and genesis, mutually nourishing each other.

Trends in Derived Epistemologies

Let us recall that an epistemology derived from a science seeks "to determine the respective roles played by the subject and the object in the particular mode of knowledge specific to that science" (p. 1239). The principle of classification is thus provided by the data themselves: either knowledge is derived from the object (physical object or ideal object in the platonic sense), or it is derived from the subject (physical subject or transcendental subject), or it is derived from an interaction between subject and object, the result of which synthesizes the necessary contribution of both. If we apply this triad to the currents of thought that are common to internal epistemologies, we obtain a double-entry table (Table 3) whose columns correspond respectively to anti-reductionism (structures without genesis), reductionism (genesis without structure) and constructivism (structures and genesis). The rows then correspond to the sources of knowledge, depending on whether one considers knowledge comes from the object, from the subject, or from the interaction between the two.

The first triad (1–3 of table 3) is characterized by its recourse to transcendental realities. For example, Platonism refers to a world of pure Ideas which have an existence independent of any subject. It is thus a transcendentalism on the side of the object. As for Kantian apriorism, it refers this time to a transcendental subject with its *a priori* intuitions: space, time, and causality. Finally, Husserl's phenomenology uses both at the same time: phenomenological reduction and eidetic reduction make it possible to pass from empirical subject and facts to transcendental subject and pure essences. This triad thus differs from the other two (4–9) in that the latter does not call upon any transcendental reality.

The second triad (4–6) refers to various types of reductionism. Either knowledge is considered as originating in the object, i.e., is reduced, as in classical empiricism, to a "given" independent of the subject's actions; or it is recognized, as in conventionalism, that the subject's intervention is not limited to receiving external data but also consists in expressing them through a cognitive activity of a logical-mathematical type specific to the subject. "But, following the internal logic of reductionism, notes Piaget, this intervention of the subject is then 'reduced' to its minimal form, which is that of an exclusively linguistic activity consisting in coordinating conventional signs" (p. 1242). As for variety 6, which Piaget calls "identification," he reserves it for Émile Meyerson's conception. One could spontaneously situate logical empiricism, which claims to combine physical empiricism and linguistic interpretation of mathematics, but Piaget refuses to do so, because, according to him, this current of ideas only juxtaposes the two previous theses without making a true synthesis of them.

Table 3. Classification of epistemological trends in science.

	ANTI-REDUCTIONISM (Structures without genesis)	REDUCTIONISM (Genesis without structure)	CONSTRUCTIVISM (Structures and genesis)
OBJECT	1. Platonism	4. Empiricism	7. "Dialectic of nature"
SUBJECT	2. Apriorism	5. Nominalism and Conventionalism	8. Historical relativism
INTERACTION SUBJECT × OBJECT	3. Phenomenology	6. Identification	9. Dialectic

Source: Piaget, J. (dir.) (1967), *Logique et connaissance scientifique*. Paris, Gallimard. Encyclopédie de la Pléiade, p. 1240, 1241.

As for Meyerson's interpretation, it consists in "reducing the activities of the subject to the exercise of the principle of identity, in conceiving the act of knowing objects as the progressive reduction of the complex to the simple," pursues Piaget (p. 1242). Cognitive activity is thus always presented as an interaction between the "rational identical" and the diversity reflected in facts, an activity that is never fully realized.

The problem with the third triad, constructionism (7–9), is that one should be satisfied with box 9 since, as notes Piaget, truly constructivist approaches result "sooner or later to an inseparable interaction between the inputs of the subject and those of the object in the mechanism, not only of knowledge in general but of all the particular varieties of scientific knowledge" (p. 1243). However, constructivism, it is noted, also oscillates between the three tendencies – realism, idealism, or inseparable subject-object interaction – even if, for all these tendencies, the subject and the object are no longer separated, as in anti-reductionist or reductionist approaches. In the latter two cases, the knowing subject either reproduces in thought a copy of the outside world or draws from himself his knowledge of the world. For constructivism, and all dialectizing epistemologies, knowledge is primarily linked to the action of the subject who modifies the object, and it is through the transformations introduced by this action that the object is reached.

Despite this commonality, therefore, some types of constructivism lean either towards the object or the subject. For example, the "dialectic of nature" as set forth by Engels (Box 7) is more object-centered. According to the latter, science illustrates that dialectics is embedded in nature and lies at the heart of its own development. And science, by following the path of dialectics, accounts for that. However, the intervention of the knowing subject in such a conception is minimized, since objectivity resides more in a natural datum that is to be attained by a dialectical process. One has to wait for the discoveries of microphysics to see how the intervention of the knowing subject in observed reality leads to a constructed objectivity instead of a simply dialectically discovered one.

As for cell 8 of the table, Piaget reserves it for the idealism of Léon Brunschvicg, in whom he sees two points in common with dialectical approaches: the role of action and the constant overcoming of opposing theses. Brunschvicg's "[...] essential thesis is the rejection of any a priori structure and empiricism in favor of interactions that are constantly changing in the course of history and exclude any speculative absolute", notes Piaget (p. 1245). According to the latter, Brunschvicg's constructivism remains idealistic in that his historical relativism fails to really decentralize the subject's knowledge.

That leaves cell 9, which Piaget describes as dialectical constructivism. We will pay special attention to this epistemological position, of which our approach constitutes a kind of extension. A more thorough epistemological reflection would lead us to discuss the relative value of each of the positions[76] and also to further develop the horizontal dimensions of the table. That would mean further exploring *realism* whose various tendencies emphasize the object, *idealism* whose various kinds place the origin of knowledge in the subject, and *subject-object interactionism* which leads to constructivism as such.

Instead of following that path, however, we will explore the latter category in greater depth, first by going somewhat beyond the Piagetian framework, and occasionally introducing a critical viewpoint on certain epistemological positions as they appear relevant in the current discussion.

Constructivism

As mentioned in the previous paragraphs, constructivism involves an interaction between subject and object. It avoids having recourse to some transcendental reality and places itself at the heart of the interaction. Nothing is given at the outset, neither on the side of the subject nor that of the object. Piaget then sets out to observe how from birth to adulthood the subject manages to build the world as we know it by increasingly coordinating his or her actions, and simultaneously constructing the structures by which he or she assimilates this world effectively. Notions of space, time, and causality are not given at the outset but constructed. The psychological subject gradually shifts from an egocentric perception to a decentration that allows him or her to reach the knowing subject in general, the epistemic

---

76. Jean Piaget's discussion in this regard can be found in the same book (1967) from pages 1246 to 1271.

subject. The object is no longer the thing in itself, perceived "as it is or through structuring glasses" (p. 1244), but rather the result of a construction which is simultaneously a self-construction.

For the egocentric subject, who has not yet achieved epistemic decentration, the object says more about the subject than itself. I enter a room and feel it is warm. My neighbor, in the same room, finds it is cold. The object "temperature" is then a projection of the characteristics of the egocentric subject. But if I say, after reading the thermometer, "it's 20 degrees Celsius in the room," I switch from a self-centered subject to a decentered subject; in other words, I leave my personal point of view and adopt that of the knowing subject in general. However, this new object "temperature" is invested with many characteristics that belong to the subject: first, the numbers, appearing on a scale at intervals (and not proportionally, which makes me understand that 4° is not twice as hot as 2°), then matching of this scale with the variations in the volume of a column of mercury in a glass tube, etc. The number as such does not in itself belong to temperature, nor does the type of scale on which this number is placed, nor the correspondence established between the scale and the physical properties of mercury. And yet, these inputs from the subject into the object are the only way to speak objectively about temperature. The object "temperature" is, therefore, a constructed object, but not one built in an erratic manner. Throughout its construction, the subject has had to accommodate to the constraints of reality and coordinate his or her actions effectively. This is what Piaget calls adaptation, which is at the origin of the construction of increasingly complex action structures.

Varela, for his part, develops a vision directly inspired by the Piagetian conception and also by the oriental philosophies of Zen Buddhism. His epistemological model is called *enaction*, from the verb "to enact," which means to generate, to make something happen or emerge. Here again, nothing is pregiven, neither on the side of the subject nor on that of the object. Universe of subject and universe of object are co-created; they make each other simultaneously emerge through the history of the various actions of the living unity considered. Within this historical journey, the questions that arise are not problems predefined by a pregiven environment but are *enacted* through a "know-how dependent on the context [...], knowing and known [...] standing in relation to each other through mutual specification or dependent coorigination."[77]

In such a perspective, one no longer finds, as in idealism, a permanent and stable "self" that would form the basis of our experience of the world, nor, as in realism, a pregiven world that would represent the basis of the emergence of our self: the two are reciprocally generated.

From such a situation, Varela concludes, strangely enough, that there are no foundations. According to him, one must abandon the philosophical project of finding foundations and learn to live in a world without foundations. He quotes, in this respect, Hilary Putnam:

> *Science is wonderful at destroying metaphysical answers, but incapable of providing substitutes ones. Science takes away foundations without providing a replacement. Whether we want to be there or not, science has put us in the position of having to live without foundations. It was shocking when Nietzsche said this, but today it is commonplace; our historical position – and no end to it is in sight – is that of having to philosophize without "foundations."*[78]

Now we are back to the heart of the debate. Are there foundations? Let us recall that one of the objectives of this reflection is to show how the paradigm of self-reference, as developed here, would force us to come up with an answer other than those proposed. But we will have to take into account the difficulties encountered historically in the search for foundations, both in science and in philosophy. We will also have to resolve the question of the famous "self" as the foundation of our experience, something that has turned out to be so problematic.

Let us begin by revisiting this last epistemological category, which includes the dialectical constructivism of Piaget and the enaction of Varela, and from which our approach originally stems. The preceding description of this position gives rise to unease.

---

77. Francisco J. Varela, Evan Thompson, Eleanor Rosch, *The Embodied Mind*, Cambridge, MIT Press, 1992.
78. Hilary Putnam, quoted by Francisco J. Varela *et al.* (1992), p. 218.

Let us take, for example, the Piagetian statement that "the object is known through the modifications that the actions of the subject exert on it, while the subject only ever becomes aware of himself through the transformations that the object provokes in his actions."[79] The meaning of the word "object" is not univocal in this quotation. If we refer to the above example of temperature, the object, quite obviously, is constructed. It is, therefore, the result, the culminating point of an interaction. But between what and what? If one answers, "between subject and object," one must assume an already pre-existing object somehow endowed with its own action in that it forces the subject to adjust, to accommodate to its requirements. What, then, is the status of the "object" before it is constructed, since it precisely obliges the subject to construct it? And what is also the status of the subject? These questions have obviously not escaped Piaget:

> *Objects do exist, and they have structures that also exist independently of us. However, since objects and their laws can only be known by our operations that are applied to them for this purpose, and constitute the framework of the instrument of assimilation that allows us to attain them, we reach them only by successive approximations,* **which means that they represent a limit that is never reached**.[80]

Regarding the *subject*, we find a similar phenomenon. It is clear that the constructions elaborated by the subject do not start from 'nothing' and suppose internal preconditions. From this point of view, Piaget agrees with Kant but adds :

---

79. Willem E. Beth, Wolfe Mays, Jean Piaget, « Étude d'épistémologie génétique. » I. *Épistémologie génétique et recherche psychologique*, Paris : Presses Universitaires de France, 1957.
80. Jean Piaget, *L'épistémologie génétique*, Paris, Presses Universitaires de France, Coll. « Que sais-je » 1399, 1972, p. 119. "*Certes, les objets existent et ils comportent des structures qui existent elles aussi indépendamment de nous. Seulement, les objets et leurs lois ne pouvant être connus que grâce à celles de nos opérations qui leur sont appliquées à cet effet, et constituent le cadre de l'instrument d'assimilation permettant de les atteindre, nous ne les rejoignons donc que par approximations successives,* **ce qui revient à dire qu'ils représentent une limite jamais atteinte.**" (Emphasis added.)

> *However, [Kant's] a priori forms were much too rich: he believed, for example, in the necessity of Euclidean space, whereas non-Euclidean geometries reduced it to the rank of a special case.*[81]

This is the case of *group* structure, considered by Henri Pointcaré to be necessary at the outset, but whose construction was also shown by Piaget to be progressive.

> *The result is that to achieve an authentic a priori, one must reduce ever more the "comprehension" of the initial structures, and that, in the end, what remains as a prior necessity is reduced to mere functioning [...]*[82]

Piaget's formulation concerning the prior existence of objects with their structures seems somewhat imprudent and could lead one to believe that he inadvertently falls into *realism*. Such is the opinion of Varela (1993, pp. 239–240) who criticizes Piaget for this, even though he acknowledges relying heavily on the latter's thinking. It is also the opinion of Ernst von Glasersfeld (1988, p. 27) who notes Piaget's "penchant for metaphysical realism."

However, we do not find the above criticisms to be well founded. But let us begin with a brief comment on the *enaction* of Varela.

Varela's perspective of enaction attempts to solve the problem by suggesting that subject and object simultaneously come to life. But if one examines the genesis of this co-creation, one must admit that subject and object cannot be distinct at the beginning of the process; otherwise, they would already be in the world as distinct pre-determined entities. Now, how can one imagine this subject-object co-creation without implicit reference to an original state in which they are undifferentiated? Can one ignore this horizon or backdrop from which they mutually emerge? Neither Piaget, Varela, nor von Glasersfeld manage to go without this "background of reality" to develop their thesis.

---

81. *Ibid.* p. 120: "*Seulement, [les] formes a priori [de Kant] étaient beaucoup trop riches : il croyait, par exemple, l'espace euclidien nécessaire, alors que les géométries non euclidiennes l'ont réduit au rang de cas particulier.*"
82. "*Il en résulte qu'à vouloir atteindre un a priori authentique, on doit réduire de plus en plus la « compréhension » des structures de départ et que, à la limite, ce qui subsiste à titre de nécessité préalable se réduit au simple fonctionnement [...]*"

What I took the liberty of calling Piaget's *imprudence* lies in the fact that the author speaks of a world of already structured *objects*. Piaget is not a writer of micro-precision, but a writer of context. The full meaning of a statement is rarely fully contained in the statement itself. If we look at his entire work, both as an epistemologist and as a scientific observer, nothing suggests that he is not a constructivist; in this respect, he is indeed "the father of us all." It would suffice to correct the Piagetian formulation while preserving the essence of the message. One could thus rephrase it approximately as follows:

"Certainly, reality exists, of which one can postulate an implicit coherence, which manifests itself, among other things, through the appearance of a living totality (which we are) which constitutes a unity capable of distinguishing itself from the rest. It is in the interaction of this unity with that which is not it that a world of objects is created at the same time as the knowing subject is structured."

This world of objects is not reality as such, which would have been discovered as it is, but simply the story of an interaction between an entity whose natural functioning has been permanently disturbed by *that which it is not*, and which it has had to construct as a distinct environment, while at the same time constructing itself through a process of adaptation to this environment.

In constructivist epistemologies, but at the other end of the continuum, one has learned to fear being stigmatized as a *realist*, to the point of wanting to believe and make believe that reality comes into the world downstream from an interaction between that which must, of course, somehow constitute parts of that very reality: the living being and its environment. The refusal to recognize upstream a prior horizon of reality leads to a confusion that makes it challenging to specify the various types of epistemological constructivism, whose plural character has been illustrated by Le Moigne (1995).

Even constructivist epistemologies need, in other words, what might be called this "ontological hypothesis" of reality. The fundamental difference between constructivist and realist mindsets lies in the fact that for the latter, it is the world of pre-existing objects as such that one must discover as they are, whereas, for constructivists, the horizon of primitive reality is undifferentiated and does not constitute a world of prefabricated objects. It is the progressive differentiation of subject and object that will create the constructions that we inhabit as our world. Von Glasersfeld, for whom the radicality of constructivism lies in eliminating all forms of metaphysical realism, may take offense at this. But it can be illusory to link the radicality of constructivism to collusion with idealism.

Experiencing and the "Self" Issue

Let us now come to the foundations of experiencing and the 'self' issue. Considerable energy is spent by Varela and the Eastern approaches to which he refers, to show that no "self" exists that would serve as a stable foundation for one's experiencing. We will discuss this question in greater depth, but we can already provide some elements of an answer.

First, every living being represents a totality that constitutes a self-referential unity, which is a unity that distinguishes itself from its environment through its own autonomous functioning. Contrary to what is sometimes heard, this distinction is not an illusion. It is the very condition of the existence of this living being. But, however differentiated it may be, the living being is not separated from the environment. It is in the environment.

And, as already indicated, the self-referential cycle cannot take place without the living totality differentiating one of its parts as an internal agent of a particular operation. This notion of "agent" is entirely consistent with that proposed by Minsky in his *Society of mind*. Local action structures (Minsky's agents) are set up to solve local problems. These agents coordinate with each other to form "agencies", or, one might say, complex agents, capable of acting at a higher level. The agent at the highest level is precisely the tool of action of the living unity as an autonomous totality in its environment. If the living unity is a person, some traditions will speak of the Ego, a Latin reference to the form of language that refers to the self-indicated subject of the action, "I."

We, therefore, have a totality and a differentiated part within this totality which is the agent of the highest level. It is then that one sees the common-sense theorist emerge who seeks the foundation of the totality in this agent. Finding nothing valid at this level, he looks for another, deeper anchorage point and so he turns, as is most often seen, to the various forms of personal pronouns, hoping to find there a natural expression of this hypothetical instance that can serve as a foundation. Will thus be proposed a Self, a Me... and other characters that populate the inner universe of the person and that some will feel the need to qualify as deep, profound or superior, etc.

One can thus build a whole pyramid of alleged foundations, a process reminiscent of the myth, from a primitive culture, according to which the earth rests on the back of a turtle, which in turn rests on the back of yet another turtle, which... and so on. To the interlocutor who would want to go immediately to the end of the story, one could simply answer: "Don't waste your energy, they're turtles all the way down!"[83] This risk threatens the Ego that would want to lean on the turtle of its "deepest self"... and so on "all the way down." And it is this deep and desperate attempt to cling to something that would establish the legitimacy of the Ego that Varela, in continuity with oriental traditions, rightly attempts to combat.

A confusion remains, however, which could easily be dispelled by making the distinctions called for here: "*I*, a living person, *am* indeed myself, but I *have* no self. "My-self" is not something I have: I *am* myself." Therefore, when I say "myself," I am only referring to the totality that I am, within which the agent "I" who is speaking to you stands apart or, in other words, "is differentiated." This agent "I" is very real, but it is only a part of "myself," the totality, which is also very real, but directly inaccessible as a totality to the differentiated agent that is a part of it.

Normative Implications for Theory

This is where the conditions required by the self-referential paradigm come into play. For a totality, there is no foundation to be found in the parts of that totality. There is no internal

---

[83]. Abbreviated version of an anecdote experienced by Williams James and presented by Isabelle Stengers at the 1981 Cérisy colloquium on self-organization, published by Le Seuil in 1983 under the direction of Paul Dumouchel and Jean-Pierre Dupuy under the title *L'auto-organisation. De la physique au politique*. The metaphor is also taken up by J.-L. Le Moigne (2003) and developed, however, in the context of another problematic.

ingredient that alone would make the totality be a totality. That there is no internal ingredient in a totality, be the latter an individual person or a society, that can be regarded as the definitive point of reference for that totality has, for example, considerable ethical and political consequences. No element is the ultimate truth of that totality. Nor can one find a foundation in an element external to that totality, since it is by nature self-referential. Should we thus conclude with Varela that no foundation exists?

The only way to be consistent in a self-referential context concerning this issue can be expressed in the following statement: "Totality is for itself its own foundation." But then we may have the impression, because of the paradox inherent in the statement, of dealing with a vicious circle. Of being plunged into the Cretan paradox which, should our objective be choosing between true and false, we would find repulsive. However, this latter objective is one option among others. Indeed, the circularity of the statement may appear to us instead as a richness to be exploited, as Varela himself suggests on page 23 of his 1989 work. In this case, it is a question of placing the presence and absence of foundation on two successive levels that are mutually engendered. Referring to the statement, let us see how we can answer the following questions:

Question 1: Is there a foundation?

Answer 1: Yes, the *totality*, which is at the origin of a process that presides over the differentiation of an agent subset that initiates the foundation process by exerting its action on the *receptive*.

Q2: Is the founding *agent* the foundation?

A2: No, because it is a part of the totality.

Q3: Is the *receptive* the founded object that will then become the foundation?

A3: No, because it is a part of the totality which should then owe its founding character to another part of this same totality.

Q4: Given that the dichotomy *agent/receptive*, in this case, *founder/founded*, covers in extension the entire field of the whole, is there a foundation?

A4: No. The totality cannot be whole either in the founding or in the founded agency, so the foundation disappears in the founding act itself.

Q5: Can a particular type of interaction between founding and founded agencies restore the totality?

A5: Yes, if a hierarchical reversal of the founding process gives rise to a paradoxical agent that integrates the forces at work and regenerates the totality in a state of greater coherence.

Q6: Is there then a foundation?

A6: Yes, the totality is for itself its own foundation: it is upon its own functioning that it has relied to continue to be what it is and to enrich its identity.

Q7: Is there a methodological expression of such a foundation?

A7: Yes: the self-referential process is the foundation of a living unity, etc.

In this way, the two poles of the alternative – foundation/absence of foundation – can be developed in turn in an oscillation that enriches the process. The circularity of the process is a means of highlighting the reality that founds it. This reality is the *totality* as a self-referential unity. The dichotomy generated by differentiation allows a third party to emerge that has meaning in relation to the two poles, but which is not reducible to either of them. Such a dichotomy thus escapes the restrictive logic of an exclusive distinction that would imply the exclusion of the third party. The self-referential dynamic is thus that of the *included third party*, which makes it possible to pass through successive planes from one pole to the other and to regenerate the totality in a state of greater coherence.

In short, when a pertinent question, relative to a particular reality, comes up in a dichotomic fashion, the answer is never to be sought in one of the poles of the alternative to the detriment of the other, but rather, as just illustrated, in a dynamic integration at the heart of the self-referential cycle.

This may call for a certain caution as to the type of question to be asked. For example, posing the question, "Does reality have a foundation?" would project us into the metaphysical world of ontology. Suffice it to say here that should we be unwise enough to engage in such a reflection, we would have to, on the basis of the present paradigm, proceed as we have just done.

This being acknowledged, and without pretending to indulge in a rigorous ontological reflection, let us attempt, as a kind of exercise, a *thought experiment*. More precisely, let's examine the question of "being."

Spencer Brown (1969) has made it clear that something exists ("there is something") if it can be distinguished from what it is not.

First hypothesis: being comes forth against a background of nothingness. If this were the case, the nothingness that serves as a background would itself be something, it would be part of being. Thus, being cannot arise as differentiation from nothingness. If being cannot distinguish itself from nothingness, it merges with it and cannot emerge from it. In the absence of any other hypothesis, one would have to invalidate this one and conclude that there has never been and never will be anything, which would be the simplest and most probable hypothesis.

But it seems that this latter hypothesis has not been retained, given that we observe that there is something rather than nothing. There is only one way out: the only way for *being* to be is to distinguish itself from itself, making a founding instance emerge from itself on a background of being to be founded. At this level of the process, the foundation disappears. We find here the self-referential cycle with the same contours and paradoxes as when we apply it to any living totality. It is only through the founding process and at its end that "*being* once again becomes for itself its own foundation." But let us quickly move away from this playful digression, intended to highlight the imperative linked to using the paradigm of self-reference in dealing with any level of reality.

In sum, Varela's choice of rejecting one side of the alternative in favor of the other, namely the absence of foundations, appears, from our perspective, to be a methodological error. The author's insistence on making this absence of foundations a stable, fixed, and absolute point of view appears inconsistent since, should this be the case, it is this absence of foundations that becomes the foundation itself, a position that Varela himself with the same insistence defends himself from taking. If such is not the case, what is the status of this fundamental truth (absence of foundations) from which one cannot depart without being anathema? Is it not thus this truth that founds discourse, that founds behavior, that founds reality? What does Varela rely on to decree the absence of foundations? On the other hand, if one admits the absence of foundations, what does he rely on to deny the status of foundation to this "absence of foundations"?

In the binary logic in which Varela positions himself, the choice of one pole to the detriment of the other leads to a dead end. While Varela's solution places us before an insoluble contradiction, the solution proposed here – a dynamic oscillation between the two poles – places us before a paradox that is manageable, consistent with the self-reference paradigm, and consistent also, let us emphasize, with the foundation of Varela's thinking.

Self-Reference and "Construction"

These reflections lead us to the epistemological proposal underlying the present book. Let us take as our starting point the further elaboration of epistemological constructivism, which we referred to earlier. We will first examine the various meanings that the word *construction* can have when one speaks of constructing one's world. For the purposes of the present proposal, I will reduce the various types of construction to a limited number of categories.

The first category would be that of *constructed knowledge of natural objects*. The meaning given to the words *natural objects* here is very broad. It refers to the case where the knowing subject does not himself or herself give birth to the reality that gives rise to cognitive construction. For example, no knowing subject has the pretension of creating the reality *temperature* by the mere fact of measuring or defining such a reality. Thus, the object of knowledge, *temperature*, is constructed, but it is rooted in a pre-existing reality from which subject and object are differentiated. This first category includes the objects of the sciences of matter (physics, chemistry, geology, etc.) and the processes that can be associated with them (thermodynamics, mechanics, etc.) Next, the life sciences (biology, psychology, etc.) and finally the sciences of this particular object that is the *knowing subject* in the construction of the cognitive structures by which he comes to construct all these natural objects previously mentioned. This last element was the object of Piaget's genetic epistemology.

The second category of cognitive construction concerns what I will call here *artifacts*, or if you like, man-made objects that give access to a whole realm that Herbert Simon has called *the artificial*.[84] It is, so to speak, the domain of a pragmatics that generates all prospective simulations, such as artificial intelligence, for example, and to which we will return later.

The third category concerns *self-constructing objects* of a level of complexity equal to or higher than the knowing subject. This is the central focus of this reflection.

There exists an obvious break between the first category and the other two. And this break manifested itself more clearly historically from the end of the 17th century with Vico, whose method was opposed to that of Descartes.[85] Vico proposed the theory of *Verum Factum* which states that "the 'true' is what is done and that only he who has done can know the result of his operation". He proposed the principle of *Ingenium* as an alternative to the principle of analysis which is the basis of Cartesian methodologies. This is where the expressions *engineering sciences* or *engineering design process* come from. Rather than endlessly separating and atomizing, the approach rather tries to link, to join, to associate. Thus, it is fundamentally creative capacity that is emphasized instead of analytical capacity. Realistic epistemologies have always wanted to reduce this path to an *application* of the so-called basic sciences, whereas it has more to do with what Simon called the *sciences of design* or *design sciences*. In this perspective, the *engineer* is more a "designer of constructible projects" than an "applicator of physical knowledge" to use the expressions of Le Moigne.[86]

---

84. Herbert A. Simon, 1969. *The Sciences of the Artificial*. MIT Press, Cambridge, Mass.
85. This opposition could be traced back to the Greeks. On this subject, see Jean-Louis Le Moigne: *Les épistémologies constructivistes* published in 1995 by Presses Universitaires de France and *Le constructivisme. Volume I: Les enracinements* published in 2001 by L'Harmattan. In addition to this source, one can consult G. Vico's book *La méthode des études de notre temps* presented, translated and annotated by Alain Pons and reproduced on the site ric-mcxapc@wanadoo.fr. Retreived April 15, 2019.
86. Jean-Louis Le Moigne, *Les épistémologies constructivistes*, Paris, Presse Universitaires de France, 1995, p. 50.

The most striking achievements in this area are computer simulations. One might wonder how these simulations can advance our knowledge. Indeed, a simulation can only be as good as the assumptions on which it is based, and a computer only does what it is programmed to do. Nevertheless, Simon (2004, pp. 46–56) points out that despite this, simulation can provide one with new knowledge in two different ways. The first is that it is always difficult to see all the implications of one's premises, however correct they may be. The power of the computer thus allows one to analyze, starting from complicated initial conditions, the interactions of a large number of variables. For example, our knowledge of the mechanisms governing the behavior of gases allows us to produce simulations that make it possible to establish a climate theory allowing us to make short-term weather predictions.

The second way in which simulation can further our knowledge concerns cases where we have limited knowledge of the laws that govern the internal behavior of the system. Let us take an example: we don't have a completed theory that would tell us the processes underlying Johann Sebastian Bach's art of composition. Attempting to produce an artifact that is a clone of the musician would be absurd. The author of a simulation, which was actually carried out, thus had to abstract the aspect of musical production in the composer and create an artifact, a program in this case, capable of composing "Bach music." The first results, in the ongoing construction, failed to meet the desired goal. So, the behavior of the artifact had to be observed empirically, and this observation made it possible, by successive approximations, to gradually enrich the fragments of the theory that guided the design. At the end of the process, the computer was given the order to create a *"Bach composition."* Once produced, this composition was auditioned and compared with a real Bach composition, both pieces being performed by the same pianist.[87] All listeners with minimal knowledge of the music recognized Bach in both cases and many could not determine which of the compositions was truly by Bach. Clearly, the artifact could not have produced masterpieces such as the Art of Fugue

---

87. The experience was performed on Radio-Canada with pianist Louise Bessette.

or the Mass in B minor, but it greatly enriched the knowledge of the paradigm underlying Bach's art of composition.

Before moving on to the third category, let's clarify the fundamental difference between the second category and the first. This second category related to artifacts brings us to an interesting crossroads concerning the fact of *construction*. We see the latter's meaning differentiating itself and following two different paths: first, the systems to be observed must be *built*. Secondly, they must then be *observed* empirically so that knowledge can be gained from them. This second step is also a construction, but distinct from the first. This second construction is of the same type as the one specific to the first category concerning *natural objects*: indeed, the knowledge of the artifact will be the result of construction as was the knowledge of *temperature* in the previous examples. On the other hand, this *cognitive construction* is distinct from the *construction of the artifact* itself, which becomes the *reality* from which emerges an object of knowledge for a knowing subject. It is therefore ultimately the *cognitive construction* of a *reality* that has been previously *constructed*.

The two constructions followed, so to speak, two different paths, one that could be described as pragmatic and the other that always remains cognitive in the sense of the first category. It is the *interaction* of these two types of construction that is peculiar to this second category. We note here that despite the distinction made between the cognitive dimension of the first category and the pragmatic dimension of the second category, this second dimension, pragmatic, is also essentially of a cognitive nature. For example, the simulations produced are in fact manipulations of symbols using a computer. But to simulate an act of creative design in this way, as in the previous example, we nevertheless note the need for a particular accommodation of the cognitive tool: we can no longer rely on a process subject to the rules of formal logic from which we would somehow hope to obtain a valid result by deduction. The act of conception can be seen, in the words of Le Moigne (2001), as "the act of seeking – through an exercise in symbol manipulation – that which does not exist, and yet finding it: creating it." In the previous example, the researcher develops a theoretical knowledge of an artifact by which he sets out to search for a piece of music (Bach-sounding) that does not exist and yet finds it: creates it.

In this field of the conception of "design," one can call upon heuristic procedures and all kinds of non-standard logics such as the recursive logic of the self-reference calculus of Varela (1975), for example. In this perspective, it is interesting to welcome Le Moigne's proposal concerning a recursive interpretation of the symbol linked to "the possibility of conjunctive formalisms, capable of manipulating *at once the operator and the operand, an operand which, when operated, produces the operator that operates it again*" (op. cit., p. 240).

Let us summarize the characteristics of this second category: an artifact is constructed to simulate by successive approximations another reality that does not yet exist. The researcher makes an empirical observation of the behavior of the artifact and constructs a knowledge that tends towards a theoretical expression of this behavior. As we have just said, we then have two construction paths: one, pragmatic, which is that of the construction of the artifact itself, which then becomes the *reality* to be observed, and the other which is a cognitive construction of this artifact. By proceeding in this way, one comes to discover, while creating it, the desired result. This is how a design artifact can be distinguished from a machine running a program according to a pre-programmed algorithm based on a defined result. Le Moigne cites as an example Karl Marx's metaphor concerning the bee and the architect: "What distinguishes from the outset the worst architect from the most expert bee is that he builds the cell in his head before building it in the hive." And Le Moigne comments: "Building in one's head before building in the hive is perhaps the most satisfactory definition of design as an intelligible act of computation" (op. cit., p. 242).

Let us now begin the transition to the third category which, while being an extension of the second, is at odds with it. The third category has been said to be that of *objects in self-construction*. Let us take a further step along the pragmatic path. At the previous stage, the constructed artifact simulates a reality other than itself, which we will call the reference reality (a program simulating a musician's art of composition, an artifact simulating market reactions to an intervention in the economic field, an artifact simulating intelligence, etc.). The artifact is distinct from what it produces, but it is also distinct from its creator. Moreover, the objective is clearly defined and can be achieved through some type of symbol manipulation.

In the third category, however, it is the reference reality itself that is self-constructing. There is no longer a constructed artifact outside of constructor and constructed product. The self-constructing unit is, so to speak, called to become its own artifact and this artifact will not produce anything other than itself.

The first imperative that presents itself to this unity is not knowing the construction process, but rather putting it into practice. At each level, the human being is from the outset his own, initially unbeknownst laboratory. The ingredients to be manipulated are then no longer symbols, but human entities: individuals, groups, and societies. Here we find ourselves in the field of ethics and politics since the latter develop in the here and now of action, and not primarily in the field of a knowledge that one would have gained from them. If we return to the metaphor of Marx, the human being is initially in the same situation as the bee without having the advantages in the sense that he is launched into construction before he has even thought about it, but this time without benefiting from an already assembled tool: it is from experience that he realizes that he is forced to become his own project.

Contrary to what it has done for the bee, nature has certainly gone a long way in assisting humans in the process of their construction, but it leaves them high and dry, more deprived than the bad architect, who at least has the advantage of being at a distance from his work and, as a result, of being less directly questioned. The void facing the human being is thus more daunting than that of the architect, for this void is the first image to which he has access when he becomes aware of himself as a project. Everything happens as if, at this stage of the self-referential cycle, the ground was being pulled from under one's feet, the absence of a foundation of the approach thus appearing as a yawning abyss.

Pragmatics then takes on a new meaning and plunges to the roots of being to merge with the recursive processes that maintain the unity in question in existence and that push it to realize itself as a self-referential entity. At its base, this pragmatics is cognitively empty and will have to deploy itself through a communicational process before the cognitive arsenal developed on the adaptive axis comes to the rescue.

On this axis of cognitive construction, the observation of the successive states of this self-construction is subject to a second accommodation, which this time pushes the observer into his last retrenchments. There no longer exists any external reference to judge the validity of the product. In the second category, one had a predefined symbol of the product sought, that is, in the example given, the works of Bach himself, which served as pre-existing reference realities with which one could judge the value of the simulation. Here, the reality of reference only appears at the end of the construction on the pragmatic axis and merges with the finished product. Deprived of direct access to a predefined symbol of the sought-after product, the cognitive construction then turns to the observation of the internal coherence of the self-construction process that takes place on the pragmatic axis, a process that is itself evaluated in the light of an independent cognitive version, itself under construction, of the self-referential process. This yardstick must be quite modest at the outset, given that, being forged along the way with the means at hand, it must be able to question the ongoing action in the field, while accepting to be itself shaped in return by its various frequentations. In other words, does the hands-on process put in place respond to what is known, at this stage, about the self-referential process, and can this knowledge in return be enriched and made more coherent by this process?

The peculiarity of the present constructivism then lies in the reversal of perspective that brings the construction process back to its source by zooming in on the methodologically unexplored space of the *precognitive existential*. So far, it is knowledge that represented the edifice to be constructed and pragmatics constituted but a subsidiary of this edifice. Here, the edifice to be built is the human being – the individual person as well as society – and knowledge is only a necessary scaffolding, so to speak, temporary and second, at the service of a pragmatics that is no longer, at its source, of a cognitive nature, but rather of an *existential* nature and which unfolds in the communicational process. The success of the approach established on the cognitive axis comes more from the fact that it fosters the blossoming, on the pragmatic axis, of the human self-construction process, than from the fact of developing true statements about human beings independent of this context. Such is thus the lieu outside of which speaking of radical constructivism would, in my opinion, seem abusive.

But to remain in the line of constructivism, we will have to coordinate the aspects of genesis and structure. For example, the absence of the aspect of genesis could lead one to believe that there exists a pre-established structure, either as an underlying *a priori* to one's functioning or as a pre-existing ideal reality that one must free from its hidden space for it to then appear in its full truth. In Piagetian terms, one would then speak of an anti-reductionism, or transcendentalism, where ready-made structures are deemed to exist without one having to create them.

In contrast to this vision, one could choose to introduce time – thus take genesis into account – but avoid seeing in development any kind of order that would tend towards a process of totalization from which something new would emerge. According to this perspective, the totality would be a mere result without the addition of new properties. This is the vision of reductionism.

As noted previously, the constructivist point of view adopted in our approach synthesizes the above two currents of thought in the paradoxical relationship of a unity with itself, which depends on a process of totalization that is constantly recommenced and linked to a circular interaction between the parts. But such a point of view can easily draw criticism both sides: the reductionists will accuse the constructivists of being preformists who ignore that they are, and conversely, the preformists will accuse them of being reductionists.

Certain criticisms of Piaget were made in the preceding chapter. Let us reformulate the whole matter within the present problematic: if it is constructivism, how can one explain the fact that the development of intellectual structures invariably leads to structures which are identical for everyone? Does this not suggest that what is happening is the unfolding of pre-formed structures? And could this not also be the case in the approach that is being set forth here? If the human being develops by reaching levels of equilibrium from which general characteristics can be deduced, could this not be a sign that everything is there at the beginning and that the pseudo-construction is but the revelation of a pre-formed reality? And furthermore, does not presenting the model of *self-referential totality as a cognitive void*, a void inaccessible to the action of internal agents, constitute a new transcendentalism?

To this, one can answer, regarding intellectual structures, that if there existed, for example, beings made of antimatter which had to adjust to reality as it is presented to us, it is probable that they would not lead to these same structures. But the beings whom we are, subject to the human condition of having to adapt to the physical world of our planet, can only do so through their own action on this world. And to acquire greater mastery of their condition, all humans must adjust their action to this world, abstracting from their own action ever more efficient structures. It is this identity of condition in front of the world, which leads to the identity of results, according to an increasingly complex ordered sequence. Of course, there is a potential provided at the outset by biology, which is not the same for all species. The plasticity of humans is greater than that of other species, but common adaptive processes can be described in the same way since they all derive from the action of a biological organism on its environment. For example, the same sensory-motor constructs can be observed in other mammals as in humans.

The reasoning is analogous concerning the present approach. The condition of an entity that must maintain itself and become complex as a unit must necessarily be based on internal processes of totalization, that is, processes must themselves become the indirect object of their own action to restore the totality to a generally greater state of coherence; otherwise the unit will crumble into multiple unintegrated parcels. In other words, the living being is made up of recursive processes whose results, by a hierarchical reversal, become agents that produce these same processes.

Can one then say, from a Platonic perspective, that one is dealing with a matrix of which reality is made, and of which we would be imperfect images that we would have to perfect? One could reason this way, and this would not be devoid of meaning; however, such is not the meaning of the present statement. To be convinced of this, let us return to an example given in the first chapter, whose lightness may paradoxically contribute to give more weight to the argument: a cat grooming itself. If the animal operates as it does, it could be argued that it has access, through a kind of animal telepathy, to the world of universal essences where one finds the archetype of hierarchical reversal. It is much simpler to say that it is the very nature of the situation that leads the species, through the mechanisms of evolution, to invent such strategies so the cat can reach the totality of its coat, as long as complete grooming has acquired importance for this species.

In another order of example, this is the case with any living organism, which cannot be maintained and become more complex without a constant re-entry of its constituent processes into their own field of application. This cannot be done through the continuous, linear action of an agent on its object, but necessarily through a circular, discontinuous process, which the self-referential character of the condition calls for. It is therefore of necessity, and not by an intervention of the transcendental world, that one finds this same character in all living beings, whatever their level in the hierarchy.

The same type of reasoning applies to the constituent agents' inaccessibility of the totality. If an agent cannot access the totality, it is not that the totality belongs to a transcendental world, but simply that it is inaccessible to that agent because of its position as a constituent element.

There remains the opposite objection of the preformists or anti-reductionists: if one rejects their approach, one should, according to them, be satisfied with observations that respond to the canons of epistemological empiricism, the results of which can be presented through a more or less structured language. A certain form of behaviorism, in short, applied to the random cobbling-together of the adventurer that is the human being. To that, one can reply that even if structured totalities are not preformed – and therefore constitute the constructed result of a process of totalization – they cannot be reduced to behavior alone. The totality is an outcome that goes beyond the characteristics of the agents whose interaction is necessary to maintain it in existence. Here we agree with the idea, recalled earlier, of a certain type of transcendence of the totality with respect to its components, linked to their very condition as components. This relative transcendence makes it possible of doing away with the need of a pre-formed transcendental world, while at the same time avoiding reductionism.

We are, therefore, in the process of trying to see what kind of regularities occur in the development of unities subject to the self-referential cycle. We can expect to observe a sequence of stages, some of which constitute levels of equilibrium. The notion of stage is taken here in the strict sense: their sequence is invariant, the contributions of a stage are necessary for the appearance of the following one, the latter integrating these contributions in a new coherence. This anticipation of a sequence of stages is based on the fact that the elements which are the constituents of the self-referential cycle do not appear randomly. For example, the hierarchical reversal cannot occur before the initial action carried out by the agent. The development of this aspect of genesis will be the subject of the following chapter.

Always in view of specifying more precisely the change in perspective inherent in the present approach, it would be worthwhile to take a closer look at what Morin (1991) refers to as the Western paradigm.

The Western Paradigm

The distinction between the *existential* and the *adaptive*, which gives rise to the unfolding of the corresponding processes of communication and cognition,[88] is at the heart of the present approach and puts the spotlight on the so-called Western paradigm, the name given to the structuring background characterizing Western civilization's main productions. Morin (1991, pp. 211–238) pointed out its main characteristics: for example, the tendency to dissociate, disjoin, analyze, reduce, and simplify in the hope of mastering and dominating the world ever more; and, also, the opposite though not dominant tendency to associate, unite, synthesize, and apprehend complexity in the hope of living in harmony with ourselves and nature.

While agreeing with this point of view, we will attempt to further circumscribe this notion by placing it in the context of

---

88. Let us recall that in the present perspective, communication includes a cognitive dimension, but that it is rooted in an existential process that is, for the unity under consideration, cognitively empty.

the present approach. In the terms of the present model, what characterizes the Western paradigm is the primacy given to the adaptive over the existential, that is, to cognitive activity over the self-generative loop that poses and maintains the human being in existence. The unfolding of this existential process gives rise to a production site that must be set in motion, the lieu of production of the multiform artifact necessary for human self-creation. It is to the evolution of this artifact on the pragmatic axis that science must thus accommodate its methodology.

A few examples to illustrate how the *cognitive* dominates over the *existential* in our culture. Varela (1989) states that "the immunological system can be viewed as a network of cellular interactions which, at each moment, self-determines its own identity". Such a statement sounds reasonable, but he then adds: "If the organism does not know itself, how can it detect the presence of something foreign?".[89]

We fully understand the purported meaning of the text and do not intend to question it, but the expression remains symptomatic of our natural tendency to give primacy to knowledge. Taken literally, the expression implies that the living system in question receives a stimulus that it relates to the knowledge it has of itself and thus determines the foreign character of that stimulus.

Returning to the present perspective, let us recall that the living being does not know itself in the very roots of its existence: it exists! Let us once again paraphrase Merleau-Ponty who asks where, when, and how there ever was a knowledge from within. It suffices for the living being to *be* what it is for the intervention of the stranger to represent a disturbance; it need not *know*, for this to happen, what it is. The primitive disturbance of the living unity is related to its existential reality and this unity is, at this level, as blind as the reaction of the physical particle subjected to an experimental condition. The difference is that in the living being, this primitive disturbance sets in motion an adaptive process that then generates "knowledge of an object." Knowledge is then produced downstream and is not a precondition, as Varela states.

---

89. N. Vaz, F. Varela (1978). Self and non-sense; an organism-centered approach to immunology. *Medical Hypotheses 4*, p. 10.

Within the Western paradigm, any project of importance must give primacy to knowledge. We could give many other examples, including this statement by de Béchillon (1997) for whom the fundamental project of transdisciplinarity would be to remain strictly in the realm of science, that is, as he puts it, "limiting oneself to science!" But if intellectual work begins and ends in the field of knowledge and not in a self-constructing ethical and political worksite, we are operating resolutely within the Western paradigm. In fact, whether we like it or not, this worksite pre-exists intellectual pursuit. The latter is not its product. To paraphrase the previous quotation, one could say that the imperative of the project is not "limiting oneself to science!" but rather "opening oneself to human creation!" The intellectual process applied to this latter endeavor becomes more of a methodological and, so to speak, provisional support tool facilitating its implementation and coherent development. But, as we have seen, this cognitive tool will then have to transform itself to accommodate its schemas and practices to this paradoxical process of human self-construction which will have primacy.

If we address the same problem using Piaget's approach, we find that we remain trapped in the Western paradigm. The intellectual structures, as noted earlier, constitute, according to Piaget, the structures of the person, everything else only representing the energetic aspect fostering the functioning of these structures. An examination, even superficial, can lead us to doubt these premises. Let us take the case of a person suffering from a severe personality disorder such as paranoia. This person is dysfunctional in his or her relationship to himself or herself and to others. However, he or she can nevertheless be quite intellectually productive. The relationship that is disrupted is communicative, not intellectual.

Let's go back to the source of the problem. If we examine more closely the origin of the intellectual process as observed by Piaget, we find that the basic tools of the subject are biologically endowed. These are the reflexes, present at birth, which are sucking and grasping (palmar reflex). This is the only empowerment the subject has on disturbances from the environment. Children construct their world through the adaptation of these two reflexes to their environment; they coordinate their actions more and more efficiently and internalizes these actions of coordination. The resulting structures are thus structures of adaptation to the environment. When we say that subjects construct themselves by constructing the world, it must be clear that they develop themselves as beings-in-process-of-adaptation-to-what-is-not themselves, that is to say, they construct themselves as knowing subjects. But in doing so, we are leaving aside the construction of the subjects' relationship to themselves, which is a prerequisite for their construction of the world.

As a hypothesis, we could try to see what tools biology initially provides to newborn infants to establish their first relationship with themselves. The most obvious is the crying reflex linked to a state of discomfort, which in fact constitutes an expressive reflex behavior that an organism associates with the state in which it finds itself. It is the first empowerment that children have on their relationship to themselves. Out of a chaotic set of felt states emerges a behavior linked to the specificity of some of these states. Order appears in the relationship to oneself, an order that will be able to develop gradually, at the same time as order appears in the relationship to what is not self through the reflexes of adaptation to the chaos of disturbances coming from the environment. Here we have the origin in newborn infants of the two great trajectories that will lead, on the one hand, to the edification of their existential relationship to themselves through a communicational process and, on the other hand, to the edification of the adaptive relationship to their environment through a cognitive process. Needless to say, these processes are radically distinct, even if cognitive elements are an integral part of the communicational process and communicational processes enrich cognitive development.

Obviously, the preceding description is incomplete. First of all, other expressive behaviors play the same role as the one already mentioned, and which develop later, such as smiling, for example. Moreover, only the point of view of the newborn is taken into account here, even though we know that their expressive behavior also constitutes elements of a higher-level unit of communication, the mother-child couple, a unit that is also self-constructing.

In short, the Piagetian conception, which can be seen as the first great contemporary breach in the Western paradigm, would nevertheless tend to maintain us within that same paradigm by giving precedence to the adaptive and ensuing organization over the existential, and this to the point of confusing them with it. In the perspective defended here, however, the cognitive apparatus is not the primary fact of the self-referential totality and cannot, at the cognitive level, by itself completely carry out the self-referential cycle. Rather, the cognitive apparatus is the tool of the hetero-referential relation to reality, and in this sense, it is understandable that it cannot be the basis of the human self-construction process and that it undergoes a paradoxical distortion in such a context.

Construction and Hierarchy

In the introduction, we discussed hierarchically organized *levels* of reality. The term *hierarchy* here is conceived in terms of unities that encompass successive sets of sub-unities, constituting so to speak a tree structure. It is the relationship of a totality to its parts which is highlighted in this kind of hierarchy. This concept excludes the idea of power or control. It is thus totally different from that of hierarchical power; in the latter case, one is not dealing with a relation of the whole to its parts but with a relation where authority links together two parts of the same whole. To avoid confusion, we will thus speak here of a tree hierarchy.

As far as the human being is concerned, the most encompassing level of the tree hierarchy is that of the human species as a whole. Societies constitute units of a lower level and individuals would constitute units of the lowest level. One can identify many intermediate levels between these. The level of the individual is held to be elementary if we consider the unities as totalities. However, the totality that is the individual can only be considered a totality if one acknowledges a lower level and possibly a sub-level, as we have already suggested when discussing the *internal agent*. These subunits, however, will never be studied in themselves as totalities, but always in relation to the level of the individual. Moreover, it will not be necessary to search for the biological correlates of these subunits, any more than it is necessary to do physics to study biology.

Simon (2004, pp. 319–371) points out that among all possible complex forms, *tree-like* forms are those that have time to evolve, as they are made up of a set of stable and relatively autonomous subsystems, each influenced only by the inputs and outputs of the other subsystems. The system is said to be quasi-decomposable. To illustrate this relative autonomy of subsystems, we can refer to an experiment in which the heart of a chicken embryo was isolated and placed in a separate solution. The heart continued to beat on its own for some time, thus detached from the embryo. To obtain a chicken, if one had to wait until the entire animal was built from a single, non-decomposable process, such an animal would probably never be born. It is this characteristic of quasi-decomposability that renders complex systems viable and allows them to evolve more rapidly.

Simon (*Ibid.*) highlights the fact that links within subsystems are stronger and more frequent than links between subsystems. In other words, the further down the hierarchy one descends towards elementary forms, the more the internal dynamics of the units bring into play high-frequency dynamics. The processes are denser and take place on shorter time scales. This is what happens, in physics, with nuclear forces relative to electromagnetic forces and finally gravitational forces. In the human realm, forces of cohesion within an individual are more intense than those within a group or a society. Individual time is much more compact than societal time and the latter is more compact than that of the entire species.

One of the consequences of this property is that units intervene at their level in an aggregated manner and need not take into account all lower-level interactions. In order to study the interactions of two nations, it is not necessary to take into account all the interactions of individuals between and within these nations. In the present approach, it will suffice, to describe or construct a totality of any level, to consider the interaction of the unities of the level immediately below. For example, to describe a dyad as a totality, one need only consider the interaction of the two people who are part of it.

Another consequence is that the development of low-level units is likely to be much more advanced than that of higher-levels ones. If one compares the development of humankind with that of an adult individual, one sees that the stage of evolution of humankind, which extends over thousands of years, is in its infancy, whereas at the individual level, a large number of people have, within a time scale of less than a hundred years, come close to the optimal development of their human potential.

Simon (*Ibid.*) points out that complex structures are redundant, and that this property makes it easier to describe them. For example, the multiple varieties of proteins are made from only twenty amino acids. It is, therefore, the same subunits, in fairly small numbers, that constantly recur in different combinations. In the present approach, this redundancy is further enhanced when applied to units of different levels from which the self-reference characteristic is abstracted. We have seen that the self-referential matrix is made up of a limited number of ingredients that form structures that become ever-more complex as they interlock from level to level. But the characteristic of quasi-decomposability of complex systems allows us to work at one level without necessarily taking into account all lower-levels interactions.

If we draw a conclusion synthesizing these remarks, we first note that the quasi-decomposability of complex systems allows us to work at one level of the hierarchy without necessarily explicitly including all other levels. Secondly, that time scales are shorter and maturity levels greater in lower-level unities of the hierarchy. Finally, that there is redundancy at each of the levels since the units found therein are postulated to all tend towards a self-referent functioning. There is indeed no reason why Vico's assertion that "humanity is its own work of art" should be applied restrictively to a particular level.

The first consequence of all this is that in all probability we will not be able to observe, if only in an embryonic form, the manifestations of the self-referential process in the higher-level unities. This is why doing will have to take precedence over observing, and artifacts will have to be created to allow these unities to gradually become self-referent, hence the primacy of the *project*. The second consequence is that as achievements in lower-level units are more advanced in their development, these will be able to inspire us to build our artifacts at higher levels since they are called upon to manifest, in their construction, the same self-referential process. The third consequence, complementary to the previous one, is that the degrees of freedom of higher levels are much greater since they are built based on increasingly complex sub-unities. The relevant elements are more easily manipulated and constitute the equivalent of a microscopic magnification of lower-level elements. This will be an important methodological tool from a pragmatic point of view.

Any element of the process observed at one level must, of course, be reinterpreted to adapt to the reality of another level, even if the overall structure of the process is isomorphic from one level to another. For example, the notion of *operational closure* must be found at all levels, but it will then take different forms. In biology, for example, the cell is endowed with a physical symbol of what separates internal processes with their own coherence from what is external to them: it is the membrane. At the level of societies or micro-societies, it would be inappropriate to look for such physical symbols. It will thus be necessary to see what meaning should be given to the boundary distinguishing a societal unity, for example, from its environment, and what is the recursive play of the processes that are generated within this boundary.

To Conclude

Finally, this corollary by way of conclusion: all cognitive or pragmatic constructions will have to result from the combination of the fundamental ingredients of the self-referential process. One will thus find at all levels the notions of *totality, identity, operational closure, agent, receptive, paradoxical agent, differentiation,* and *integration.* However, given the particular interpretation given to these basic notions at each level, new notions and new objects will be introduced. It will thus be necessary to encroach on the fields of all disciplines, while retaining only the transdisciplinary aspect and leaving aside the essential objects specific to these disciplines. Furthermore, since this book purports to set forth the outline of a model, not a completed version of it, certain levels of human reality will hardly be mentioned.

Let us begin with a temporal interpretation of the self-referential process when applied to humans.

Chapter III

Temporality of Self-referential Process

We have mentioned the fact that the self-referential circle that characterizes the living includes a dimension of *time*. Even at a microscopic level, each moment experienced as presence to oneself is home to a microgenesis. We could speak metaphorically of a "genetics of the instant," of an ever-being-renewed presence to oneself. These instants that follow one another are the "atoms of time" which interlock to form longer time spans. We will nevertheless have to address the issue at a level of complexity greater than just the immediate instant, a level where longer time spans allow the process to reveal itself more clearly.

The situation presents us with a twofold challenge: whatever the order of magnitude of the cycles, they must first respond to the same general model, because it is always the same process of self-production, of self-creation, of self-invention, on a more or less large scale; the other challenge is to know how to set up these elementary blocks among themselves to create larger structures that are, so to speak, the self-referential unfolding of this same model.

Let's start by recalling the time-ordered sequence of the parts of the basic cycle identified in chapter one. To do this, let us reduce the cycle, independently of orders of magnitude, to a simple formula using the metaphor of personal pronouns:

<u>Me, I am developing myself</u>

In the cycle's development, we first have the *totality*, still in an undifferentiated state: *Me*. Next comes the *agent, I*, which differentiates itself as the subject of a development action, thereby distinguishing the *receptive* as the object [implied 'me'] of this action. If there was a pronominal form to identify the *paradoxical agent*, we could insert it here. Let us recall that the paradoxical agent, having no linguistic counterpart, is not part of our mental habits. But it nevertheless comes into play by bringing the initial agent to let go in order to be itself carried away in its action, thus marking the integration of all the parts in a new state of the totality: *myself.*

Let us complete with a table portraying this self-reference process:

Table 4. The self-referential process of self-creation over time.

Time:				
	Stage 1	Stage 2		Stage 3
Totality	Pre-differentiation Me	Differentiation	Integration	Identity Myself
Parts	Unorganized sub-units	I → [me] Agent → receptive	I [me] Paradoxical agent	Related sub-units
Dimensions	Receptive	Active	Active paradoxical	Identity

Recapitulating the above timeline described, we have, in stage 1, the undifferentiated state of the totality, *Me*, in which the parts function in an unorganized manner and are so to speak juxtaposed relative to the forthcoming operation. All parts are, therefore, regarding a potential organization, in a state of receptivity.

At stage 2, we have a structuring agent, ***I***, which differentiates itself and places the other parts, the receptive ***Me***, in a state of receptivity towards this agent. However, for this agent to become itself structured in return through its own action, a hierarchical reversal of functions takes place, and an agent, this time a paradoxical one, coming from the receptive, will make it possible to complete the operation and, in stage 3, to close the cycle to restore the totality in its own identity.

We see that stage 2 is separated into two parts corresponding to two different operations: the action of the agent and the reversal of the paradoxical agent. This second part of stage 2 could be considered in itself as a distinct stage since it is a fundamental transition at the end of which the totality is restored, which would then give a sequence of four stages. In contexts where it will be relevant to highlight this second part, we will use the four-stage sequence. However, when we want to highlight the basic consistency of the model, we will see that it is preferable to consider these two parts as a single stage, which then brings us back to a sequence of three stages.

The person, constituting a hierarchical level halfway between biology and society, is chosen as the appropriate level of unity to be observed. We will have the advantage of benefiting from the direct influence of the biological processes governing the development of the person, while not being restricted to them, since personal development goes beyond the biological processes by prolonging them, and always bears the mark of the social context in which it takes place. We will also have access to many important works in psychology describing the process of personal development, a process we will then examine from the perspective of the present paradigm.

An Empirical Model of Human Development

In psychology, many empirical observations have been used to describe various stages or phases of a person's development. Examples include Sigmund Freud, Erik Erikson, Margaret Mahler, Daniel Levinson, and others. All these observations, obviously, are not perfectly congruent but they do suggest trends. As a starting point, let us briefly examine one of these theories: that of Erikson.

Needless to say, this book does not purport to situate the model it proposes in relation to the work of all authors with important contributions to these themes. The few authors mentioned here, including, more specifically, Erikson and Levinson, are used to highlight the present thesis, both in terms of content and method. In terms of content, we will show how a self-referential vision of development differs from that of these authors. And in terms of method, we will also at the same time show how a theory like that of Erikson, when confronted with itself – in other words schematized by the self-referential matrix – can prove to be more coherent, while keeping its own identity. But in return, we will also point out that applying the self-referential matrix to Erikson's theory enriches this matrix, while also preserving its basic coherence.

Erikson's Theory

Our choice of this theory is based on the facts, first, that the description of the development cycle covers the entire life cycle, then that the model has an epigenetic character, i.e., each stage integrates the achievements of the previous ones and builds the foundations for the following one. Furthermore, the theory is of a psychosocial type, i.e., at each stage, the individual is related to a social unit of a particular level in the hierarchy of complexity, from a single significant person at the outset to the whole of humanity at the end. Finally, the author shows a constant preoccupation to make explicit the construction principles of his model. We shall see the limits of the results of this last effort, after having presented the model succinctly.[90]

In the chapter "Eight Ages of Man" in his book *Childhood and Society*, Erikson (1950) presents eight stages, each of which triggers a developmental crisis that brings into play the dynamic balance to be found by the individual between two opposite poles, one positive, the other negative, between which there arises a creative tension. Beyond the presentation of each polarity, this first version provides general indications on that which can promote adaptation and on the forms maladjustment can take. For example, the polarity of the first stage involves *trust* or *mistrust*. Regular and consistent quality maternal care develops in infants a basic level of confidence that enables them to trust their environment and experience. Despite the suffering and discomfort felt in this first stage of life, infants can thus optimally develop their receptive capacities. In a less supportive and

---

[90]. The presentation of the model will be mainly based on the following works by Erik H. Erikson:(1950). *Childhood and Society*. W. W. Norton & Co, then *The Life Cycle Completed*, published in 1982 in New York by Norton and finally, *Vital Involvement in Old Age*, published by the same publisher in 1986 in collaboration with Joan M. Erikson and Helen Q. Kivnick.

functional social context, suffering and discomfort tip the balance towards the pole of mistrust, and the pathology associated with such mistrust is apparent in schizoid and depressive adult personalities.

This is how the author initially develops each of the stages defined by a specific polarity, which are listed below: 1) trust/mistrust, 2) autonomy/shame or doubt, 3) initiative/guilt, 4) industry/inferiority, 5) ego-identity/role confusion, 6) intimacy/isolation, 7) generativity/self-absorption, 8) integrity/despair. The first three stages cover the period from birth to about the age of 7. The fourth stage goes up to adolescence, where the question of identity arises. Then comes the stage of young adulthood, the stage of parenthood which marks the interest in the next generation, and finally the stage of old age.

In his more recent works, Erikson has attempted to complete his model and, by making the underlying pattern at all stages explicit, to render the presentation more systematic. The first thing he makes explicit concerns the dialectical aspect of the model. It is not a matter of choosing between positive and negative poles – which he now describes as a pair of *syntonic* and *dystonic* predispositions – but of achieving their integration. For example, developing a certain amount of mistrust can be positive because, when balanced by a healthy dose of trust, it avoids one from indiscriminately accepting all situations, something that could prove destructive. The author then identifies this place of integration for each stage. For the polarity *trust/mistrust* for example, it is *hope*. He states it clearly in the collective work of 1986:

> *Trust... can only exist positively if it is juxtaposed with "sensitive" mistrust – as necessary in life. It is only within a kind of creative balance between these two tendencies that hope can develop.*

The author and his collaborators also clarify the dysfunctional dimension of poor developmental conflict resolution. They discuss maladaptive conflict resolution, which leads to what they call maladaptation, and pernicious resolution, which leads to what they call malignancy. According to the authors, overdevelopment of the syntonic pole to the detriment of the dystonic pole leads to *maladaptation*, which they clinically associate with neurotic disorders. Conversely, overdevelopment of the dystonic pole leads to *malignancy*, which they associate with psychotic disorders. These new developments are presented in Table 5. The reader may refer to the above-mentioned works to complete the description.

Criticism of Erikson's Model

Despite all the systematization efforts made by Erikson and his colleagues, the approach leaves one with a feeling of unease. The basic content and its extensions were indeed placed in a structure whose rigor and consistency can clearly be seen, but the content itself was not questioned and the principle of their construction remained dependent on an intuitive process.

At the outset, the first stage is built on the enunciation of a predisposition and its opposite: *trust* and *mistrust*. This is an interesting principle of construction for a content which, given the observations we have been able to make of the child's situation behavior, also seems fairly accurate. We find ourselves in the second stage with *autonomy* versus *shame* and *doubt*. As far as I know, shame or doubt is not the opposite of autonomy.

We thus already have another construction principle: consequences triggered by an absence of the first dimension. The same thing is repeated in the third and eighth stages: the opposite of initiative is not guilt and the opposite of despair is not integrity. These are possible consequences, and probably not the only ones.

Furthermore, stages two and three do not reflect very well what one actually observes. *Initiative* is about action. It is much more characteristic of stage two than stage three. In the second stage, it is clear that intuitively and at first sight, the fact that children want to do things by themselves evokes autonomy, but it is only a very incomplete component of autonomy. The reference is still largely external. Children's *no* to others is still predominant and the initiative they take is only the very beginning of the active component of autonomy which, overall, is much more the result of the third stage. The canonical statements of these stages are clear: the "I can do it alone" of the second stage reflects someone who decides to take the initiative of the action rather than leaving it to someone else.

Table 5. Summary of Erikson's model revised by the author and his collaborators (1986).

MALADAPTIVE TENDENCY	Syntonic Pole	ADAPTIVE FORCE	Dystonic Pole	MALADAPTIVE TENDENCY
I. Sensory distortion	Trust	Hope	Mistrust	Withdrawal
II. Shameless willfulness	Autonomy	Will	Shame and doubt	Compulsion
III. Ruthlessness	Initiative	Purpose	Guilt	Inhibition
IV. Narrow virtuosity	Industry	Competence	Inferiority	Inertia
V. Fanaticism	Ego-Identity	Fidelity	Role-confusion	Repudiation
VI. Promiscuity	Intimacy	Love	Isolation	Exclusivity
VII. Overextension	Generativity	Care	Self-absorption	Rejectivity
VIII. Presumption	Integrity	Wisdom	Despair	Disdain

Source: Erikson, E., Erikson, J., Kivnick, H. Q. (1986), p. 45,

In contrast, the "I'm myself" of the third stage is an affirmation of identity that manifests the hard-won autonomy gained in a synthesis of the previous stages. It is a synthesis of *trust* in what comes from outside and inside oneself, and, at the same time, it is an affirmation of what comes from one's own initiative concerning action, the reference for both now being interior. This is precisely what autonomy is all about.

It's quite amazing that the psychoanalyst Erikson did not highlight the link between this third stage and that of adolescence, which is defined initially by identity. It is recognized in psychoanalysis, it seems to me, that the turbulence experienced in adolescence has something to do with how the Oedipus complex was experienced in the third stage. Not only are these two stages twins, but they are also of the same nature as the very last, the eighth, based on *integrity* and that Erikson (1982) describes as the "sense of being coherent and whole." This, however, is simply a definition of identity: when the child says, "I'm myself," it is in fact asserting that it is a coherent whole; and it is this same coherent unity that the adolescent is seeking. In the eighth stage, not feeling this coherence indicates that one, in not knowing who one is, feels scattered, which exactly evokes the role-confused mindset of the adolescent who has failed to make a satisfactory synthesis of who he or she is.

Here we are referring to the stages related to *identity*, but we could carry out a similar analysis starting from those stages related to action, such as the second and fourth, for example. We'll come back to that. For the time being, suffice it to say that the terms used by the author as well as his intuitive method of construction totally conceal the profound coherence of his model. The content added in the subsequent developments[91], constructed in the same way, often leaves one with the impression that the first function performed here is that of filling in the cells of the new schema, rather than shedding more light on the initial contents: *wisdom* becomes a synthesis between *integrity* and *despair*, which is somewhat puzzling, and if this second pole ends up dominating, it becomes *disdain*. Let's admit that such a combination does not at all appear to be immediately obvious.

One of the phenomena that seem to have had a major impact on the development of this theory has more to do with the sociology of science than psychology: such was the ever-

---

91. See Table 5.

enduring impact and popularity of Erikson's psychosocial approach, set forth in his book *Childhood and Society* in the 1950s, that the idea of revamping it in depth became virtually unthinkable. Not only was the author the first victim of his success, but that was also the case for his critics.

Carol Gilligan (1986), for example, questions the universality of the sequence proposed by Erikson. It would not be the same, she argues, for women and men. For example, the stage of *identity* (5th stage) is first reached by men while it is that of *intimacy* (6th stage) that is first reached by women. Though the argument developed by Gilligan seems to be extremely rich and relevant, she fails, curiously enough, to question the reality of the stages in their initial definition. She takes for granted that the stages exist as described and only questions the universality of the sequence.

If one takes the time to take a closer look at this socio-historical paradigm, one rapidly notices that its construction is basically flawed. Why would *intimacy* constitute the sixth stage? Quite obviously because one intuitively sees that after adolescence the young, at least in our culture, start a family and that relationships of young couples necessarily involve intimacy. But this type of observation remains anecdotal. Could it be that *intimacy* is an essential ingredient of *identity* for both men and women and that one cannot conceive of one without the other? Successfully building one's identity means developing an intimate relationship with oneself, which renders possible developing an intimate relationship with others. We are often inclined to see identity as the result of one's *separation* from that which at the outset constituted one's external reference and intimacy as the manifestation of one's *attachment* to that reference. However, neither *identity* nor *intimacy* is achieved by limiting oneself to such a description. If the identity process does not achieve intimacy, it remains unrealized. Conversely, attachment devoid of distancing leads to identification with the reference rather than intimacy. Identity and intimacy are two sides of the same reality. It is clear, however, that such a reality may come about following different paths, as seems to be the case for men and women. From this point of view, Gilligan's argument remains quite relevant.[92] But *identity* and *intimacy* will have to occur at the same stage, the one called adolescence in the West. So, the next stage will have to be redefined.

In short, because Erikson refused to call into question his model's initial contents, which would have allowed him to discover their internal coherence, one ends up with a syncretic amalgam concealing the implicit power of this model. Subsequent developments certainly add interesting information, but the need to fill in the numerous cells of the new container sometimes appears more as a decorative process than a response to data and observations. This is why in our summary scheme of classification of the theories presented in the introduction, Erikson's would fall into the category of empirical-intuitive theories. We will now try to see how it would be possible to put the core of this theory on new foundations.

Sketch of a Self-referential Version of Human Development

The primary purpose of this essay is to present our approach, not rehabilitate that of Erikson. While it is unlikely that enthusiasts of Erikson's theory will find complete satisfaction in our model, I am nevertheless convinced that it does justice to the basic insights that guided the development of his theory.

As we have already mentioned, the construction principle underlying this project consists in creating the elementary units constituting the fundamental ingredients of the self-referential process, and to interlock these units to form units of higher complexity. For example, the three primitive dimensions of the present model are *Receptive*, *Active*, and *Identity*, the *Paradoxical* dimension being derived from the other three. These three dimensions will fit into a temporal framework to form a cycle, which will be followed by another cycle encompassing the first one, etc. The construction will thus take the form of a fractal.

We will then have to manage to determine more precisely, by successive approximations, the general temporal structure of this interlocking of cycles. To do this, we will have to start by questioning ourselves about the observational data, however approximate these data may sometimes be, and then abstract

---

92. For a summary of this argument, see Renée Houde, *Les temps de la vie*, Boucherville, Gaëtan Morin, 1991, pp. 61–67.

from them a general principle of construction. Let us recall that at this stage, the exercise is limited to the level of the development of the person, an exercise whose results will have to be generalized to be adapted to other levels.

Time Structure of Cycles

In Erikson's model, as well as in other psychological models of development such as Freud's, for example, we first note that the early stages have durations belonging to a certain order of magnitude. For example, the first three stages end at the age of around six or seven. Freud talks about the oral, anal, and phallic stages. Erikson talks about *trust, autonomy*, and *initiative*. So, we have stages that each last, on average, about two years.

However, in the fourth stage, we observe a quantitative leap in which the scale changes, and this change remains until a new leap is made. For example, the fourth stage brings us to about the age of eleven and the following to about seventeen or eighteen. So, we have now shifted to stages lasting an average of five or six years. But curiously enough, we also find that the first cycle of three stages (0 – 6 or 7 years) is, in its entirety, of the same order of magnitude as each of the following stages, i.e., more or less six years. Thus, the first cycle as a whole could be seen as the first stage of a higher-level cycle. The latter would be similar in all respects to the first three stages constituting the first cycle. We could more precisely say: this higher-level cycle would be in every way similar to one of its parts, that is to say, its first stage, made up of the first lower-level cycle.

But first, let us see if this principle is empirically confirmed in the observation of the subsequent stages. And to do this and advance in the stages, let us turn to other authors who have been more precise than Erikson in the delimitation of the adult stages. Such as Levinson (1978), who also developed a psychosocial theory that is completely compatible with Erikson's. Levinson suggests a stage he calls *the early adulthood*, which goes from 17 to 45 years old and includes a significant transition at the age of 28. The average order of magnitude of the stages is then increased to more or less fifteen years. Once again, we find that the order of magnitude of the stages adjusts to the duration of the complete cycle of the lower level, that is, the sum of the three stages leading to late adolescence.

Let us refer to Figure 5 below. The first cycle as a whole (0–6 years), for example, could be seen as the first stage of the higher-level cycle (0-6-11-17). Thus, this higher-level cycle would be similar in all respects to one of its parts, its first stage (0–6), which is the first lower-level cycle (0-2-4-6). The same phenomenon is repeated at a higher level, with the entire second cycle (0–17 years) being the first stage of the higher-level cycle (0–45 years). We then have the cycle 0 – 17 – 28 – 45. If we examine in the figure the lines preceded by Cycle 1, Cycle 2 and Cycle 3, we see that Cycle 1 of three stages is the first stage of Cycle 2, and so on.

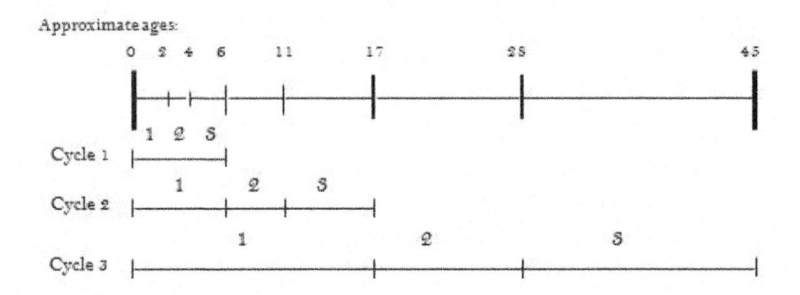

Figure 5: Diagram of early stages of human development.

From these observations, we can infer as a first approximation the following principle:

> *Development takes place through an interlocking of cycles composed of three stages, each cycle in its entirety constituting the first stage of the higher-level cycle.*

The Basic Dimensions of the Process

As mentioned earlier, the three dimensions identified, namely *receptive*, *active*, and *identity*, can be said to be primitive and occur sequentially in that order. They thus constitute the framework of the stages that make up a self-referential cycle, a cycle in which a totality finds itself at the end of a process of which it is the origin.

In order to render the general nature of a cycle more explicit, we will thus use a single cycle as a typical example: the zero to seven-year cycle, which we will call for the purpose in hand *first cycle*, with its three stages. We will see later how this description applies *mutatis mutandis* to all other cycles.

The first stage concerns the RECEPTIVE component. This is based on the fact that no living being is responsible for the fact of existing. It is therefore initially placed in a receptive mode relative to the forces that constitute it as well as those in its surrounding environment. Such is the position in which we find ourselves before being called upon to make a change. As long as an action is not initiated, we are in receptive mode concerning possible change. The totality that we are is endowed with this change as a potentiality, but at the outset, we are in a waiting mode.

In newborn infants, for example, we observe that the internal agents that differentiate themselves to trigger action are not yet sufficiently developed to become responsible for the infants' life. The only relevant agents provided by biology are reflexes – crying, sucking, grasping – and are not initially under the infants' control, even though they will gradually gain such control with time. At the outset, infants receive the effect of the actions of these agents in the same way as they receive the effect of the actions of the social agents who provide them with the basic care necessary for their survival. Thus, the dominant underlying experience of this stage is RECEPTIVITY.

It is then that the *active* dimension comes into play and an internal agent differentiates itself to initiate action. This action places the rest of the totality in a receptive mode. We have precisely called this space the *receptive*, which, it should be noted, is in a mode analogous to that of the initial totality. In fact, following this structuring intervention of the agent, a differentiation of the receptive leads to the emergence of another agent, then called *paradoxical*, which will extend the action undertaken by the initial agent to encompass the latter, which ends the active dimension. At this stage, the underlying dominant is therefore ACTIVITY.

Following this hierarchical reversal, the totality then emerges in a renewed identity. It is the expression of self as integrated totality. This third stage, therefore, highlights the dimension of IDENTITY.

Experiencing Under Each Dimension

As we said at the beginning of this chapter, here and now experiencing is not static; rather, it is the process of an ever-renewed presence to oneself. Each atom of experience contains the same basic ingredients as the longer cycles, but on a microscopic level. It is thus possible to discover in this micro-cycle the trace of the primitive dimensions mentioned above. The exercise then consists of naming the three dimensions one finds in the micro-cycle of here and now experiencing. This will result in categories that will take on a particular color at each stage. These will constitute, so to speak, the basic contents of the stages.

For the time being, we are limiting our reflection to the level of the individual person. Extending this reflection to other levels – communities, societies, the entire species – will oblige us to adapt the concepts to these levels and will undoubtedly also lead us to correct and improve the general model.

Let's revisit here and now experiencing. If one puts oneself in a position of receptivity and deep listening, one feels things. The receptive component can then be called *feeling* or, if you like, *felt meaning*. Indeed, *what one is feeling* represents an aspect of experience that one does not create, that one does not construct. What one is feeling in the present instant comes up by itself, is a mere 'happening'; no responsibility is attached to the very fact of feeling. Otherwise put, "feeling is something that happens to me: I am in a position of receptivity and listening relative to this something."

The active counterpart of *feeling* refers to *behavior*; one is always reacting to experienced feeling, even if only internally. Therefore, it is *behavior* adopted in relation to *feeling*.

From this *feelings-behavior* interaction emerges my *identity*, that is to say, "who I am in this instant": it is the *identity* component. At the outset, we will try to keep this term in its primitive meaning: fundamentally, identity is the very fact of *being oneself*. This notion evokes the idea of the *integration* of the parts into a coherent unity: *oneself*. It is both the origin and the synthesis of the other dimensions. It is only in a second phase that identity becomes the fact of *being this rather than that*. For example, identity in the first stage of a cycle takes on a different color from identity in the second stage. Although the identity process remains basically the same, *the way "I am myself" differs at each one of the three stages*: Active, Receptive and Identity.

Stages of Personal Development

Using the three elements – *feeling, behavior,* and *identity* – we will now describe experiencing as it occurs at each stage of development. Each element will be presented on a continuum from positive to negative. Keep in mind that the examples are taken from the zero to seven-year-old cycle.

- *The First Stage: RECEPTIVITY*

For the developing entity, let us recall that the first stage involves the challenge of RECEPTIVITY concerning a diversity of elements whose coherence is not yet built and over which the entity does not yet have control. For example, newborn infants are bombarded with stimuli to which they will gradually have to learn to adapt. When the process involves the very existence of the entity, survival depends, let us bear in mind, on facilitating elements in the environment in addition to pre-formed internal biological agents or reflexes. The quality of the external intervention will depend on the type of RECEPTIVITY that the child will develop.

To designate the basic **feeling** developed at this stage, we will borrow directly from Erikson's continuum of *trust/mistrust*. If the facilitative intervention from the environment provides essential survival tools with regularity, consistency, and attention, infants develop a *basic trust* in the process in which they are engaged. With regular and loving care, they learn to develop basic confidence in life; otherwise, they develop *basic mistrust*.

At this same stage of RECEPTIVITY, **behavior** will oscillate between *opening* and *withdrawing*. If the care received by infants is such that it fosters their confidence in the process in which they are engaged, they will actively *open up* to this process. If, on the contrary, trust is not established, the ensuing result will be *withdrawal*. Note that trust and openness are two dimensions influencing each other: I will open up if I feel that I have reasons to trust and, reciprocally, feeling trust fosters openness. On the contrary, I will withdraw if I feel mistrust, and reciprocally, this withdrawal feeds mistrust.

The question now is what kind of *identity* results from this interaction, always at the stage of RECEPTIVITY. What results from being open and trusting or withdrawing and being mistrustful? In other words, how is my identity – "who I am" – expressed in relation to the process I am engaged in? It is on the continuum of *engagement/disengagement* that **identity** is established at this stage. "I am someone who is *engaged* in the process or someone who is *disengaged* from it." The diagram in Figure 6 below summarizes the first stage.

Stage 1: RECEPTIVITY

Feeling (receptive pole): Trust / Mistrust ↔ Behavior (active pole): Opening / Withdrawing

Engagement / Disengagement

Identity (Identity)

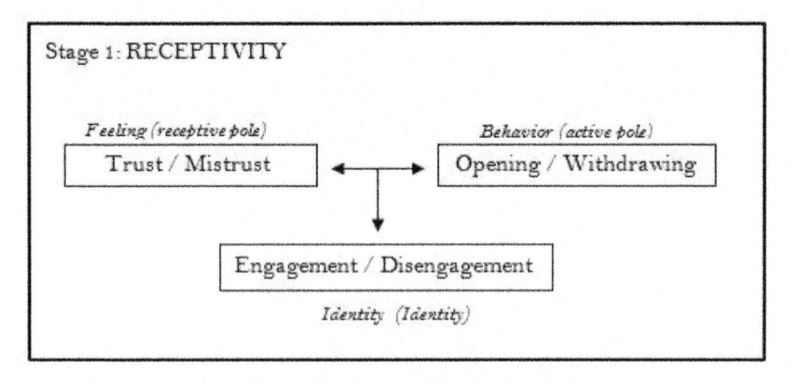

Figure 6. General description of the first stage of a cycle in a person.

René Spitz (1945) observed that some children suffering from what he called the *hospitalism* syndrome even went so far as to let themselves die. They were completely *disengaged* from life. Conversely, in an environment providing regular and quality care, children become *engaged* in their process of development and learning. Regardless of the level of complexity to which the developmental process applies, the challenge for any practitioner is to ensure that, at the end of the first stage, the developing entity *is engaged in the process*.

TEMPORALITY OF SELF-REFERENTIAL PROCESS

- *The Second Stage: ACTIVITY*

The second stage has to do with the ACTIVE dimension. It is when developing children start taking over and controlling processes which were, in the first stage, partially ensured by external intervention. When they start saying, "I can do that by myself". The **feeling** is then that of the *capacity* or *incapacity* of doing. This feeling will affect **behavior**, more precisely taking or not taking the initiative of action, which forms the couple *initiative/inertia*. The result of this interaction is an **identity** evoked by the notion of *competence* or *incompetence*.

External facilitating here takes another form. It is no longer a matter of providing children with tools, but rather accompanying them in their appropriation of tools. The diagram in Figure 7 summarizes the second stage.

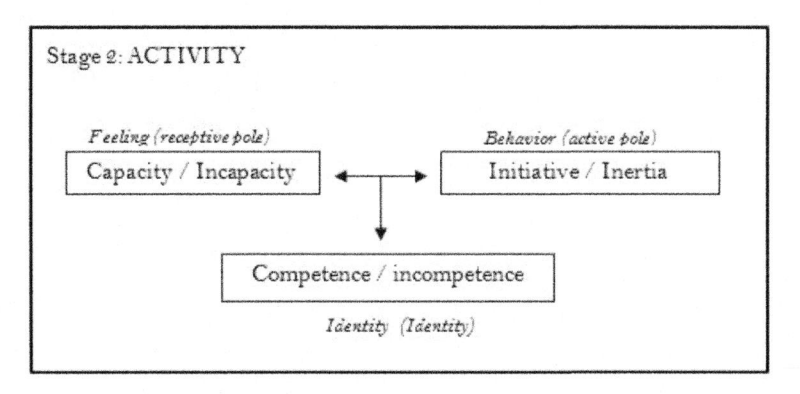

```
Stage 2: ACTIVITY

   Feeling (receptive pole)              Behavior (active pole)
   ┌──────────────────────┐              ┌──────────────────────┐
   │ Capacity / Incapacity│ ◄──────►     │  Initiative / Inertia│
   └──────────────────────┘              └──────────────────────┘
                          │
                          ▼
                 ┌──────────────────────────┐
                 │ Competence / incompetence│
                 └──────────────────────────┘
                       Identity (Identity)
```

Figure 7. General description of the second stage of a cycle in a person.

- *The Third Stage: IDENTITY*

The third stage has to do with the IDENTITY dimension. Now the child says, "I'm myself." Identity is linked to a **feeling** of *integrity*. All pieces fall into place, so to speak, creating a new unity. Conversely, a child, because of internal conflicts in which various aspects of oneself are incompatible with each other, may experience a feeling of *dispersion*, of being scattered and lacking cohesion.

From a **behavioral** point of view, identity gives rise to *expressive behaviors* that emerge all the more spontaneously if the person has a strong feeling of integrity and which, conversely, can go as far as complete *inhibition* in the event of chaotic dispersion. Behavior is thus established on the continuum of *expression/inhibition*.

As for the **identity** component, one notes that it is linked to the interactive synthesis of the other two dimensions. More precisely, at the first stage, the engagement in a development process supported by an external force; and, at the second stage, the appropriation of a skill allowing one to engage in the process by one's own means. Thus, identity at the IDENTITY stage is linked to the notion of *autonomy*, that is to say so to speak, "being myself by myself." At the pole opposite to autonomy, however, one finds *alienation*, that is to say a state where the *other* remains the reference for one's own definition; this, because one has not managed to become one's own locus of personal integration.

The diagram in Figure 8 below summarizes this third stage.

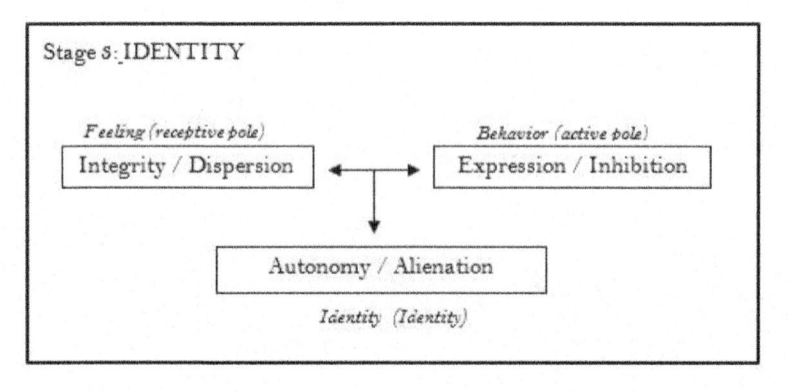

```
Stage 3: IDENTITY

  Feeling (receptive pole)              Behavior (active pole)
  [ Integrity / Dispersion ]  ◄──►     [ Expression / Inhibition ]
                               │
                               ▼
                    [ Autonomy / Alienation ]
                        Identity (Identity)
```

Figure 8. General description of the third stage of a cycle in a person.

The following table presents a global picture. The columns indicate the stages designated by the dimension that characterizes them. The rows indicate the same dimensions as they apply to experiencing in the here and now.

Table 6. Experiential contents of the stages of the general cycle in a person.

Stages Experiencing	1- RECEPTIVITY	2- ACTIVITY	3- IDENTITY
Basic feelings	Trust/ Mistrust	Capacity/ Incapacity	Integrity/ Dispersion
Basic behaviors	Opening/ Withdrawing	Initiative/Inertia	Expression/ Inhibition
Identity	Engagement/ Disengagement	Competence/ Incompetence	Autonomy/ Alienation

From these reflections and observations, we can infer a second principle:

> *The three stages of development within a cycle have to do with the dimensions considered to be primitive: RECEPTIVITY, ACTIVITY, and IDENTITY respectively. Experiencing within each stage is analyzed in terms of these same dimensions, whose interpretation at the level of the person is presented in the terms of* **"feeling,"** *"behavior" and "* ***identity*** *"*

Specificity of Cycles at Various Levels

If the stages of each cycle, at whatever level, can be described using the previously developed schemas, the question arises as to what distinguishes each cycle from the others. The distinction comes from the order of magnitude of the process under consideration and the social frame of reference in which it is embedded. It is clear that the second stage of the first cycle will be described differently from the second or third cycle. What a person learns around the age of two, or between the ages of seven and eleven, or between those of seventeen and twenty-eight, is very different. However, in all three timespans, this person takes the initiative for action in new ways and develops new skills. We will try to compare the same stages belonging to different levels, starting with the second and the third. We reserve for the end the comparison of the first stages with each other. Let us begin with the second stages for what we will call the last four cycles, the [0 ± 6 years] cycle, the [0 ± 17 years] cycle, the [0 ± 45 years] cycle, and the life cycle.

Comparison of Stages 2 for the Last Four Cycles

For the cycle from zero to more or less six years, the active stage, i.e., the second, is for the time being delimited with a certain degree of vagueness. Later, when the core of the model is fully constructed, we will define it more precisely. For the moment, let us situate it between the ages of two and a half to four [2 ½ to ± 4]. We see that the *competence* that children develop is related to the control of their body, their movements, and the control of their motor skills. They experimentally explore and discover their immediate environment. These competencies are obtained within the family environment or any other substitute for this environment, in which adults take constant care of children and accompany them in their discoveries. In this context, children will develop more complex social relationships. Of course, the social context in which this basic care is provided to children may vary from one culture to another.

In the second stage of the following cycle, from seven years of age to eleven or twelve [7 to ± 11], children learn to master the tools that the culture has given itself to adapt to its environment. One immediately thinks of basic handicraft instructions in the field of sewing, carpentry, mechanics, cooking, etc. In some cultures, hunting or fishing skills, for example, may be of primary importance. In our culture, one thinks of school where children learn the three Rs – reading, writing and arithmetic – and of leisure where they learn team sports. The social reference goes beyond the family and extends to the local community, an extension which, of course, can take various forms in different cultures.

In the second stage of the cycle that follows, from approximately seventeen to twenty-eight years of age [17 to ± 28], young adults go on developing and using skills in the society to which they belong, with all possible cultural variations. In our culture, finding a job in a certain field is what

TEMPORALITY OF SELF-REFERENTIAL PROCESS

allows young adults to break away from their dependence on society and, should they so desire, start a family.

The second stage of the life cycle, from about forty-five to old age [45 ± 75], presents a new challenge in the development of competence. People in this stage start wondering not just about what *competency* they can perform as members of a given society, but as human beings! About the competency Paulo Coelho refers to in *The Alchemist* as one's "Personal Legend."[93] The "who am I" as a *competent* person no longer has the same color in this new context. The challenge no longer consists in merely showing that one masters those skills society expects one to have in a given social position. It also consists in choosing, among those skills already acquired or yet to be developed, those best corresponding to what one perceives *as the person one is called to become.* Though, of course, somewhat present at all stages of one's life, this fundamental quest takes on particular importance at this stage.

We can see that it is basically the same question that arises in stage 2 of all cycles, but it arises in a very original way and very different contexts. Let us now try to see how the question arises in the various third stages.

Comparison of Stages 3 for the Last Four Cycles

The autonomy characterizing the third stage of identity takes the following form in the period from approximately four to six years of age [4 to ± 6]: children exhibit expressive behavior in play and fantasy. They like to express themselves, tell stories, invent games, and practice their sexual role as little boys and girls. Basically, children invent and express who they are.

In the third stage of the second cycle, which in our culture corresponds to adolescence [11 to ± 17 years], these same functions of self-expression are manifested in a broader framework. Adolescents try to find the best version of themselves to move into adulthood. This quest can be more or less tumultuous, depending on one's difficulty in achieving an autonomy providing coherence and identity.

---

93. Paulo Coelho, *The Alchemist*. Translated from the Portuguese by Alan R. Clarke and illustrated by James Noel Smith. HarperOne, 2014 (first published in 1988).

During the third stage of the following cycle – from the turn of the thirties to about forty-five years of age [28 to ± 45] – adults define who they are in society. Their dream in life starts coming true, their ambitions are taking shape, and they are becoming the central figure in their social journey. If the third stages of the previous cycles have been traversed with some turbulence, similar challenges may resurface in the early forties. It is sometimes said that some people of this age begin to look like teenagers because of the disturbances that occur at this stage of identity. We then talk about the midlife crisis.

The last third stage is that of old age [75 and over] and, as we have already mentioned, the question of "who am I", of one's integrity and coherence, arises once again as in adolescence, but this time the questioning concerns one's entire life and, inevitably and in a more or less distant future, one's death.

Comparison of Stages 1 for the Last Four Cycles

As for the first stages, it is difficult to treat them separately, since the previous cycle constitutes the first stage of the cycle being considered. We can then simply assess the difference between each cycle taken as a whole. In the cycle from about zero to two years of age, children learn *to open up* to what the environment offers them and to engage in the vital process of development in the context of a privileged relationship with the reference person, the mother or another person who plays that role. In the zero to six- or seven-year-old cycle, the context widens to the family. In the next cycle from zero to seventeen, one's community of proximity becomes the reference, and from zero to forty-five, one's society. In all cases, however, it is a question of trusting and opening up to one's milieu so as to be able to commit oneself to this milieu and then move on to the second stage of the cycle and take responsibility for action. We then observe that the first stages contain all the others which belong to the preceding cycles. Thus, this *trust*, this *openness*, and this *engagement* are always considered in relation to the active stage that follows, in which the person takes the initiative of a new activity in order to master a skill exceeding the requirements of the previous cycle. Each cycle is thus a preparation for the second stage of the higher-level cycle.

Precisions on Temporal Logic of Cycles: in Search of a Heuristic

In addition to a coherence observed in the development of the content of the cycles and stages, the first observation led us to a structure that also manifests a coherence, that of *nested ternary cycles*, whose relative orders of magnitude do not seem to be a matter of chance. We note the self-referential nature of this development. Indeed, a completed cycle becomes the model on which the higher-level cycle is built, while becoming one of its parts. There is a particular relationship between the whole and the part: the structure of the whole is found here in the part. In the natural development of living processes, would there be a constant relationship between the length of the cycles when the latter are compared to one another, and thus between the whole and its parts? Would there be a constant relationship between the parts within a cycle?

The challenge would be to discover a heuristic device that would allow us to automatically generate a structure of nested ternary cycles outside of empirical observation and then confront this construction with observation. Should such a procedure allow us to obtain results in terms of the development of the person, we could then ask ourselves whether this heuristic approach could not be equally fruitful when applied to any self-referential process of development, whatever its order of magnitude.

The result of a first exploration leads us to suggest that this model corresponds to a mathematical structure whose first characteristic is to be a geometric progression. A geometric progression is a series of numbers whose value is obtained by multiplying the previous one by a constant number called a *common ratio*. The first number in the sequence is given at the start. For example, if the common ratio is 2 and the starting number is 3, the second number is $3 \times 2 = 6$. The next number is $6 \times 2 = 12$, and so on. So, we have the following 3, 6, 12, 24, 48, etc. So, if we divide a number by the common ratio, we get the previous one: $24/2 = 12$. If we divide a number by the previous one, we get the common ratio: $24/12 = 2$.

Using the approximate ages presented above from the authors' observation, we can try to see towards which value the common ratio for the progression moves. If we divide 45 by 28, we get 1.607. If we do the same for 28 and 17, we get 1.647. Now,

1.6... is the beginning of the number *phi* (1.61803399), usually called the golden ratio. Let's try to generate the progression from the end of adolescence, which the authors place around 17 or 18 years old. Let's use 17.5 as a starting point. If we divide this number by the common ratio *phi* and do the same for the numbers obtained, we have the following result: 17.5 – 10.8 – 6.7 – 4.1 – 2.6. If we do the same upwards, this time multiplying each number by the common ratio *phi*, we get 17.5 – 28.3 – 45.8 – 74.2 – 120.

To simplify, let's use this number 120 to reversely generate all the ages that separate the stages by dividing 120 by the number *phi* and so on for each of the numbers thus obtained. The following figure illustrates the result.

Figure 9. Reverse application of the algorithm starting from 120 as a possible end of the life cycle.

Surprisingly, we end up with all the milestones of the stages as described by the above-cited authors. We thus see that life develops according to a self-referential logic: a microcycle is developed that serves as a model for the higher-level cycle while constituting the first part of this new cycle. It is a bit as if the living were telling itself: "I'm copying myself as an extension of what I already am." The living thus develops, this suggests, according to the fractal principle.

Let's note in passing that this progression also has the characteristic of constituting a Fibonacci sequence, that is to say, a sequence in which each value is obtained by adding the two preceding values. For example, 17.5 + 28.3 = 45.8 (We can also see that for any Fibonacci sequence, the ratio between a number and the one preceding it tends towards the golden ratio).

It is, therefore, possible to reformulate our first principle as a second approximation:

> *Development takes place by interlocking cycles composed of three stages. Each cycle in its entirety constitutes the first stage of the higher-level cycle. The relative length of the stages and cycles is obtained by constructing a geometric progression having* phi *as*

common ratio. The progression also has the characteristics of a Fibonacci sequence.

Anchoring the Model

When faced with observable reality, one cannot arbitrarily apply the structure of the progression from any observed value. We must thus proceed to what we will refer to as *anchoring the model*. The principle of anchoring is the following: if we take the example of human development, the first step is to arbitrarily place oneself at an age corresponding to what we claim to be an empirically observed turning point, which we will call the initial anchor point. Another age is then generated by applying the algorithm, namely by multiplying or dividing by 1.618 the number corresponding to the anchor point. If the deployment of the progression does not reveal other significant turning points, we must conclude either that we have chosen the wrong anchor point or that this reality does not fit the model. We were able to see that for human development, the anchor point chosen generated all other turning points empirically identified by researchers. The model, as coherently structured, has undeniable heuristic value. It makes it possible to predict what one is entitled to observe from a given moment, in general terms as described by the stages.

Prediction Test

Let us bear in mind that the cycles are composed of three stages, the last of which is of the *identity* type and the second of the *active* type, the first *receptive* stage being the lower-level cycle. Since we are reversely generating the cycles and stages, we see that the first number generated from the end of a cycle marks the beginning of the identity stage and the second number generated the beginning of the active stage. For example, in the cycle from 0 to 17.5 years, the first number generated is 10.8 which marks the beginning of the identity stage, and the second 6.7, which marks the beginning of the active stage of this cycle.

We will then attempt, on a trial basis, the following deduction:

If, starting from the stage ending at 6.7 years, we reversely generate four new numbers using the indicated algorithm, we theoretically find ourselves at the beginning of the active stage of a cycle located at the lower level. We should then empirically observe the child's entry into a stage where we observe the appearance of a new activity.

$$0 - \mathbf{0{,}98} - 1{,}6 - 2{,}6 - 4{,}1 - 6{,}7$$

In terms of months, 0.98 of one year corresponds to 11.7 months. If we consult the reference work on child development *Lifespan Human Development* by Ann Gormly and David Brodzinski (1993), we can see that 11.7 months is exactly the age when children start walking on average, i.e., when they can then take at least three steps. It is thus an *active* stage in which the child starts learning a new activity. However, this activity is only just beginning. A few weeks later, of course, it becomes easier to observe the fuller manifestations of the activity characteristic of this stage.

We can then hypothesize that this heuristic process allows one to predict the main articulations of the development process and what kind of observations one would be entitled to make at a given age. Furthermore, that is precisely what any theory should really do: allow one to decide in advance what one should be able to observe. Something that could be particularly useful in infancy where identifying the ages which constitute turning points in development is not at all obvious.

Primary and Secondary Levels

We will describe as primary the various levels of cycles generated by the application of the algorithm starting from the upper limit of a cycle. This algorithm quite naturally subdivides the first stages of all cycles. But it is also possible to subdivide stages 2 and 3 according to the same proportion. These substages thus generated will be said to be of secondary level. To do so, one need but apply the algorithm to the value of the distance between two points and to add these values to the lower bound. For example, the distance between 45.8 and 28.3 is 17.5. Applying the algorithm to this value gives 10.8 and 6.7. By first adding 6.7 and then 10.8 to 28.3, one gets 35 and 39.1. More simply, one need but add to the value of the lower bound, in this case, 28.3, the third and second preceding values in the list of primary values, namely, 6.7 and 10.8.

These three sub-stages have the same characteristics as the primary stages, but they basically express the specific characteristic of this particular stage. For example, if the sub-stages are those of an active stage, the first sub-stage constitutes a preliminary mastering of the action, like the first three steps of walking, in the previous example. The second sub-stage is most likely the one where the action is most obvious and most revealing of the stage itself: the child, in the same example, can move from one point to another over short distances. Finally, the third sub-stage manifests the expression of the acquired competence.

As for the sub-stages of an identity stage (stage 3 of a cycle), it is the third sub-stage which is the most meaningful, but it is possible that upon observation, it is the second which appears more clearly because observation focuses but on behavior, which is precisely characterized in the third stage by *self-expression*. Whatever the stage, therefore, it is possible that for the outside observer, the active stages and substages appear more obvious, because they manifest an explicit behavior by definition.

This phenomenon can be seen, for example, by comparing this model with Margaret Mahler's (1980) observations for the phase of child development she calls *separation-individuation*, and which spans the ages from approximately 5 months to 2.5 years. The four stages of this phase are referred to as Differentiation/Hatching, Practicing, Rapprochement, and consolidation of individuality with emotional Object constancy. These stages begin at 5 months, 9 months, 14 months, and 24 months respectively (of course, Mahler rounds fractions of months to the nearest whole number). If we relate these various turning points observed by Mahler with the stages that are generated by this model, we see that all these ages correspond at the start of the active substage of each of the stages thus generated, as shown in the diagram in Figure 10.

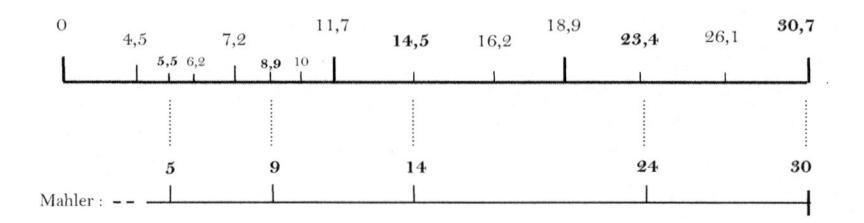

Figure 10: Comparison of the stages generated by our model with Mahler's separation-individuation stages

Thus, over a period spanning the ages of four and a half to thirty months, we find, and this without exception and consistently, the ages identified by Mahler which correspond, according to her observation, to the manifestation of a new activity and one that coincides with the *active* sub-stage of each of the stages of this model.

The model then allows us to focus observation on the primitive stages where traces of actions are still embryonic. In the 0 to 4.5-month period, for example, can one observe clues showing the onset of activity at 1.7 months and identity expression at 2.8 months? If so, we thus have a heuristic procedure that is of definite interest for research by orienting observation.

The model itself, of course, needs to be further explored and developed. For example, what is at stake when one moves from the first to the second stage, which at the same time constitutes the passage from one cycle to the next? And what challenge presents moving from second to third stage? What are the consequences of a negative synthesis in each of the stages on the whole cycle? What are the consequences of a negative synthesis of one stage on the equivalent stages of the other cycles? These are all questions that have not been addressed and that open up promising avenues of research.

Commentary on the Phi *Heuristic*

One would think that the significant results obtained using the phi heuristic would argue in favor of a platonic conception of development: there would be a pre-established model to which real development would try to correspond. This question arises for all correspondences one manages to find between our mathematical models and reality. The constructivist conception is, once again, more down-to-earth, while giving the phenomenon a more elaborate explanation than does a conception calling for a predefined transcendental universe.

One must acknowledge that mathematics and logic are formal expressions of our own intellectual structures. Yet, these structures have been built from our interaction with the environment. More precisely, they originate from an abstraction drawn from the coordination of our own actions on this environment, the latter having obliged us to adapt to it in order to assimilate it effectively. Any assimilation of any dimension of reality by these structures bears their mark and the result is a constructed object in which the subject (epistemic and not egocentric) recognizes himself or herself. It is therefore not a mystery that one can see a correspondence between this object and the structures by which it was constructed.

One must rule out any mystification about the constant phi as such. At the beginning of the 16th century, for example, Luca Pacioli (1509) liked to talk about divine proportion (*Divina proportione*). This call to the divine does not seem necessary. Let us take as an example the arrangement of the scales of a pinecone as it grows. The scales are generated from the center, the apex. As they grow, they repel each other and move away from the apex to migrate to the periphery at a constant angle called the angle of divergence. The arrangement of the spirals thus obtained responds to the Fibonacci sequence and the golden ratio. The explanation can be found elsewhere than in an inscription of the golden ratio in the plant's genes: it may be more simply that the constraint of physical space linked to the plant's need for light leads to such an arrangement. In short, "the plant seeks to optimize its exposure to light and the arrangement that gives the best result is the one whose angle of divergence is close to the golden angle [...] The golden ratio via the golden angle is thus part of the solution to a complex geometric optimization problem" (Cyril Jacquier and Kévin Drapel, 2005). This minimal explanation probably does not exhaust all the reasons why the golden ratio is widespread in nature. The self-similarity of patterns in fractals seems to favor a self-referential development characteristic of living beings.

The structure of the nested ternary cycles and the constant phi (golden ratio) that applies to them are not causes, but consequences. It can be hypothesized that the intervention of the constant phi in the nesting of the ternary cycles is linked to the problem of optimizing the self-referential cycle as it unfolds over time.

Having said that, it is important to first note that these regularities do not determine the particular events that will occur. From this point of view, the future is unpredictable. Yet we can observe, for a given unity, a natural tendency to favor certain types of activities that are more in keeping with the characteristics of the stage of development in which that unity takes place. However, we can just as easily observe in particular cases a discrepancy between the type of activity observed and what is expected. It then becomes interesting to see what is the effect on the activity of the gap between the type of activity observed and the type of activity expected. For example, a woman who decides to have her first child at the age of forty engages in a very challenging enterprise, while she is in the identity part of an identity stage. On the other hand, from a pragmatic point of view, the ability to situate a unity in its stage of development makes it possible to adjust an intervention to the characteristics of that stage, which then serves as a background for the development of that unity.

Another point to consider is that the model presents an optimum whose various values are averages that do not take into account individual variations. The same is true in empirical observations: for example, it can be stated that children take their first steps on average at 11.7 months. However, some will take their first steps before, others after. The anchoring of the model could then be adjusted to individual cases if regularity is found in the time lags of stages.

Prospects for Generalizing to Long Cycles

The research hypothesis underlying this approach is that any human entity – individual or collective – that is engaged in the process of developing its own identity does so according to the coherence inherent in the self-referential process. The challenge has been to discover by successive approximations the temporal contours of this coherence. We have at the outset a basic image of this process, a matrix, as we have called it, which guides the ordering of the observation data. Everything happens as if we had to reconstruct the world from the few primitive dimensions of this process, which span out over time, fitting into each other to form increasingly complex units. The observation of a particular level of complexity of human reality then provides an interpretation of this construction, while also enriching the process. This construction is temporary and must remain open to the contributions of other interpretations, this time derived from the observation of other levels of human complexity.

In this case, the model was described in the context of the level of complexity corresponding to the development of the person as a self-referential entity.[94] The extent to which this model applies to other contexts with different levels of complexity will need to be explored. This will eventually make it possible to distinguish between what is general and applicable at all levels and what is specific to the level under analysis. To do this, we will proceed "naively" as if what we have built were integrally applicable to this global level, a bit like Piagetian children who apply integrally to new objects a scheme they already master. Little by little, they then learn how reality forces

---

94. Brief reminder: three main stages have been described, which are repeated and enriched from one cycle to the next. The first stage, related to *receptivity*, is the locus of *engagement* in the process of development that emerges from *trust* and *openness* to the forces of life that are present in oneself and in the environment and that preside over this development. The second stage, related to the *activity*, is the locus of the development of a *competence* that emerges from the *capacity* to take the *initiative* for action concerning one's own development. The third stage, related to *identity*, is the locus of *autonomy* that emerges from *self-expression* as a unit forming an *integrated* whole. The observation oriented us towards a heuristic process which consists of a geometrical progression of reason phi, which at the same time has the characteristics of a Fibonacci sequence. This progression fully reproduces the structure of the nested ternary cycles corresponding to observation.

them to adapt their scheme to the requirements of the new objects.

The first step is to assess the order of magnitude of the process studied and to anchor the model in this process. The heuristic process is then applied to the entire period under study. Considering, however, that humanity is still in its prehistory and that no civilization has yet truly and clearly manifested the collective human identity as a unity with an operational closure and manifesting the self-referential cycle, it is not obvious that we can empirically observe a complete and convincing example of this result. We can nevertheless hope that whatever the civilization studied, the natural tendencies to optimize the process provide traces of a framework, underlying historical events, which at least evokes the model presented. For illustrative purposes, we will attempt to produce a first sketch of the application of our model to the Dionysian era of Western civilization, in other words, to the development of our civilization in the Christian era.

Preliminary Observations

To prepare the anchoring of our model, let us carry out a first intuitive analysis of our era. To do this, we will draw from general historical treatises as well as a work by Pitirim Sorokin (1941), an American sociologist of Russian origin who, in the middle of the 20th century, believed he had discovered cycles in the development of civilizations. Though we will not use Sorokin's model as such, given that his categories are not very articulate and lack generality, we will nevertheless draw on his observations to determine some decisive turning points in the development of our civilization.

Let examine, therefore, the great periods of the past that have characterized Western civilization, keeping in mind the characteristics of the stages we have identified previously. More precisely, let us take a look at the early Christian period from this perspective. According to our model, we should observe in the first period a situation in which one is essentially in a *receptive* mode regarding an external force, and over which one has no control.

The culture specific to this period constitutes a unified system based on the principle of a force that is beyond the senses and reason and which constitutes true reality and true value. All important sectors of medieval culture are articulated around this reality. The Christian Creed sums it all up: *"I believe in God ... and am waiting for eternal life."* What really matters takes place elsewhere than here on earth, in the concrete world of the senses. Sculpture and architecture are but versions of the Bible in stone. And the same is true of music, painting, and thought. Priority is given to promoting the development of faith, that is to say, *trust* in and *openness* to this reality of another order and to all the intermediaries who can represent it. Thus, every manifestation that one can directly link to God provokes one's *engagement* or commitment.

The next stage would be when human beings become aware of their *capacities* and take the *initiative* for the action for which they become responsible, thus motivating them to develop their own *competences*. A new principle then gradually asserts itself and leads to the development of a new culture in which the reality of reference is essentially the human reality, a reality to which the human being has direct access. Thus, the arts, sciences, and philosophy become detached from the supernatural world, as does the social, economic, and political organization of society. The human being is, so to speak, placed back at the center of human matters. People become increasingly interested in discovering the world, in knowing its laws; they develop tools, and utilitarian values occupy an important place.

This characteristic, which begins somewhere at the end of the Middle Ages, is later affirmed with more evidence from the 16th to the 18th centuries and leads to a constant redefining of modernity that brings us to the present day, with a focus on *doing* and on competence in action. Concerning the first stage, we find here the same characteristics as those of the second stage of the cycles of development of the person, that is, the emphasis placed on developing *competence* in *responsibly assuming* one's own reality and one's relationship with the environment.

The identification of these two major trends corresponding to two distinct stages provides the material needed to find the point of transition from one to the other, which could then serve as an anchor point for the model. Since this concerns the transition from the first to the second stage, this point will, on the one hand, delineate a whole cycle with its three lower-level stages, and, on the other, the second higher-level stage.

Anchoring of Model and Its Deployment

It is thus a matter of finding, according to the previously mentioned criteria, a transition point that corresponds to observation and that illustrates the end of the first stage and the announcement of the second. P. Sorokin places the arrival of the new culture corresponding to what has been called a second stage in the 13th century. There are, moreover, various signs of this in several fields: for example, the birth of universities, the introduction of Greek and Arab thought, the promotion of reason, and the introduction in England of the Magna Carta, all of which are manifestations of the emergence of new values linked to the re-appropriation by human beings of the control of their condition.

From a heuristic point of view, observation of the evolution of governance in Europe leads us to choose the middle of this century, the year 1250, as the anchor point of the model. For the sake of clarity, we thus anticipate the results of a more elaborate analysis of the historical currents present at that time, which will support this choice.[95] Let us now try to see what kind of breakdown would result from the application of the process described above, starting from this anchor point.

Values before 1250 belong to the first stage, which in itself constitutes a complete cycle, itself made up of three stages of the primary level. The higher values will divide the second and third stages. Also, the second and third stages will be divided into three sub-stages according to the principle of secondary stages described above. The first cycle will be presented on a first line at a magnification of phi^2 compared to the second line. This is illustrated below in Figure 11.

---

95. See note 96. Note that this choice is based on historical observation and not on the elucubrations of the "fanatics of the Apocalypse" inspired by the illuminations of the Calabrian abbot and hermit Johaquin de Flore (1145 – 1202) (see Norman Cohn 1970). Moreover, the present model is built on an algorithm that has nothing to do with this kind of tradition.

TEMPORALITY OF SELF-REFERENTIAL PROCESS

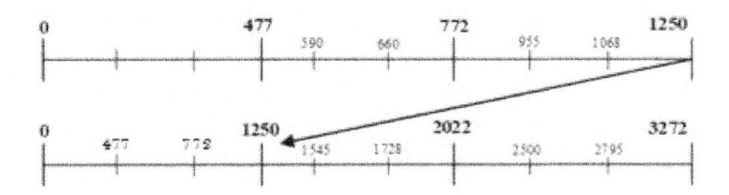

Figure 11. Temporal breakdown of Western civilization according to the principle of nested ternary cycles based on the phi heuristic and the year 1250 as an anchor point.

Let's start with a brief description of the three stages of the first cycle (0–1250) by highlighting the third, this in order to confirm our anchor point. In the first stage, we observe the decline of the Roman Empire until its fall in 476 with the deposition of the emperor Romulus Augustulus. The establishment of the first ingredients of the new civilization then coincides with the decline of the previous one.

The next stage corresponds roughly to what historians have called the Upper Middle Ages, witness to the rise and development of the Merovingian dynasty. At the fall of the Roman Empire, antagonisms due to the multiplicity of barbarian peoples interacting with each other and remnants of imperial Gaul on the same European territory, called for the differentiation of an agent capable of taking the initiative of a structuring action within this diversity. It was Clovis who succeeded in this operation (481–511), facilitated by his conversion to Catholicism. The religious question at that time was indeed more important than the racial question. This hegemony of the Merovingians continued in the Kingdom of the Franks until Pepin le Bref. We thus have here, in terms of our present model, the establishment of an *active stage* characterized by the differentiation of an agent who, in terms of governance, succeeds in distinguishing himself and in making the other agents move into receptive mode. However, the mode of transmission of power to descendants created a division with each generation, which gradually led to a dislocation of the Kingdom of the Franks.

The next stage, always according to our model, should place us before an effort of synthesis, successful or not, on the part of a unit seeking to assert itself as an *autonomous* entity based on its own *identity*, and that is repugnant to *chaotic dispersion*. Let us see what observation suggests.

If we consider the great movements of this stage,[96] we can observe the affirmation of the new Carolingian dynasty with Pepin le Bref in the middle of the 8th century. His son Charles, who will be called Charlemagne, will start reigning in 768. Through his conquests, he transforms the Kingdom of the Franks into a real continental empire that covers almost all of Western Europe. In short, he succeeds in uniting the entire Germanic and Latin world in a new political entity. Western Europe is awakening to its own political, cultural and religious *identity*. Now it is the kingdom of Charlemagne, not the Byzantine Empire; Latin-speaking, not Greek-speaking; and Roman Catholic in terms of religious practice. We can thus interpret this period as a frantic attempt to achieve a synthesis of all civilization forces involved, based on an expression of *identity*.

However, the empire is fragile and the difficulty of keeping it together, due to external pressures and internal succession problems, leads to its collapse. The 843 Treaty of Verdun divides the Empire into three parts, heralding the future great political divisions of the modern states at the heart of Europe. In 870 a new division takes place which, except for the temporary reunification achieved by Charles le Gros from 882 to 887, ends up being final, the imperial dream having been overthrown by regional forces. However, in the broken Germania Otto I succeeds his father, Henry of Saxony, in 936 and dreams of restoring Charlemagne's empire. He will be at the origin of one of the main political organizations of the Christian West, which will take the name of the Holy Roman Empire of the German Nation. Yet this power extends neither to France nor England. Thus, the Western world is no longer politically united after Charlemagne's era. The Empire collapses upon the death of

---

96. Bernard Dionne, Michel Guay, *Histoire et civilisation de l'Occident*, Laval, Études vivantes, 1993. This description is directly inspired by this book.

Frederick II in 1250 and imperial power remains vacant for 23 years. Hence the choice of the year 1250 as an anchor point. Obviously, when dealing with such large time spans, the choice of a specific year must not be considered absolute.

It is thus not in the form of a unified empire that the synthesis of the period leading to the middle of the 13th century will finally manifest itself. Instead, the renewal expressed and manifested in the medieval civilization of the 12th and 13th centuries originates from the political consolidation of the states of Western Europe. The relative stability of the states made possible the construction of great cathedrals, the revival of literature and the arts, and the development of schools and universities. It is the consolidation of the power of the Anglo-Norman, French and German kings that makes all this possible. In short, at the end of the 12th and the beginning of the 13th century, political leaders set up true secular states, though the religious reference remains present.

The second half of the 13th century represents the beginning of the following period. Thus, as early as the fourteenth century, we see the appearance of what was already known at that time as *humanism*, the beginning of a period in which human beings become aware of the power they have over themselves and nature, and start developing their knowledge of the world through observation and the mastery of increasingly efficient technologies. From the sixteenth century onwards, this trend becomes more marked with great discoveries and humanist thought ever more strengthened and based more on facts and evidence than beliefs or dogmas. This brings us to the Age of Enlightenment that gives rise to the deployment, over a few centuries, of what could be considered the most advanced expression of this cultural principle linked to *competence*, the art of doing, a progression that leads us to the present day. Mankind develops tools in a way no other civilization ever managed to do. Science and technology allow people to attain the world like never before, and this from the infinitely small to the infinitely large. Yet, though we owe such results to values based on efficiency in means and ways of doing, on competence, we nevertheless feel that we are losing control of ourselves, that we know less and less who we are and where we are going. The great certainties have collapsed. This feeling of emptiness seems to be a characteristic of the passage from a second to a third stage. The crisis we are now experiencing should thus lead us to the development of a new culture, one based more on *being* than *doing*, one where expressing our human *identity* would take precedence over putting into practice our *competence*.

Commentary

Noteworthy is the fact that this heuristic method has the advantage of immediately placing us in coherent temporal orders of magnitude. We might be surprised, for example, that the second stage brings us all the way from the Middle Ages to the present era with the same backdrop. But it should not be forgotten that it is the whole first cycle which serves as the first stage at this level. However, this cycle includes twelve centuries. It is normal that the second is of a comparable order of magnitude. The observation data are, moreover, consistent with the general characteristics of this stage.

A second observation concerns the correspondence between the breakdown obtained and the historical data. Let us first note that in our model, the first stage of the first cycle of this era overlaps with the decline of the previous era within which the new logic was gradually appearing. It is also striking that the deposition of the last Roman emperor in 476 and the advent of Clovis in 481 correspond fairly exactly to the transition our model predicted would take place in 477. That is also the case with the transition between the Merovingian dynasty and its replacement by the Carolingians, in particular with the advent of Charlemagne who was crowned king of the Franks in 768. Our model predicted a transition to this period would take place around the year 772. The year 1250, as well as the transitions to the sixteenth and eighteenth centuries, have already been discussed, not including the outbreak of the present crisis, an issue that we will revisit at the end of the chapter.

However, as mentioned earlier, the characteristics described for each primary or secondary stage are meant more as a backdrop or ideal than a real achievement. For example, one observes that Charlemagne wanted to give his new empire its own identity. And to a certain extent, he succeeds. However, the expression of identity as the realization of a self-referential process requires more than that; it cannot result from imperial domination. A dominant power within a unity cannot be the self-referential expression of that unity.

In short, the model allows us to give an interpretation of history that has its own coherence. However, it is not the only valid interpretation. Other breakdowns can highlight other aspects, according to the intention of the observer.

Let us bear in mind that whatever the model, the object "*civilization*" is always a constructed object. The heuristics used here facilitate the decentration from an egocentric subject exposed to the biases of perception. However, we see the contribution of the subject, as in any constructed object. For example, the introduction of the constant *phi* in the production of a Fibonacci sequence. These elements do not exist as such in nature, but they can help us to gain an objective, approximate knowledge of a phenomenon, a bit like the interval scale of a thermometer and its correspondence with the variations of a column of mercury could help us to gain objective knowledge of temperature.

The hypothesis explaining the relative adequacy of the model with observation has already been mentioned: the discomfort linked to the lack of maturity of the unity under consideration, in this case, civilization, leads to various reactions depending on the state of development of this civilization, in the hope of reaching a more satisfactory state. A civilization can only improve its state from within, by taking responsibility for itself through the initiatives of the various agents that make it up. The hypothesis is that efforts to optimize this self-referential process, whatever its level of application, will produce regularities that can be observed through the proposed model. This is the working hypothesis to which the previous reflection leads us. Such is, therefore, the first approximation of what emerges from the introduction of time into the self-referential process.

The Present Time

Sorokin criticized his contemporaries for not seeing the extent of the current crisis, which marks a unique turning point in the history of our civilization. We could address the same criticism to him, for if he is right to see in the present turning point a repetition of what has been observed in other civilizations, he could not foresee what is unprecedented about this turning point: indeed, it involves not only the living forces of one civilization but those of the whole of humanity. It is the first time in history that the same crisis affects all nations at the same time. What happens in China, India or Japan affects us in America or Europe as directly, and sometimes more, than what happens in our neighboring countries. The turning point of our Western civilization coincides in time with a distinct turning point that affects all humanity. Everything is now connected. We can be instantly in communication with any point on the planet. States are overwhelmed by transnational forces no longer guided by the classic principle of power as we know it. What kind of agency will differentiate itself from all the forces at play to ensure humanity's transition to the next stage? That is the big question. It seems that the power models invented to lead states are not the feasible and desirable way to achieve this.

If we look at the present critical turning point within the framework of the present analysis, we see that Western civilization is entering a third stage, one of *identity*, while humanity is entering a second, *active* stage, where it would be a question of such a unity, the human species, this time covering the entire planet, giving itself the means to take charge of itself effectively and responsibly.

This discrepancy in the stages of development of contemporary entities suggests the possibility of the emergence of a particular process, of which the educational relationship would be an example. We will discuss this further in the fourth chapter.

In short, this chapter has allowed us to describe the self-referential circle as it stretches over large time spans. It is the dimension of genesis. We had previously discussed the general workings of the self-referential process at the heart of the existential relationship that a unity maintains with itself. This process, according to the fourth founding statement presented in the first chapter, is at the source of communication. The next chapter is devoted to an exploration of this statement.

Chapter IV

Communication

The conception of communication developed within the paradigm of self-reference defies common sense. As mentioned in the introduction, we are used to seeing communication as an outward-going process that puts us in contact with others. This conception is not false, but it is incomplete. If two people are in contact, we forget that the couple they form, which we will call the dyad, has its reality in its own right and that its influence precedes, so to speak, the interaction that the protagonists will have with each other. We also forget that when we are alone, we are in constant contact with ourselves, and therefore in the middle of a communication process. Communication is thus not essentially an outward-going process.

Let's go back to the dyad. We have all experienced a situation where we inadvertently find ourselves with another person, for example in an elevator, and wonder how to react. The origin of the communication is in the dyad, in the fact of being two people. This is why the authors of the Palo Alto School[97] state that as soon as one is in contact, "one cannot not communicate." In other words, communication takes place before anyone has spoken. Even if one decides not to intervene, one communicates this intention indirectly. So, the very fact that there is a dyad puts pressure on people to engage despite themselves in an interaction, either to make clear that it is unwanted or to go ahead with it. It can, therefore, be said that fundamentally it is

---

97. The *Palo Alto School* refers to the current of thought initiated by Gregory Bateson and perpetuated in particular by Paul Watzlawick and his colleagues, the best known of whom are John Weakland, Richard Fish, Janet Helmick-Beavin and Don D. Jackson. The content of the various references to this School can be found for the most part in the work of Paul Watzlawick, Janet Helmick-Beavin, Don D. Jackson. Jackson, *Pragmatics of Human Communication*, published in New York in 1967 by W.W. Norton & Company.

not primarily individuals who communicate: they are the cogs of a process that begins upstream of their interaction. This is partly in line with N. Luhmann's point of view[98] that it is not individuals, fundamentally, who communicate.

However, our present model rapidly distances itself from Luhmann's, given that the latter eliminates the reference to totality, whereas in our model, the paradigm of self-reference should, on the contrary, represent the advent of this totality, as discussed in chapter one. In Luhmann's world, for all intents and purposes, there would no longer be anyone present at any level. Who would then be communicating? Communication itself! It would be communication that would be communicating! It would be like walking but with no one really walking. Walking itself would be walking! Luhmann basically replaces the founding self-referential relationship of totality with the self-referential illusion of a process floating above human realities, these being reduced to servile supports whose only hope would be losing any illusion about the role they might have in communication.

In the model we are setting forth, totality constitutes the reference of communication. It is the self-referential cycle that establishes and maintains this totality in existence as a unit. If we return to our example of the dyad, we are in the presence of three universes of communication: that of the dyad and the two universes of the individuals involved. It is the dyad that is the primary referent of the process, the interaction between individuals being only a cog in this process.

The source of communication lies therefore in the dyad, deemed a unity in its own right. And if the interaction between two individuals runs smoothly, the dyad can also be found at the end of the process. Two individuals, for example, can feel themselves buoyed along by the couple they form. The dyad has its own identity and, like any human unity, it tends to become self-referential. Basically, communication then designates this process by which a human entity seeks to build itself, to reinvent

---

98. Niklaus Luhmann, *Theories of Distinction. Redescribing the Description of Modernity*, Stanford, Stanford University Press, 2002.
Niklaus Luhmann, *Essays on Self-Reference*, New York, Columbia University Press, 1990.

itself, to create itself. It represents the self-referential process that, from the outset, we have been trying to explain.

The primary impulse underlying communication is thus existential and emerges from the entity encompassing the agents, before being a motivation pushing these agents to achieve a result. For this global entity, it is the question of *being or not being* that is at stake. Yet, though the identity of the whole is the alpha and omega of the communication process, it remains dependent on the interaction of the parts. We must, therefore, see by what mechanism this vertical communication is fed by the (horizontal) interaction of the components, communication by which the communicating entity, which includes this interaction as one of its constituent processes, regenerates its identity in a self-referential cycle.

In this context, the interaction between people is somewhat instrumental in the self-referential process of the dyad. What triggers people to interact is the will to participate in the creation, the co-creation should we say, of a human reality, which precedes and encompasses them, but for which they have full responsibility. The interaction between people can be seen as the engine room of a larger process, that of the self-production of the totality they form, in this case, the dyad. Communication is thus first the construction of an interior before being an exit to the exterior. It is when we look inside the dyad that we see that each person interacts with the other and thus turns towards the outside of his or her own universe. In short, every communicative interaction between the parts of a totality is a cog in the relationship that this totality tries to establish with itself.

In short, communication is that self-generating loop by which a totality is maintained in existence through the interaction of its constituent parts. If the totality is a person, it is the various components of the person that interact and become in turn the subjects of internal actions that continuously generate and regenerate him or her. If the totality is a dyad, the parts are the two persons whose interaction regenerates this totality. If the totality is a society, they are the latter's various constituent groups interacting with each other. We thus once again find our initial schema of a totality within which an intervening *agent* is differentiated, thus cutting out a *receptive* from which a *paradoxical agent* will emerge, which ideally will encompass the initial agent in its intervention. From there, another agent will do the same, and so on. The question now is to see how this diagram can serve as a basis for the explanation of the main aspects of communication. In the context of communication, the general term *agent* will now become *intervening agent*. And if the *receptive* refers to a unity that is already fully constituted, such as a person for example, we will then use the term *receiver*. To simplify things, let's continue with the example of the dyad.

Communicational Zone

Whether one is dealing with a person, a dyad, a group, or a society, the boundary distinguishing the inside and outside of each of these totalities delimits a zone within which the entire communication process will take place. We will thus speak of the *totality* as a *communicational zone*. We have also noted that by the mere fact of being in the presence of each other, and therefore of constituting, intentionally or not, a dyad, two individuals feel impelled to interact. We have chosen to call this dynamic aspect of the communicational zone the *communicational field*, by analogy with the situation of two magnets whose magnetic field, disturbed by their coming together, "incites" them to generate an electromagnetic wave that induces a current. [99]

At this deepest level of the process, we are faced with the most basic identity of this totality – the dyad in this case – an identity which, expressed in words, could boil down to: "I, the dyad, exist as a unity distinct from what is not me." Let's revisit the example of two strangers who happen to be together in an elevator. They have no choice but to form a dyad, however short-lived it may be. Yet, the same two would have crossed paths in a crowd and may not even have noticed each other. In the context of a crowd, they would not have been led to stand apart as being "WE" relative to "that which is not WE." This standing-apart WE represents the dyad considered from the point of view of the people who compose it. We can represent this zone by an oval

---

[99]. This is the slightly anthropomorphic (hence the quotation marks) expression of the principle that a varying magnetic field generates an electromagnetic wave that induces a current in a conductive body. Here, the variation of the magnetic field is caused by the coming together of two magnets that evoke two persons meeting each other.

that marks the border of this unit which distinguishes it from its environment (Figure 12).

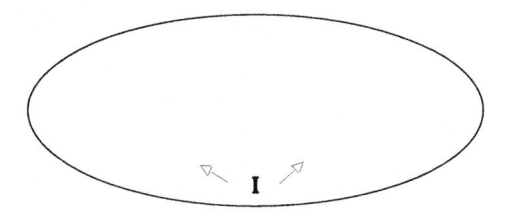

Figure 12: Identity of the dyad delineated by the boundary that distinguishes this unit from its environment. The communication field is symbolized by the arrows.

Differentiation of an Intervening Agent in the Communicational Zone

We have seen that the communication field of the dyad incites people to start interacting. One person usually decides to intervene. We will see later on that such interaction involves a complex superimposition of messages. For the time being, however, let us simply note the characteristics of the intervening agent himself.

At his own level, the intervening agent – referred to as **A** in figure 12 below – is also a totality, which is, of course, more complete than the nascent dyad of which he is a part. He also constitutes a communicational zone with his own identity, which makes him a distinct unity in his environment. However, his identity – "Who am I?" – takes on a particular color in the elevator. Am I someone who wants to be an enabler, who wants to ease the tension by giving the stranger the impression of wanting to carry on a conversation? Or am I someone showing no interest whatsoever in such an eventuality?

This implicit identity (I') of **A** will elicit the action of the internal intervening agent (A'), an action that will first modify him (R'), generating an appropriate attitude, and then directly target the receiver **R**. This action may just be saying "hello" (A'), but if the identity that the intervener wants to convey or make explicit is that of a dominating character who is in a bad mood, the "hello" will first modify him (R') by generating an attitude of tension and dryness and an unfriendly tone of voice, and it is this complex intervention that will reach the receiver **R**. In our example, to simplify things, suppose that the "hello" simply expresses a cordiality whose warmth invites the other person to be open to continuing the interaction. The diagram in figure 13 provides a general outline of an *intervention*, regardless of its content.

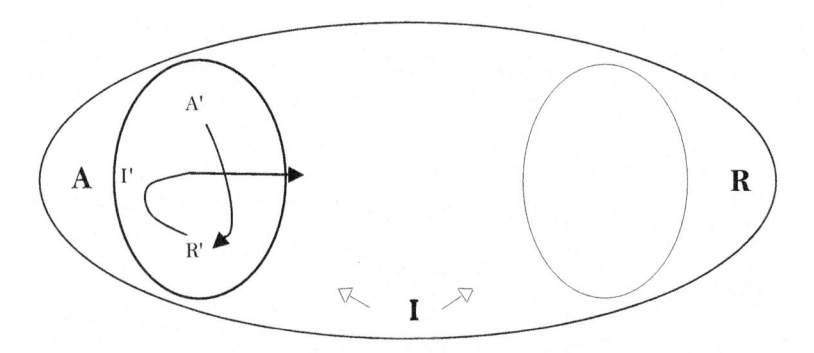

Figure 13. The intervening agent **A** whose personal identity (I') leads him to differentiate the inner agent A', which first modifies the internal receptive R', and then aims at the other unit of the communication zone **R**, which is then in receptive mode.

We can then imagine that the receiver, in turn, takes the position of agent **A** and that the initial agent places himself in receptive position **R**. Suppose that this second intervening agent also responds with a "hello" by showing openness. The interaction of the two identity messages of the intervening agents then gives a more defined form to the identity of the dyad. When confronted with the choice, "to be or not to be," the dyad leans more on the side of "to be." It shows signs of moving in the direction of self-creation rather than self-destruction. This is shown below in the diagram in Figure 14.

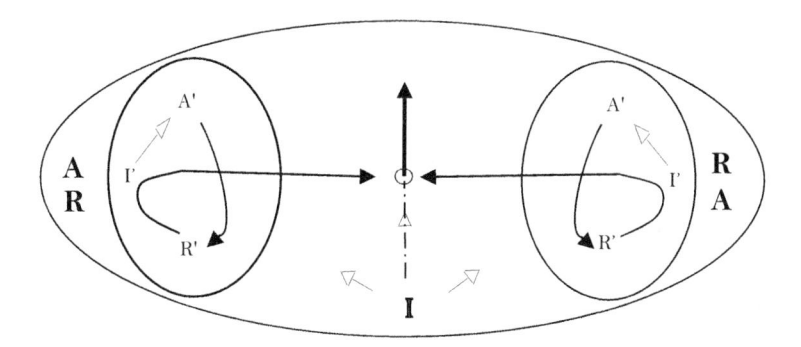

Figure 14. The dyad's identity, **I**, pushes the two individuals to manifest their own identity, I,' whose interaction gives a more defined form to the initial identity of the dyad.

Complex Message Structure

As we have already pointed out, communication itself flows from the implicit identity of the dyad, which tends to become explicit as it is constructed. It is therefore at the end of an *interaction* between the two protagonists that we can speak of an *identity message of the dyad*.

The same is true of the implicit identity of the intervening agents who are at the origin of the interventions. Each intervention is made up of a hierarchy of messages whose structure reflects the structure of the intervening agent himself. It is only at the end of an *intervention* that we will have access to the *identity message of the intervening agent*.

The first explicit message of the intervening agent comes from the internal agent A' which, in humans, is expressed essentially through language. In other animals, it will be the species-specific cry, meowing in cats, barking in dogs, etc. It is, in short, the tool with which nature has endowed each animal to intervene symbolically with its fellow creatures.

Human language is special in that it is a code made of *conventional signs* so that the same object will correspond to different sounds according to the implicit conventions specific to the language of those speaking. The message delivered through language will be called the *spoken message*. It is characterized by a strong referential function: language makes it easy to know *what one is talking about*.

Yet this message first modifies the intervening agent himself (R') who receives this message in a way that depends on the identity that is at the origin of the intervention. In the example given above of a "hello" from an intervening agent whose implicit identity takes the form " *I'm a dominating character who is in a bad mood,*" it is voice intonation – dry and abrupt -, bodily attitude – tense and rigid -, etc. that would convey this. But it so happens that this result on R' itself becomes a message, one that helps the receiver to interpret the *spoken message*. The "hello" in our example would then take on the meaning, "I find your company aggravating." Palo Alto School theorists emphasize this aspect of the spoken message, referring to it as the metamessage, in other words, a message about a message. In the model we are setting forth, we will highlight the fact that the metamessage defines the relationship by indicating the relative *position* of the intervening agent in relation to the receiver. Such a metamessage will be called a *relational message*.

The *relational message* is conveyed through codes with *analog signs*, i.e., codes whose signs have a natural meaning, regardless of conventions. For example, anger expressed by screams and violent posturing is immediately understood as such without the help of any prior convention. The semantic function of this message is therefore strong, but its referential function is weak: the message does not say what it is about. We will see that the positions defined by this message can be classified according to the categories "high position (H), center position (C), low position (L)". We will come back to the various combinations which indicate the position that the intervening agent takes and that which he attributes to the receiver, positions that we can list here: HH, HL, CC, LH, LL.

The interaction between these two explicit messages, *spoken* and *relational*, reveals the *identity message of the intervening agent*.

This identity message, initially implicit and at the origin of the other two, then becomes explicit in their interaction. In other words, it is the intervener's implicit identity that leads him to generate the two explicit messages, *spoken* and *relational*, and it is the interaction of the latter two messages that in the end reveals – makes explicit – the identity of the interv ening agent. The *intervening agent's identity message* is therefore not directly emitted as such. We will thus refer to this type of message as an *emerging message.*

Let us now assume that in response to this intervention, the receiver takes on the role of intervening agent. The process then goes through the same steps: implicit identity → spoken message ←→ relational message → intervening agent's identity message. The identity message of this intervening agent then interacts with that of the first intervening agent and it is finally from the interaction of the two identity messages that emerges the *identity message of the dyad.* Let's sum it all up in Table 7.

In short, this whole process of interweaving messages of various kinds aims to make the virtual identity of the dyad, and indirectly, the virtual identity of each participant in this specific situation, real. It goes without saying that in the example of Table 7, the verbal interpretation of the relational and emerging messages is approximate.

We see here that the present model has simply pushed the Palo Alto School model to its conclusion by making the *totality* the instance of reference for communication, whether it be the person in his or her relationship to himself or herself, the dyad, the group or society. It is the implicit identity of the totality that is actualized and constructed through the *identity message* of that *totality.*

Table 7. Diagram of an interaction involving an intervention and its response. Italics are not pronounced and are interpretations.

Operations	Messages	Examples		Examples	Messages	Operations
Intervention 1	Spoken	"Hello"	→	"I don't accept being approached in that tone"	Spoken	Intervention 2 (response)
	Relational	[Dry, tense tone...] "I find your company aggravating" H→L	↓ ⇢	[Dry, tense tone...] "It makes me angry" L←H	Relational	
	Identity of the intervening agent [Emerging]	"I am the authority"	↘ o ↗	"I'm challenging your authority"	Identity of the intervening agent [Emerging]	
			"We are at war" Identity message of the dyad [Emerging]			

198

The simplified schema could appear as follows:

Spoken message		Spoken message
Relational message	⇐⇒	Relational message
Identity message of the intervening agent	⇓	Identity message of the intervening agent
Identity message of the dyad		

A more in-depth presentation would lead to more precision concerning the relationships of the various positions precisely defining the relational message. We could draw inspiration this time from Thomas Harris (2004) who defines, within Transactional Analysis, the various types of interactions he calls transactions. In the example we have just given, the first participant takes a high position – "I'm a dominating character" – and places the other in a low position (H→L). The interlocutor retaliates by also taking a high position and places the first participant in a low position (H→L). If we graphically represent this interaction, we get what Harris calls a crossed transaction:

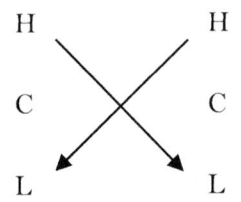

```
H           H
 \         /
  C   ✕   C
 /         \
L           L
```

We can now try to see how this basic scheme can reproduce – or not – the self-referential cycle. In other words, how this schema can be the locus of self-creation – or the locus of self-destruction – of the communicating entity, in this case, the dyad. In the example provided in Table 7, the dyad, based on the interaction shown, is not heading towards a bright future.

Let us go through the cycle of the self-referential process step by step to see how this communication pattern can be its vehicle.

To sum up: we have posited communication as the expression of the self-referential cycle of self-production, whether it be of the individual, the dyad, the group, society, or humanity as a whole. This process is oriented towards self-realization achieved through successive approximations. Some individuals, who are said to be wise, have reached a high level of self-realization. For such individuals, the self-referential process unfolds naturally: there is not a moment that is not creation, self-creation, novelty so to speak, and this flows from and at the same time regenerates their own identity. Some couples have been able to reach this level of realization as couples, and this has even been the case of some societies that have stayed out of the orbit of empires and have been able to develop such collective wisdom far from conquerors.

This overall process can unfold at the microscopic level of a single interaction in the dyad. Let's briefly review the stages. First, we have an undifferentiated state of the dyad concerning the intervention to come before the interaction begins. This is the initial state of the *totality*. Next comes the differentiation of an *agent* that carries out an intervention on the *receiver* through a complex message. The receiver is then placed in receptive mode concerning this intervention. It is here that the key but usually missing piece in the communicational process intervenes: the *paradoxical agent*, which is, in this case, a differentiation of the receiver. Thus, the receiver will have to perform three distinct functions in turn: first, receive the intervention, then release the paradoxical agent, which will perform a hierarchical reversal based on the initial intervention to verify whether the understanding is adequate, and finally to switch from receptive to intervening mode.

Acting in paradoxical mode is not part of natural reflexes, especially since language does not distinguish between the simple posture of the initial intervening agent and that of the paradoxical agent. The characteristic of the latter is to prolong the intervention of the first agent by echoing it so that this agent is placed in receptive mode compared to this particular version of his intervention and that he recognizes himself there from this receptive point of view. The intervening agent assesses the conformity of the two distinct versions of his intervention so that it includes himself as a receiver, making the intervention coextensive with the totality, in other words, covering the whole dyad. This done, the receiver shifts into an active mode of his own right, and the interaction occurs this time in the other direction, according to the same process.

We note that the intervention of the paradoxical agent, in this context, is marked by empathy, a type of intervention that humanistic psychology has largely developed. Indeed, the response of the paradoxical agent is not produced with reference to the receiver, but with reference to the intervention of the initial agent. The paradoxical agent is not involved in the content of the interaction, but he aims to facilitate its progress. He judges the content neither positively nor negatively. He allows the intervening agent to assess whether his intervention has been received for what it is from his perspective. It is then up to the receiver to move from the position of the paradoxical agent to the position of agent, this time operating from his own frame of reference.

It is interesting to note that in its early days, humanistic psychotherapy made almost exclusive use of this type of intervention, that is, empathic understanding, which corresponds to the function of the paradoxical agent. In short, this therapeutic approach consisted of completing the natural process of communication by introducing the missing piece, i.e., an intervention resulting from what has been called the paradoxical agent. Of course, since the methodological framework of psychotherapy was not a natural communication situation, the therapist was limited to playing this role of paradoxical agent in communication.

We examined the structure of messages within an intervention and interaction between people. According to the basic principle of the approach we are setting forth, one should find the same structure at the lower level, the intrapersonal level, and at the higher level, the societal level.

Intrapersonal Level Messages: First Approximation

The intrapersonal spoken message. On the intrapersonal level, spoken messages are the product of the whole system of idiosyncratic representation that accompanies here and now experiencing. Some would call it the mental dimension of experiencing. It is, so to speak, the ongoing semiotic function constantly generating signs and symbols, and which constitutes one's ever-active inner voice. Much of this level of expression is borrowed from interpersonal language: indeed, part of a person's experiencing is expressed internally in words.

The intrapersonal relational message. In terms of relational message, the question is always, "what am *I* doing to *myself*." For example, if I'm feeling guilty about my behavior, I will place myself in a high position relative to a part of me that is somehow "punished," and thus in a low position. An internal verbal message often accompanies such a situation. The relational message is therefore made up of the various positions that *I* take concerning myself and which place *me* in one or the other of the complementary positions.

The identity message of the intrapersonal intervening agent. In the previous example, the differentiation of a blaming intervening agent can be interpreted as an attempt to avoid reducing the totality to the identity evoked by the denounced behavior that causes shame. It is as if the intervening agent is asserting his or her identity as a "redresser of wrongs" or an example of "good behavior," which generally tends to produce the opposite effect and provoke a response in the agency being blamed in which reproached behavior is reinforced. As at the social level, experiencing within a person is the scene of multiple actors who do not always agree on the drama to be staged. Thus, any internal intervention will result in a response made up of the same structure of messages.

The identity message of the person. Thus, the interaction of all these internal actors transforms a person into a more cohesive and coherent unit or, conversely, one that is more conflictual and in loss of integrity.

Societal Level Messages: A First Approximation

Societal level spoken messages. At the societal level, the paradigm of the spoken message is evoked by what R. Petrella (2007) calls the *narrative* that a society gives of itself. Every society expresses *itself to itself* and *expresses the world* through its customs, its founding texts, its ideologies, its theories, its artistic expression, the speeches of its freely chosen or imposed leaders, etc. It is the conversion of social experience into conventional signs. According to Petrella, the dominant narrative in today's Western societies is characterized by faith in technology, confidence in capitalism, and the conviction that there are no alternatives to this vision.

Societal level relational messages. The relational message says what the intervening agent is *doing* to the other person by placing him or her in a particular relative position. If we refer to the dominant narrative mentioned above, survival depends on competitiveness. One must, therefore, be the best. The intervening agent, in such a context, will try to place himself or herself in a *high position* in order to reduce the other to a *low position*. In various societies, the higher-level actor, the state, adopts various measures to compensate for the devastation that such an approach produces, such as providing services to those who are victims of a survival-of-the-fittest society. On the other hand, some social actors are trying to see if it is possible to shift the dominant narrative towards a functioning promoting a *central position* more favorable to cooperation between actors. The relational message in society is thus made up of the actions people take towards one another, and that places them in particular complementary positions with one another.

Identity messages from societal-level intervening agents. An intervention, made up of one's actions and accompanying words, emerges from *whom one is* and, in return, defines one's *identity*. For example, state interventions under a given government and the policies through which they are expressed mean that a government, using the categories prevailing in the society in question, will be defined as progressive or conservative, *right* or *left*, and so on. It is, therefore, an implicit definition of itself that an intervening agent gives itself by taking a particular action, to which it explicitly attributes a particular meaning.

Identity message of society. From the interaction of the various identity messages of intervening agents in society will emerge the *message of social integration*, which will mean that a society will be deemed more or less cohesive, more or less self-constructing or self-destructive, etc. If the interaction of interventions is increasingly chaotic, this generates an ever-increasing state of conflict, and conversely, the more such interaction succeeds in welcoming, fostering, and harmonizing differences, the greater the social cohesion.

Internal Structure of Communicating Unities: Avenues of Research

Basic agencies within the unities were discussed: *highest-level internal agent, receptive agency,* and a *paradoxical agent* evoking the *identity* of the unity. These agencies are our only building materials. However, the functioning of these agencies is the result of an organization that has become more complex over time according to the principle developed in the third chapter. There must, therefore, be various levels of *agents* and their *receptive* complements. For example, the highest-level *agent* within a unit emerges from the interaction of a sub-agent with its receptive and thus for a third level. The same applies to the highest-level *receptive*. In short, each agency is constructed with sub-agencies that are analogous to it from level to level. If we revisit the schema of figure 13 representing a communicating agent, we can add to each agency A' and R' the analogous sub-agencies on a second level. To avoid overloading the figure, we will not represent the arrows nor the third level, nor the effect produced by the action of the intervening agent on itself.

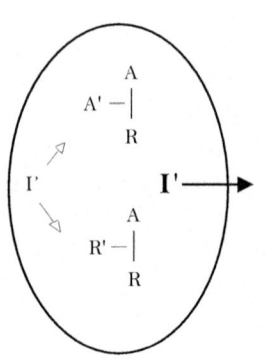

Figure 15. The implicit identity of the intervening agent I' becomes the explicit identity **I'** after manifesting itself through agent A' and the receptive R' and their sub-components.

Thus, the implicit identity I' is made explicit in the interaction of agent A' and the receptive R', each of these agencies being colored by their sub-components according to the intention of the intervener. Thus, component A can be "colored" by either sub-component A or sub-component R. We, therefore, have A'A or A'R. If the person is the receiver of the intervention, component R' can be "colored" by either sub-component A or sub-component R, resulting in R'A or R'R.

We should now see what meaning could be attributed to the elements of this construction. We will limit ourselves for the time being to the first level, A and R, as well as the second level, A'A, A'R, R'A, R'R. If none of the sub-components has a preponderance, we will only consider the first level, either A' or R'. For example, *I express myself*. This corresponds to what we referred to, in the paragraph on message structure, as the *Centre position*. This is the usual first-level operation.

At the second level, we have the explicit implementation of a sub-instance that colors the first-level action. Let us first deal with the case A'A. A *subagent* of A stands out as the predominant active element, thus also A. It is, so to speak, action being taken concerning an action, the taking over of the latter action, which gives it an orientation, which tells it how it should be. In short, it is the action's normative component.

In the case of A'R, the action of the agent is colored by a dominant receptive component at the second level. It will thus be an action of the agent including a strong listening and receptive component. It is the active component that places the *receptive agent* in the front line of the intervening agent's listening concerns.

We note that the action of agent A', thus reinforced at the second level by the sub-components, places the agent in a high position, either normative A'A or facilitative A'R. This high position may be conventional, such as that of a teacher, or natural, such as that of parents, or simply the result of a choice on the part of the person according to his or her assessment of the situation.

Let us now consider the case of the second level this time based on R', namely the situation where the person is the receiver of the intervention. First, R'A indicates that the reception is actively supported by the sub-instance A. This would be the case, for example, where a student takes possession of what he or she has received and actively appropriates it. In the case of R'R, it would be more like mere reception. All the energy is invested in receiving.

We could eventually develop a third level. Let's just mention a few avenues to illustrate this possibility. Let's take the example of an intervening agent who acts as a therapist and uses a method inspired by the humanistic approach. First of all, as an intervener, he is immediately on the A' side. But his first concern is listening to the person rather than intervening in a normative way. So, we have A'R. And if he decides to intervene, it will be from a sub-level A of R: so, we have A'RA. His intervention will not derive from the normative component AA, the latter defining the intervener's frame of reference, but rather from the receptive component, which leaves room for the frame of reference of the other and will, therefore, be of the empathic type, that is, a manifestation of the desire to understand the person from his or her own paradigm, setting aside any element deriving from his own paradigm as intervener. The expression *active listening* is sometimes used to designate this type of intervention. So, we have A'RA. We see here the emergence of the *paradoxical agent* which, as we have seen, results from a hierarchical reversal such that an active element coming from the receptive instance takes over the action initiated by the agent.

In another case where he does not intervene, the therapist manifests his empathy by a quality of presence which then corresponds to A'RR. The eight possible cases could be explored within the framework of a more comprehensive theory of communication, an exploration that is beyond the scope of this book.

Internal Structure and Transactional Analysis

In the description of the person resulting from his transactional model, Eric Berne (1971) proposes at the first level a superposition of three agencies to which he gives these metaphorical names: *Parent, Adult, and Child.* The Parent and Child agencies are subdivided into sub-agencies that reveal a second level. The sub-agencies that have been retained for the Child are the Free Child, the Rebellious Child, and the Adapted

Child. As for the Parent, the Controlling and the Nurturing Parent have been retained.

The Parent is described in a manner very similar to what is presented in this model, with AA corresponding to the Controlling Parent and AR to the Nurturing Parent. As for the Child, links can also be found, although the correspondence is less obvious. First of all, the Rebellious Child corresponds to the *one who takes the initiative of the action*; it is, therefore, the active component A. The Adapted Child is rather the one who remains in the receptive mode, which corresponds to component R. Berne has chosen to retain from these two components only the aspect according to which the Child defines himself in reaction to the Parent so that the notion of the *Child who takes the initiative of the action* is reduced to that of the *Child who rebels against authority*. This is the case of the *Child who is in receptive mode* which becomes the *Child who adapts to authority*. As for the free Child, it is the Child who expresses himself in relation to himself and not in relation to authority.

In the model that is developed here, what corresponds to the Free Child refers to the identity of the component considered as a whole, in this case, the Child. The same is true at the first level with the Adult, which in the present model would correspond not to a component, but to the unity as a whole, the person represented here by **I**, which is both the origin and the result of the interaction of the components. As with most models, there is no room within the transactional model for the totality as such. The individual is never referred to in any way other than by his or her component parts. Moreover, the metaphors used in Transactional analysis are unfortunately restrictive and lack generality. It then becomes difficult to generalize the principle of construction whose presence is nevertheless implicitly presumed. The more general terms of the present model allow such a generalization while preserving the achievements of the transactional model.

Normative Dimension of the Model

The previous description suggests but does not clearly identify the normative dimension of the model. In other words, how can one ensure that the communicative process fosters the unit's self-referentiality, thus strengthening its internal coherence and the expression of its identity, rather than causing its disorganization through self-destructive internal conflicts? These questions will be answered more fully in the context of the pragmatic dimension, but we can already provide some general indications constituting the main principles around which these answers will be organized.

The first principle could be formulated as follows: the agent who differentiates himself as intervening in a communicational zone is an essential cog in the self-referential process of the unit under consideration. Without this differentiation, the unity is deprived of its active dimension and cannot survive.

The second principle is that the self-referential process cannot unfold by taking as its center this differentiated agent carrying out the action. Any centering on the agent leads to all forms of *ego*centrism, which, on the social level, takes the form of voluntarism, the extreme forms of which are found in the various types of totalitarianism. Conversely, the receptive instance in itself cannot be the center of the process either, because it only exists in relation to a differentiated agent and at the outset does not have its meaning by itself.

The third principle is that the center of the self-referential process is the *totality* that is at the origin of differentiation and that, in terms of interaction, only the paradoxical agent can claim the capacity to represent temporarily, but effectively, this totality. Indeed, it is through the paradoxical agent that, concerning a given intervention, the agent can let go of his action and that, by a hierarchical reversal, the receptive agency can integrate in a larger synthesis the structuring contribution of the initial agent. It is then that the paradoxical agent fades away and disappears concerning this operation.

The pragmatic development of research should illustrate how these principles can be applied to various levels of human reality. We will be able to identify the elements, among known practices, meeting these criteria and help build the methodologies meant to complete the pieces of the cog that are missing at each level.

In summary…

This chapter has made it possible to trace a first approximate outline of the general process of communication considered as an existential mechanism, which enables a human unit, whether social or individual, to maintain his identity while developing in complexity. We have mentioned two dimensions of communication, one vertical, in which a totality relates to itself through the differentiation and integration of its parts, and the other, horizontal, in which the parts relate to each other. The challenge for communication agents is to know what type of interaction can either foster or undermine this self-referential relationship of the totality.

Chapter V

Power and Social Governance

Referring to society and even humanity as potentially self-referential totalities poses a considerable challenge. Although it is the question of identity (the question of *being*) that confronts these totalities, we, as components of these totalities, are challenged by the question of *doing*: "What are we going to do with ourselves?" In terms inspired by H. A. Simon, *what methodological artifact are we going to build to gradually lead us collectively out of our prehistory, to fully affirm our humanity at the highest levels of the hierarchy*? In terms of the model proposed in this book, what are we going to do to bring our societies and humanity as a whole on the path of self-reference in the construction of themselves?

As noted at the end of chapter 3, the question arises in a new way for current societies, and, at the same time, with unprecedented clarity and imperativeness for humanity as a whole. For the first time ever, we are aware that our actions can be so self-destructive as to threaten the very existence of our species. For the first time ever, the problem facing the human species presents itself in self-referential terms: *to be or not*! That is what our action will determine, save us or lose us, realize ourselves as a species or simply disappear.

As Ulrich Beck (2001) puts it, modernization in the nineteenth century took place as a *figure* set against a different *background: nature*, which one needed to know and dominate. Today, at the turn of the 21st century, modernity is no longer established on this background: "it is calling itself into question; it is questioning the premises and operating principles of industrial society. The modernization [...] of the *pre*-modern era has given way to problems of a *self-referential* modernization."[100] Though our awareness comes from knowing the ever-growing threat and risk of self-destruction resulting from our behavior, it at the same time invites us to realize that we have what it takes to turn things around, that we have the power to self-construct ourselves.

The present *internal agents* of humanity, states, were not designed to bring about this transformation. Thus, we will eventually have to reflect on the changes needed in the functioning of these *agents*. But above all, we will have to ask ourselves what instance will differentiate itself from the totality that is humanity and constitute the *highest-level agent* or authority capable of committing this totality to take control of its self-referential process. The task of tackling this issue at the level of humankind as a whole, however, goes beyond the scope of this book. For now, we will only focus on the totalities corresponding to societies organized in the form of states.

We cannot nevertheless avoid reflecting on the intermediate levels of organization between the individual and societal levels. What happens in terms of power and governance at these intermediate levels is equally relevant.

The point at issue is, "What kind of collective living will we give birth to?" In other words, how can we create social entities with an operational closure allowing them to develop by giving primacy to the internal processes that form the basis of their identity as living beings? This is the challenge we face.

It would seem that governments of states alone are not empowered to generate such entities. Thus, to determine the kind of power that would enable us to meet this new challenge, we must address the issue of *power*.

The Power Issue

Of the three primitive dimensions of the self-referential process, namely the receptive, active, and identity dimensions, power belongs to the second, the active dimension. If we situate these three dimensions in time as we did in chapter 3, power manifests itself more specifically in the second stage. This does not mean that no form of power is exercised at the other stages.

---

100. Ulrich Beck, *La société du risque. Sur la voie d'une autre modernité*, Paris, Flammarion, 2001, p. 22.

Let us recall that when in a totality, an *agent* differentiates itself to take things in hand, the structuring aspect of its action establishes previously non-existent links between the other elements of the totality. These elements are, therefore, not initially connected concerning this action, but they still exercise power at another level. But before going further, let us see how we can define power in general.

Ingredients of Power

Power is always that of an *agent* and refers to his capacity for action. However, action always takes place in an environment. The capacity for action linked to the agent's resources then comes from two sources: the agent himself and the environment. When referring to the characteristics of the agent himself, we will speak of *competent* or *incompetent*. In other words, if the agent *feels capable* of acting and *takes the initiative* to exercise this capacity, he then develops a *competence*. Otherwise, he will have to benefit from an educational intervention, which will allow him to develop this *competence* to be able to exercise his action.

On the other hand, the agent may be competent, but not find in the environment the conditions necessary for the exercise of his action. When referring to this aspect according to which the capacity to act depends on the conditions of the environment, we will speak of *freedom of action* or *obstacle to freedom of action*. We therefore have a situation with two complementary aspects of power, namely *competence* and *freedom of action*, which will be present, whatever the type of power considered.

- *First-Degree Power*

As noted earlier, power is always that of an agent. What characterizes first-degree power is that it refers to the agent's capacity to act according to his or her own nature. His power is thus merely the expression of his own activity.

For example, consider the following statement: "The community must regain its full *power* of development." In other words, it is a matter of ensuring that the community becomes fully empowered to develop according to its own identity. It may be that certain external conditions do not allow the community in question to develop its full potential: it then does not have total *freedom of action*. It is also possible that conditions in the surrounding environment are favorable, but the community does not have the expertise required to carry out this development: it does not have the *competence* to do so. Because of systemic socio-economic effects, for example, a community may be losing all its savings and thus be unable to make those investments its normal development would call for. This, of course, impedes its *freedom of action* and, in the medium term, affects its competence, as it leads to an outflow of human resources and a deterioration of the social fabric. The sudden availability of savings may not immediately resolve the issue, as one can expect that the population will no longer know how to transform savings into productive investment. Now what is at issue is *competence*, the latter having been degraded over time.

This infernal cycle provides a rough sketch of the process of *underdevelopment*: an obstacle to freedom of action leads to a blockage of normal development, which in turn results in a deterioration of competence that reinforces the initial incapacity, etc. We shall return to this in the section devoted to the analysis of present-day society.[101]

Another example. Consider the case of a person who wants to carry out a personal project. Here again, concerning this project, we have the four possible cases of a double-entry table: the person is competent or not, in an environment that is favorable or not. Here again, we are talking about the person's capacity for action concerning his or her own project.

Let's use another example, that of a group of about fifteen people who do not know each other and who find themselves in a particular situation for which they may have to take responsibility. The first stage will consist of making individuals express themselves about their own characteristics stemming from personal experiences acquired outside the group. These characteristics and skills are not initially coordinated, articulated, integrated with each other. At this very precise level, the competence of each is reduced to expressing as best as possible what he or she is and can do, while the freedom of action consists, for each one, of being granted time and space for doing

---

101. See section **Today's Society from the Perspective of the Present Paradigm**.

it. Within the framework of the temporal diagram presented in chapter 3, we could say that this first-degree power is typical of stage 1 of a given cycle. Compared to the cycle considered, it is, at stage 1, the emergence of various agents in a space where what had been at stake, until then, was not coordinating their activities, but rather each doing their own individual activity.

We could also take examples at extreme time scales. In the history of humankind, we can see that in the Paleolithic Period, humans lived in tribes made up of a few families. In an example of this order of magnitude, each tribe is an *agent*.[102] These tribes were nomadic. Of course, they occasionally bartered with other tribes and even exchanged women. But what mattered the most was the survival of the tribe, which they ensured by their skills as hunter-gatherers in sometimes welcoming, sometimes hostile environments.

As for the Neolithic Period, it required, with the appearance of sedentary life and large agglomerations, the emergence and exercise of another type of power. The complex organization of work no longer allowed a clan to simply leave and settle a little further away in case of conflict. Interdependence imposed new constraints and required the emergence of a second-degree power. The Paleolithic Period has the characteristics of stage 1 and the Neolithic Period has those of stage 2, as we will further explain in the following section.

- *Second-Degree Power*

Second-degree power is the first level of meta-power. It is the power this time relating to the power of others, more precisely to the coordination of the various first-degree powers that are exercised in a given environment. At the first stage in which these first-degree powers are used, the various agents differentiate themselves within a physical and human environment marked by diversity and they do not spontaneously

---

[102]. Note that this concept is relative to the order of magnitude under consideration. The tribe is an agent in the context of the so-called Paleolithic period of humanity. But if we consider the tribe in itself, therefore as a totality, we can find within it the three degrees of power: that of individuals and families, then that of the chief who guides the tribe for its survival operations and finally that of the sage, which can then take various forms.

have the competence to coordinate themselves so as to form an integrated whole. Insofar as these various powers are in obliged interaction, a new differentiation must then be made, introducing an *agent of second degree* capable of provoking the coordination and harmonization of these powers, capable of creating a synergy between them and making them tend towards an integrated whole.

One could speak in a general way of the power of "the chief," "the person in charge," "the leader," he who is linked to the function of orientation, direction, and command. To simplify, let us refer to "leadership". All these expressions are not perfect synonyms, but they refer globally to the same function of orientation and articulation of first-degree powers. To return to our example of the Neolithic Period, man realizes that he can and must become the object of his intervention. He must exercise this function of articulating the various existing powers. The exercise of this function is concomitant with the reversal of his position with respect to nature: he has appropriated it and now sees himself as being at the center of nature. The notion of *leadership* takes on a new meaning. It is no longer merely a matter of guiding humans in their direct relationship with nature, but instead of guiding them in the relationships they have with each other in order to achieve better control of nature. It is the responsible assumption by humans of their capacity to act, typical of stage 2 of a development cycle, whatever the level of human reality considered.

A peculiarity of this power is that the leader's intervention must encompass all the elements that are part of the initial situation calling for such an intervention. In the case of a village, for example, the leader must assume responsibility for the entire village and not just a few people.

As for first-degree power, second-degree power is also analyzed according to the two parameters of *competence* and *freedom of action*. The leader's competence is first linked to his ability to mobilize others. More precisely, he must create a climate of *trust* that will allow others to show *openness* and will ultimately provoke an *engagement* or commitment to the proposed path. For each individual first-degree power, trust will also be linked to the perception of the leader's competence vis-à-vis the other powers, i.e., his ability to provoke commitment not only in himself but in others as well. At this point, one could say that a leader is all the more competent if he succeeds in provoking a commitment fostering consensus. His *freedom of action* is then linked to the degree of acceptance his leadership manages to obtain on the part of those to whom it is addressed.

Obstacles to freedom of action may arise at the outset of the process: for example, a highly competent leader may not be perceived and accepted as such and this may not depend on him or her, but on the first-level actors to whom his or her leadership is directed. Two examples will help to illustrate this case.

The first is metaphorical and is taken from an Indian folk tale. A disciple is looking for the spiritual master who will be THE one who can guide him to ultimate fulfillment. He meets a first master whom he leaves after some time. He travels all over India and goes from master to master for ten years. Finally, he meets the one whom he finally recognizes as *his* master. The latter tells him: "I've been waiting for you for ten years; I'm the first master you met ten years ago when you started your quest." The master was just as competent then as now, but the disciple's perception represented an obstacle to the master's freedom of action.

The second example, closer to what we are arguing, is a political party selecting a leader from two aspirants in a leadership race. The winner, once in function, does not demonstrate the competence that was initially attributed to him or her and is replaced by the other candidate whose competence is finally appreciated. The latter initially possessed this same competence but had no freedom of action to exercise it, given that his candidacy had been refused. History is full of people whose genius was not recognized until a few years or even centuries after their death.

When leadership is exercised competently, it allows the first-degree powers to develop a structure of operation that manifests itself in an organization whose characteristic is to tend to become autonomous, like all living organizations. However, the second-degree power that provoked and accompanied this development becomes all the more cumbersome as, having been competent in the first instance, it seeks to maintain this same form of competence.

Indeed, it is known that leaders – second-degree powers – have a propensity to consider themselves competent and to attribute their setbacks to first-degree agents who hinder their freedom of action. Hence their big temptation to justify the authoritarian imposition of orientations and commands. It is at this end of the continuum that one thus finds various types of totalitarianism. If one locks oneself within the paradigm of second-degree power, one can but dream of the perfectly competent leader who would be justified in authoritatively imposing himself. One finds here the idea of the enlightened despot. However, if we refer to the paradigm of self-reference, everything that tends towards totalitarianism is the result of total incompetence. As we have already pointed out, this is what most radically impedes the blossoming of totality.

At the other end of the continuum, but still within the paradigm of second-degree power, there are formulas in which the constitution of binding power is the result of an agreement, as in western democracies. But in order to limit the perverse effects of the incompetence of these necessarily binding powers, they are subjected to periodic elections, which makes them somewhat precarious and provisional, thus artificially simulating the essential characteristic of competent power, namely, that its action contains within itself the conditions for its own disappearance.

Let us digress for a moment to draw an analogy between this social phenomenon and an interpretation of the biological phenomenon of phenocopy, freely inspired by the Piagetian conception.[103] In phenocopy, we find a modification of a phenotype under the pressure of environmental forces. It is, therefore, a change imposed in some way from the outside and to which the living being accommodates to ensure its adaptation. Such adaptation is fragile and unstable. However, it turns out that genetic mutations are subsequently observed, such that it is now the genes that produce a phenotype similar to the first one, without this time resulting from the constraints of the environment. The living organism subject to such mutations can then adapt quite naturally and stably to the environment. It can

---

103. Jean Piaget, *Adaptation vitale et psychologie de l'intelligence. Sélection organique et phénocopie*, Paris, Herman, 1974.

be said that this genetically based phenotype is a "copy" of the first, which is a direct result of the constraints of the environment, just as it can be said, conversely, that the first is a draft, or if you like, a copy in anticipation of the one that the genetics will produce, a bit like the evocation of an attractor towards which the organism placed in such situations tends.

If we apply the analogy to the social situation described above, we would be at the first stage of social phenocopy: the simulation of a real mutation is contained in the current democratic functioning, but this model is precarious and unstable and remains confined to the limits of the paradigm of second-degree power. A society based on this model is still fundamentally conflictual and violent and embodies a leadership reflecting this. Thus, Max Weber's statement that the state has a "monopoly on legitimate violence" still holds today. But this form of democracy is the harbinger – a sort of prerequisite *bricolage* – of the real social change that will occur when third-level power becomes the center of social functioning.

Let us further explore the conflictual dimension of this second-degree power. The legitimacy of this power lies in the degree of consensus it achieves. And since full consensus is impossible, such power will be acquired and exercised according to majority votes. The leadership agency is elected under a platform that is not unanimous and is opposed to other political platforms. It cannot, therefore, claim to be a full reflection of the conflicting mandates of the first-degree agents. Consequently, however democratic the form taken by such a second-degree agent, the latter develops an autonomous power that is the locus of an artificially constructed synthesis of the forces at work. Thus, rather than being the consensual expression of their integration, this second-degree power joins up with other first-degree powers and adds to the chaos of diversity, while having the function of maintaining this chaos at an acceptable level. Therefore, such a power must use force to achieve this.

As for the first-degree powers, they must give up some of their power in favor of a leadership authority expected to achieve an obviously impossible integration. They also expect benefits and services compensating for the part of the power they have given up by delegating it to that authority.

This deepens the opposition between agents. This time this opposition is related to the position of the agents in relation to the leadership agency, with some seeing themselves more in a *high position*, i.e., upstream, and delegating a greater part of their power to this agency without deriving equivalent benefits, and others, placed downstream, defining themselves more as beneficiaries of these services and who consider that the *low position* they occupy at the outset is not adequately compensated by the benefits they receive. In other words, some feel that they are sacrificing themselves for others, and the latter feel betrayed at the outset by the rules of the game. Such a mindset regarding electoral strategies is well expressed in this quip by Jules Michelet, which has become a popular saying: "Politics is the art of obtaining money from the rich and votes from the poor, under the pretext of protecting them from each other. »

Second-degree powers, finding themselves confronted with the challenge of squaring the circle and the impossibility of satisfying every single one of their constituents, will tend to develop, in typical Sartrian bad faith, to the benefit of those exercising such powers and their supporters, always in the name of the common good, of course! In short, second-degree powers, locked in their vicious circle, are in perfect resonance with Lord Acton's famous statement: "Power tends to corrupt, and absolute power corrupts absolutely."[104]

Throughout the process, therefore, the leaders, whatever their competence, are confronted with more or less important obstacles to their freedom of action. But it also seems that the effort to maintain their competence indefinitely in its initial form transforms it into an obstacle. Indeed, their ultimate competence would be to foster the creation of conditions enabling them, for each operation they undertake, to surrender their power to those over whom they exercise it, without creating chaos or a power vacuum. More precisely, the initial exercise of power must in itself contain the conditions for its own disappearance in favor of the complementary leadership of the agents over whom it is exercised, insofar as these agents perpetuate the logic of the initial agent, that is, to favor the emergence of the totality in a

---

104. John E. Acton, *Historical Essays and Studies*, London, N. Figgis and R.V. Laurence, 1907.

state of greater coherence. This type of reversal is generally unlikely and leads us to the need to involve a new kind of power, third-degree power.

- ### Third-Degree Power

Third-degree power is the second level of meta-power. It is the power of the *paradoxical agent* that deals with the exercise of second-degree power. Such power is fundamentally different from second-degree power because it cannot be imposed by coercion. It is, in fact, a contentless facilitator and cannot exist without the presence of second-degree power. It is thus dependent on it for its existence. Yet it is, paradoxically, the most autonomous of all powers, since, for a given operation of second-degree power, it can adopt the two complementary positions, that of agent and that of receptive. This is the essence of its competence. It is thus not reducible to either of these two positions while having its own meaning relative to this dichotomy. For a given operation, it is the only power on which the second-degree interaction can rely to allow a hierarchical reversal to take place, one in which the activity of the receptive integrates that initiated by the agent. In other words, it is the only power allowing the self-referential cycle to come to fruition. Its freedom of action can nevertheless be thwarted by a voluntarist and authoritarian second-degree power.

The main problem confronting this power – the paradoxical agent – is thus its difficulty in becoming autonomous relative to the other powers. If this power does not manage to develop an intervention originating from an original position relative to the other actors involved, it cannot play its role of mediation and will never be able to provoke a *hierarchical reversal*. In other words, its competence is directly linked to its degree of autonomy in the totality constituting the unity within which it operates.

A possible consequence of such a situation is that the paradoxical agent sides with the "Prince." This would be Machiavelli's sphere of operation. It then no longer exercises the paradoxical agent function proper to third-degree power as defined here. In short, it is only an extension of second-degree power. On the other hand, the paradoxical agent can side with the *receptive*, its lack of autonomy rendering it impotent to operate an efficient action on the current interaction. It must then limit itself to making demands, its power being only the extension of the first-degree powers composing the receptive agency.

Furthermore, a competent third-degree power, as already pointed out, may not enjoy the freedom of action it would need because a second-degree power is too rigid and wants to monopolize all power. This is what one finds, for example, in dictatorships.

The real paradoxical agent would be, in short, the Machiavelli of the *totality*, the one which, in terms of interaction, would operate in such a way as to achieve the self-referential cycle as often as possible, first within the boundaries of its own operation, and then within the unity of which it is a component. This implies at the outset the presence of a second-degree power that shows a minimum of flexibility and openness, as is the case in most western democracies.

In the proposed temporal framework, the focus on the power of the paradoxical agent is typical of the passage from stage 2 to stage 3, where the identity of the unity considered is solicited. It is the stage where the second-degree power can let go, allowing the initially receptive agent to close, as paradoxical agent, the self-referential cycle. The paradoxical agent is thus the best representative of the totality at the level of the interaction of the parts.

Educational Dimension of Human Existence

The individual human being alone cannot reinvent all the expertise developed over time by the community and previous generations. He or she must thus be the object of an intervention that we shall describe here as educational. The same is true of groups and communities. We, therefore, have, on the one hand, a learning agency L and, on the other hand, an educating agency E. Limiting ourselves to the primitive data of the model, we will try to see what kind of relationship between the learning agency and the educating agency would meet the requirements of the self-referential matrix.

We saw in chapter 3 that the self-referential process unfolds in three stages, a *paradoxical* stage occurring between the second and third stages. To acquire a minimum mastery of a desired skill, the learning agency will thus have to go through these stages. For its part, the educating agency will also be involved in this sequence of stages, but the two sequences will be out of step with each other. While learning agency L will be in stage 1, educating agency E will be in stage 2, as shown in the following figure:

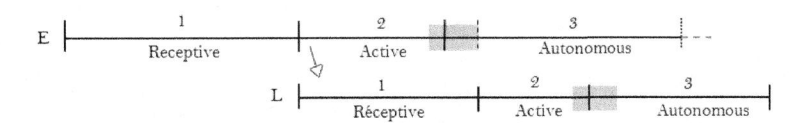

```
E |----1----|----2---▮--|----3----|---
      Receptive    Active      Autonomous
            ↓
         L |----1----|----2---▮--|----3----|
              Réceptive    Active      Autonomous
```

Figure 16. Superposition of the processes of the educating agency (E) and the learning agency (L) with staggered stages. The gray zone corresponds to the paradoxical stage. The arrow represents a structuring intervention of E on L.

In stage 2, the educator is in intervention mode and exercises second-level authority over the learner in stage 1. The educator provides the context and tools allowing the learner to *engage* in the process and eventually develop *competence*. The intervention is of a structuring nature concerning the objective sought. So, one might object that proceeding in this manner is alienating for the learner. We will see where the line is drawn between what is alienating and what is not. For the time being, however, let us simply note that depriving the learner of useful educational tools is also a form of alienation, this time by abstention.

The structuring intervention is alienating when it keeps the learner dependent on it, and adequate when it contains within itself the conditions for its own disappearance. It is at this breaking point that the paradoxical aspect of the stage comes into play. Indeed, at the end of stage 2 of the educating agency E, the latter places itself in receptive mode with respect to the initiatives taken by the learning agency L, thus supporting its sense of *empowerment for action*. Should the need arise, however, it returns to active mode to fill any remaining gaps. At the end of this transition, the learning agency L moves to the active stage and takes the *initiative* in its own learning process and develops its *competence*. From this point on, the educating agency E moves into an accompanying mode, placing itself in support of the process for which the learning agency has kept the initiative. At the end of stage 2 of the learning agency, its action has generated a product whose coherence is such that it can now let go of the action to show the autonomy of the process. Competence is then acquired. As Lao Tseu puts it when referring to this educational process:

> *Wise leaders are discreet and speak sparingly. When their task is completed, and things have been done, people say, "We did it ourselves."*[105]

We see here that the educating agent's respect for the learning agency does not consist of not acting, but rather of acting adequately, which leads the learning agency to feel that he or she "has done it by himself or herself." In short, the educating activity goes from a structuring intervention characteristic of stage 2 to an accompanying intervention characteristic of stage 3, with a paradoxical stage in between, where the agent oscillates between structuring and support, to finally move on to an interaction of reciprocity. We see here that the educational process consists essentially in methodically moving from a second-level power to a third-level power that leads to self-referential functioning. The generalization of such processes aims at transforming society into a "self-educating society" characterized by endogenous development.

Reference Actors at the Societal Level

In accordance with the announced strategy, we will initially consider the state level as the totality constituting the unit of reference. We will see what internal transformations could lead this unity to evolve from egocentrism to self-referential functioning. To do so, we will have to identify the sub-units corresponding to the basic elements of the model and also explain the correspondence of their articulation.

There is confusion about the identity of the sub-units that are part of the state. The first chapter referred to the identity of actors at the societal level by referring to three sectors: the

---

105. Lao-Tseu XVII. Élisabeth Andrès, Kyu-Yong Byun. *Les cent fleurs du Tao. La quête de l'immortalité.* Paris, Éditions Jacqueline Renard, 1991.

public sector, the private sector, and the social sector.[106] We will have to adjust the notion of *sector* to the present model and show that this choice avoids the confusion caused by other classifications. For example, N. Perlas (2003)[107] speaks of three global conflicting institutional powers: Civil Society, Governments (or states), and the Market (economic agencies). These three powers would correspond respectively to the three areas of social life: cultural, political, and economics. We would thus have three interacting units controlling a specific field, and that must in no way encroach on each other's terrain. This vision leads to unsolvable, and in Perlas' own words, pressing questions:

> *"What is the true nature of a CSO [civil society organization]? Is it a political organization? Is it cultural? Or both? Can economic institutions such as corporations be part of civil society? Aren't some people in government also 'civilians'? If CSOs are primarily cultural, how can they make a foray into the realm of the state and advocate for their causes? If they are only cultural institutions, don't they lose all power? (Ibid. p. 138)*

We must, therefore, revamp the meaning of these terms and articulate them in a radically different way. This leads us to redefine the notion of *sector*.

The Notion of Sector: A First Approximation

To remain within the logic of the model we are setting forth, we must consider that the central character of the drama is the totality constituted, in the example under consideration, by the democratic state in our Western societies. This totality could be represented by a large circle (Figure 17).

---

106. The term "social" could be advantageously replaced by "community" if the latter term did not initially have so many different meanings that could create confusion here. This is the case with the public sector, which should rather be called civic, because many things are public without being part of the public sector. We will keep here the term public as it is commonly used.
107. Nicanor Perlas, *La société civile : 3ᵉ pouvoir. Changer la face de la mondialisation*, Barret-sur-Méouge, Éditions Yves Michel, 2003.

State

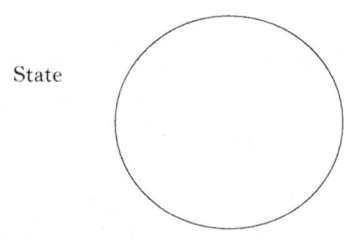

Figure 17. Circle representing the state as a totality.

The sectors will, therefore, result from a differentiation of this totality. We will now attempt to identify the ingredients of these sectors. We will first look at the composition of a sector, in other words, *what it is made up of, its specific logic, its key institution* and *its relationship to the totality.*

- *Composition of a Sector*

By indicating *what a sector is made of,* we will end up with the classic diagram of three intersecting circles forming a space of intersection in the center, as shown in figure 18 below. The public sector is made up of state enterprises and organizations and all sub-agencies of governance depending on them, such as regional and municipal governments. The private sector is made up of enterprises owned by private individuals or groups. The social sector is made up of organizations or enterprises owned by their members. The intersection of the three sectors serves as their interface. For example, a concertation table uniting representative of the public, private, and social sectors.

State-owned organizations — Public, Private, Social — Organizations belonging to private groups

Organizations belonging to their members

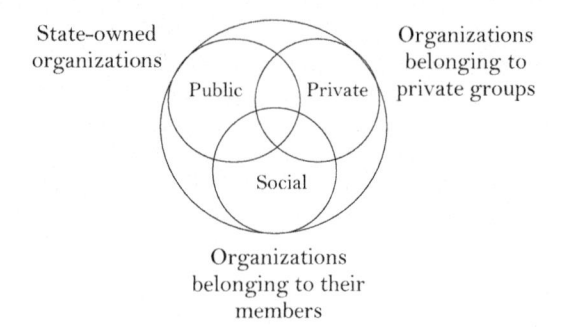

Figure 18. Circles representing the composition of sectors.

226

- *Specific Logic of Each Sector*

Each sector has *its own specific logic*. The logic of the public sector is that of collective power, previously described as second-degree power, which is basically coercive and responsible for the common good and social order. Graphically, we can represent this logic with oblique lines covering the circle of the public sector. On the other hand, the logic of the private sector is one of profit, based on competition between actors in the production and exchange of goods and services for the members of the community. This logic can be represented graphically by oblique inverted lines perpendicular to those of the public sector covering the private sector circle. Finally, the logic of the social sector is that of solidarity, cooperation, association, and mutual aid. This logic will be represented by horizontal lines covering the social sector circle (Figure 19).

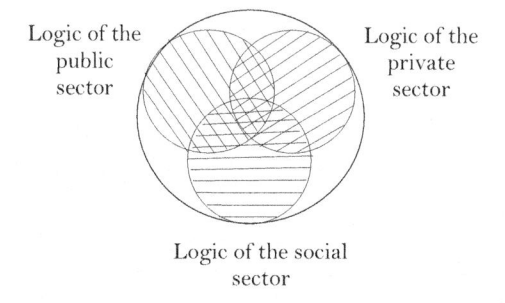

Figure 19. Oriented lines representing the logics of the three sectors.

- *Key Institution in a Sector*

A sector is represented by a *key institution*. The public sector is represented by the state, whose differentiated agent is the Government. The private sector is represented by the Market whose workings include various organizations, stock exchanges, financial institutions, enterprises, all operating in the same integrated system. As for the social sector, it does not yet have a key institution to represent it. There are, of course, ever more organizations based on the logic of cooperation and which are fostering, to varying degrees, inclusiveness and unity. However, these organizations are adding to what exists and increasing diversity rather than achieving integration. We will come back to that.

- *Coextensiveness of the Logic of a Sector to the Totality*

The *relationship of a sector to the totality* represents a crucial point. One of the characteristics of a sector is that its own logic applies, at least potentially, to the totality of the unit under consideration, in this case, the whole society corresponding to that state. We will then say that the logic of a sector is coextensive, or potentially coextensive, with the totality of the unit under consideration.

Thus, the logic of the public sector is coextensive with society as a whole. And, unlike other sectors, it is by its very nature coextensive. So, our classic three-circle diagram is completed: for example, since the public sector logic is represented by oblique lines, it is now the entire circle representing society that is crossed by oblique lines. It is all actors in society, for example, who have to pay taxes, obey laws, etc., and not only public sector actors.

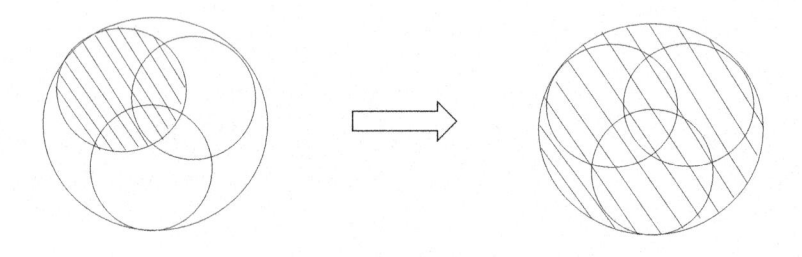

Figure 20. Coextensiveness of the public sector logic to the totality. The oblique lines representing the logic of the public sector extend throughout the society.

As for the private sector, its logic is not by its very nature coextensive with society as a whole, but it has become so. There are no longer small, self-sufficient islands in our societies that are completely disconnected from the economic system in place. If the logic of the private sector is represented by oblique inverted lines perpendicular to those of the public sector, the whole circle representing society now becomes crossed by oblique inverted lines. Even the government is subject to this logic: if it borrows on the market, for example, it has to pay interest and must pay back its debt. The government is one actor among others within this logic. The logic of the private sector is thus also coextensive with society as a whole.

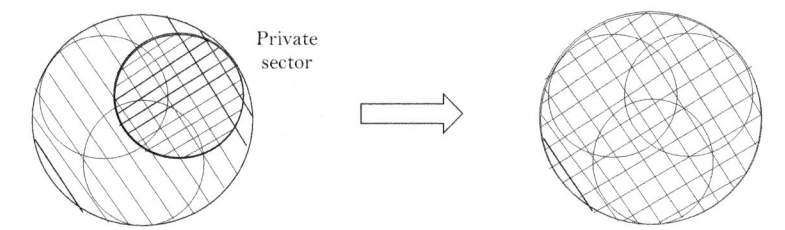

Figure 21. Coextensiveness of private sector logic to the totality. The oblique inverted lines representing the logic of the private sector cover the whole society.

As far as the social sector is concerned, we have seen that it does not yet have a key, representative institution allowing its own logic to extend to society as a whole. The logic of the social sector, represented by horizontal lines, is thus not coextensive with the whole of society. Horizontal lines are therefore limited to the initial circle representing social sector organizations. If one stays in this mindset, the "social sector" would not meet the criteria allowing it to be an authentic sector because it lacks two essential ingredients: no key institution and thus no coextensiveness with society as a whole. It would, therefore, be a misnomer to speak of the social sector if we did not foresee the possibility that it might one day acquire these characteristics. This will be the main point to be developed in this chapter.

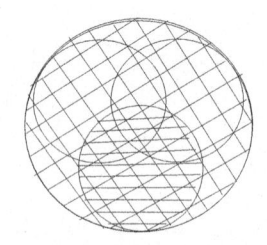

Figure 22. The logic of the social sector is presently limited to organisations of the social "sector" and is not coextensive to the hole society.

In light of this conception, wondering about the sector to which belongs a specific unity becomes meaningless. All elements making up society are members of each sector, but they are members from a particular perspective. For example, all groups and individuals in society are part of the public sector when viewed in terms of the public sector logic. They are so as *interveners* when they act, as is the case with civil servants, for example, on behalf of the reference intervener, the Government. Or they are part of the public sector in *receptive* mode when they receive services or respond to directives issued by the reference intervener. It is then that individuals are referred to as *citizens*. The foreign individual is not a citizen because he or she has not been integrated as such by the key public sector institution. The *citizen* is the individual who is basically a member of the public sector: it is the individual who has a legal link to the state. Thus, to speak of *civil society* as the third force that distinguishes itself from the state and the market is, in fact, confusing: civil society, in its literal meaning, is one imbued by the public sector logic as conveyed by the institution that is the state.[108]

Let us now turn to the private sector. All groups and individuals in society are part of the private sector. They are

---

108. This confusion in the use of the term *civil society* does not have serious consequences, since it in fact represents society when it is in a receptive position with regard to government interventions; civil society then distinguishes itself from the state through the initiatives it takes. Nevertheless, it may be preferable to stick to the precise meaning of words; thus, the expression civil society will not be used in this chapter in its current meaning of a distinct third force.

integrated in it as *interveners* if they act as producers or suppliers of goods and services within the logic of the market, or they are integrated in it as *receptive* if they follow this logic. It is then that individuals become *consumer clients*.

Finally, when the social sector manages to meet all the criteria corresponding to an authentic sector, then all groups and individuals will potentially be part of the social sector. If they are part of this sector as *interveners*, they will promote the logic of cooperation by providing support to groups and individuals who will now seek to develop as *communities* and as *persons*. That is what will happen when the social sector has acquired autonomy and coherence through the functioning of a unifying institution based on solidarity and cooperation.

In our previous graph, the horizontal lines would then cover the entire circle representing society, as shown in figure 23 below. We would thus have the image of a society imbued by three logics that would meet at multiple points of intersection in a space that would no longer be limited to the center of the three initial circles but would cover the entire circle encompassing society as a whole.

It would not occur to anyone to wonder whether a person is a citizen, a consumer, or a person. However, each point of intersection must be able to convey all three logics, and not just the first two, as is currently the case in our societies. This aspect will become ever clearer and explicit from now till the end of the chapter. On the other hand, it is impossible for the institution representing one sector to become the reference institution for another sector, since no one of these logics can be reduced to either of its two complementary logics.

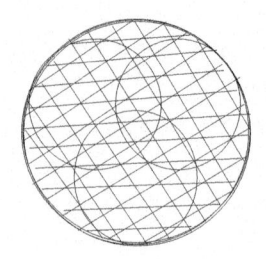

Figure 23. Coextensiveness of the logic of the public, private and social sectors to the whole of society represented by the oblique, oblique inverted and horizontal lines.

Today's Society from the Perspective of the Present Paradigm

We have already given an overview of how today's society works when viewed through the prism of the paradigm we are proposing. According to our model, power in our western democracies is assigned a conventional precariousness that artificially simulates an essential characteristic of competent power, namely, that its action contains within itself the conditions for its own demise.

This simulation has an unfortunate sequel in a similar simulation, that of *hierarchical reversal*. Initially, the framework provided by public authorities allowed the private sector to develop and maintain a very elaborate system of production and exchange as we can observe in our modern societies. The new power acquired by the private sector naturally leads it to want to integrate in return the initial action of the public authorities. Unfortunately, this integration does not prolong political action in its structuring effect on society but rather abolishes it in favor of the logic of the private sector, with all the ensuing contradictions, as Beck clearly illustrated.[109] In other words, in the absence of a third-degree power, the simulation of the self-referential process becomes a self-destructive process because it ignores the totality in favor of dominant egocentric powers. Let us examine the phenomenon in more detail.

---

109. See Ulrich Beck (2003), p. 168.

Political Dimension

Politics is about the exercise of power. We have previously identified three degrees of power. We can say that first-degree power is initially pre-political, so to speak, because the private powers involved are not coordinated among themselves.

We really enter politics when a second-degree power is exercised over first-degree powers, thus fostering the coordination of their interactions. In our societies, this is the power of the state, which is exercised for the common good; it does so by enacting laws and punishing behavior that does not comply with them. In short, the state exercises the control that allows it to provide services for the common good.

Historically, as a result of such intervention by this second-degree power, first-degree powers have developed, in a context of competition, complex and articulated exchange structures to the point of going beyond the framework of the second-degree political structures. Thus, first-degree private powers have developed ever more organizational strength and are now knocking on the doors of public authorities in an effort to assimilate them to their own logic, as illustrated by the development of current neoliberal globalization. Private sector power has thus taken over some of the second-degree power.

One might wonder, when examining the strategies of capital in today's global economy, wherein lies the origin of their ever-greater political power. Beck asserts:

> *It is through a radical reversal of the logic characteristic of classical theory of power and domination that transnational corporations are allowed to maximize their power: constraint does not come from troops of investors threatening to enter a country, but rather from these same troops threatening not to enter it or even to pull out of it.*[110]

The threat of *not doing something* replaces the threat of ordering that something be done. Choosing to invest here, not there, gives players in the global economy considerable power, and an extremely flexible one at that! The state, on the other hand, is weak given that the violence it wields is inflexible: it is

---

110. Ulrich Beck, *La société du risque. Sur la voie d'une autre modernité*, Paris, Flammarion, 2001, p. 119.

tied to a specific territory. The only thing it has at its disposal is the imposition of sanctions whose author would then be easy to identify. Not investing, on the other hand, is not attributable to anyone in particular. It is not doing something wrong, so finding a culprit is impossible.

"States compete with fellow states, each of them literally powerless before the danger of seeing the golden eggs of financial speculation hatch in a country other than its own," asserts Serge Halimi of Le Monde diplomatique. The champions of neoliberal globalization are defining the new world narrative, argues Petrella (2007). This insidious and totally illegitimate domination permeates through its mindset every single fiber of social life.

Remarkably, all this is done outside of any democratic legitimacy, in a transnational space, and by "translegal" means. In this new space, the seductive power of neoliberalism lies in the promise to reward openness to the world with wealth and to curb national egoisms, thus establishing "a principle of transnational order for the global era." However, a policy that aligns itself with the demands of the global market "ultimately accomplishes nothing but its own liquidation. One can, therefore, speak of the trap of the neoliberal conception of politics."[111] Yet it is acknowledged that no form of economy can exist without a minimum of government standardization and regulation: without taxes, there would be no infrastructure, no education or health systems, no legitimacy, no security... Yet states have allowed themselves to be gradually stripped of their power, for example, the regalian power to issue money, leaving this privilege to the banks.

Furthermore, by deregulating the market and refusing the tax on financial transactions proposed by the economist James Tobin[112], the states have put themselves at the mercy of the financial powers. We may wonder how it came to be that these powers have managed to acquire such a level of power. Let us look at the economic dimension.

---

111. Ulrich Beck, *Pouvoir et contre-pouvoir à l'heure de la mondialisation*. Paris, Flammarion, 2003.
112. Tobin tax, Wikipedia. Retrieved July 6, 2020.

Economic Dimension: The Creation of Underdevelopment

In this chapter, we have discussed the current dominance of the private sector in the transnational space and within the state. We will now further explore the dynamics of the private sector that create inequalities in the current system. We will not attempt to identify all the factors underlying the problem of underdevelopment but will rather present a general framework that will make it possible to better situate the solution proposed to this problem in this book.

- *A Structure of Nested Third-Worlds*

We will try to identify more closely the fundamental impoverishment mechanism present in the current economic system and which is undermining most self-development efforts. Let us state a general principle that could take various forms in various disciplines: "There is no development without investment, and there is no investment without savings." This elementary principle applies to all living organisms: indeed, all development involves an investment of energy, which obviously implies a reserve of available energy.

In the current economy, however, savings generated by local economies are not fully used for local investment due to a lack of sufficient guarantees. The result is a flight of savings that is not compensated by equivalent investments from outside. Let us be more precise. Let us imagine that the gross domestic product (GDP) of a country is 100 and that the economic activity of this country produces savings of 10.[113] Let us also assume that half of these savings find sufficient guarantees in the country itself to be reinvested there, but that the other half is expatriated, no equivalent amount of foreign investment moving back into this same country. (Such a phenomenon can easily be observed by analyzing the financial statements of banking organizations, whether or not these function as cooperatives or as strictly private institutions. All available funds that are not used locally are redirected to the head offices located in large urban centers and then invested for profit.) We then have a negative multiplier

---

113. The relative order of magnitude of the figures presented here is not important in itself, as the objective is only to illustrate the structure of the mechanism.

effect in the community leading to its progressive impoverishment: loss of jobs, more difficult access to resources, withdrawal of services, etc. In such a system, ever more people are excluded from the economic circuit, leading to the gradual weakening of the local economy.

The local impoverishment mechanism just described can be seen at various other levels: that of regions and major metropolitan centers. It is for this reason that we are witnessing a progressive impoverishment of local economies to the benefit of larger regional centers and of regional economies to the benefit of large metropolitan centers. And eventually of the latter metropolitan centers themselves to the benefit of a world economy which, benefiting from capital not invested in the productive economy, is developing a purely speculative type of economy. (It should be noted in passing that this same dynamic can be found at a microscopic level within a major metropolitan center if we consider the way in which rich neighborhoods develop in relation to poor neighborhoods, but also at the macroscopic level of world development: entire countries are in the process of being underdeveloped through the chronic hemorrhaging of their resources at the indecent benefit of developed countries).

Thus, all the economies of the world end up feeding this speculative economy where billions of dollars a day are exchanged, the bulk of the latter outside the real economies of production of goods and services. The laws of elementary arithmetic being implacable, we obtain the previously mentioned observation of a concomitant increase in the number of multi-billionaires and the number of extremely poor. As Bernard Estérez puts it, "this mechanism acts as a tourniquet, the pathological development of speculative circuits suffocating the productive economy and causing unemployment and underemployment. Though the productive economy does in fact experience some development, the latter is infinitely slower and more unequal than it could be, an abnormally high proportion of savings going into speculative circuits which, for their part, expand at a greater speed than they should, and this at the expense of the productive economy. Normally, there should be equality between the growth rates of the two circuits."[114]

- *Some Side Effects*

The flight of savings from level to level has three perverse cascading effects. The first concerns commercial leakage. People will buy things outside their local community where there are better services and better prices. Indeed, the absence of local reinvestment of savings leads to the development of more efficient infrastructure in regional centers and even more so in metropolitan centers. Commercial leakage follows the same circuit as savings, which constitutes an additional deadweight loss for the economies concerned.

To stem this outflow, businesses will try to at least maintain, if not expand, their access to the market by purchasing customer loyalty services. Yet a very large number of them buy these services outside their community. One of the best-known examples is the Air Miles card. It is worth insisting on this point. In an article in the August 20, 2002 edition of the newspaper Le Monde, we learn that the global stock of *airmiles* held corresponds in dollars to a number ranging from 172 billion to 765 billion depending on whether the *airmiles* are used for scheduled flights or for the most expensive flights. "This is more than the total number of euro banknotes in circulation, which makes airmiles, so to speak, the world's second currency after the dollar, even if it does not have all the attributes of a monetary currency and, in particular, does not circulate." According to calculations by The Economist, as early as 2005, "the total stock of points earned in airline frequent flyer programs and not yet redeemed is now worth more than all the US dollars in circulation around the world."[115]

This is a customer loyalty service that not only generates considerable value but is also growing at a staggering rate. Of course, corporations controlling such systems are prosperous, to say the least, but there is no economic benefit to the community. On the contrary, this kind of effort to stem commercial leakage

---

114. Personal communication.
115. Quoted by *Courrier international*, January 19, 2005.

is itself the cause of additional leakage, which is a second perverse effect of the flight of savings.

The third perverse effect has already been mentioned: the local community is weakening to the point where its members are ever less able to meet the criteria for accessing capital, though such capital does indeed exist.

One single example of this: the availability of private funds in the current economic circuit. One can see that the link between such funds and the needs of the population is broken. Which is a somewhat paradoxical situation. As far as the managers are concerned, it would seem that there are simply not enough projects (in other words, projects meeting the criteria set for these funds); yet, as far as the project promoters are concerned, it would seem that there simply are no funds available for them. This "missing link" is an integral part of the economic dynamics described above. Public and social funds also manage savings that are not their own and thus the criteria set to access them have nothing to do with the reality of the projects.

Thus, in the context of an exogenous economy as described above, operations seeking to create the conditions for an endogenous economy risk being wiped out or perverted. This is the case of the Grameen Bank, which, though a remarkable experiment, ends up reproducing the aberrations of the mainstream economic system, on the one hand, helping many individuals to get out of this system, and, on the other hand, simultaneously leaving many others in a more pitiful state than before.[116]

The exodus of resources that we have just described affects social groups all the more as they are far from the centers of power. The way of life of the people thus dispossessed is

---

116. The following references may be consulted in this regard: Connie Bruck, Millions for Millions. *The New Yorker*, New York, October 30, 2006. Aminur Rahman, *Women and Microcredit in Rural Bangladesh: Anthropological Study of the Rethoric and Realities of Grameen Bank Lending*, Boulder, Westview Press, 1999. This paper uses Jennifer Pepall's report for the International Development Research Center (IDRC), available online, http ://www.idrc.ca/fr/ev-5066-201-1-DO_TOPIC.html Retrieved June 20, 2008. See also A. Cokburn (2006) and K.Lamia (2008). A similar criticism can be found in Ha-Joon Chang's book *2 ou 3 choses que l'on ne vous dit jamais sur le capitalisme*, Seuil, 2012. Also see Marc Roesch *in* Pauline Gandré Réseau Canopé | « Idées économiques et sociales » 2012/2 N° 168 | pages 22 - 31.

considerably altered. They gradually lose control of the means by which they formerly managed to maintain their existence and progress collectively. Salvation now seems to be outside. We are thus witnessing an exodus that follows the same movement as financial resources. At the world level, entire countries that are ongoingly underdeveloped by the processes mentioned above are seeing their populations engaged in gigantic migrations to countries where wealth is concentrated. And at the national level, people are abandoning rural areas and moving to cities. For example, in Quebec, "regions farther away from major centers almost all remained in deficit in their internal migratory exchanges in 2017–2018. The net losses were particularly pronounced on the Côte-Nord, which lost about 900 residents in favor of the other regions of Quebec, or nearly 1% of its population."[117] Negative migration balances were also observed in Bas-Saint-Laurent, Côte-Nord, Saguenay-Lac-Saint-Jean, Abitibi-Témiscamingue and Northern Quebec. These departures are not compensated by newcomers, while the northern suburbs of Montreal see a significant increase in their population.

Thus, just as with savings, local populations see the human resource wealth they have produced abandoning their regions, with the ensuing drop in the level of education and professional qualifications of their communities. Achieving grassroot local revitalization thus becomes ever harder. Local infrastructure tends to become poorer in favor of growth poles closer to the geographical center and closer to the centers of power. Social fabric weakens and disintegrates. One first closes the village post office, then the school, and finally, the village itself.[118] So, the process has essentially the same structure in social terms as in economic terms: one gradually loses the means to take control of one's destiny according to one's own identity.

Faced with such a widespread and worldwide trend, one can no longer hope to overcome the current crisis by simply introducing simple corrective measures in the functioning of the system.

---

117. Institut de la statistique du Québec. https://www.stat.gouv.qc.ca/salle-presse/communique/communique-presse-2019/fevrier/fev1920.html
118. For a more detailed analysis of this topic, see Bernard Vachon, *Le développement local, théorie et pratique*, Boucherville, Gaëtan Morin, 1993.

- *Access to the Market*

We have seen that the logic of the private sector is one of profit, based on members of society competing in the production and exchange of goods and services. We see that the market does not bring about the mythical regulation that try to believe those who benefit from it. We know that the market is not one of freedom and perfect competition. And we do not see how it could be otherwise. The logic of profit and competition ensures that the most powerful agents directly or indirectly control access to the market at all levels. Let's look at what happens in terms of production, distribution, and consumption.

On the production side, an agent trying to introduce a product that creates dissonance in the action plans of a major player, such as the oil companies, will not find an investor despite the performance of the product. And if an imprudent investor tries to do so, he is quickly brought back to "reason." This is the case with any dominant product on the market. The Bombardier aircraft manufacturer found out the hard way. Having built the most innovative and highest-performing aircraft in its class, it believed it could easily enter the market. In fact, Delta was interested in buying several of them. Not to mention Boeing's intervention, which derailed the process. Faced with the impossibility of entering the market, Bombardier abandoned its aircraft in favor of Airbus, which made it its A 220 model. This new market access opportunity for this aircraft allowed shareholders to keep their stake and Bombardier to get out of a precarious situation.

In terms of the distribution of goods and services, at all levels, the most efficient suppliers have the means to spend considerable sums of money to access the market, i.e., to make themselves known, to provide benefits of various kinds to customers. Those without such means have more difficulty in gaining market share, even though their offer may be equally attractive in many respects. Others simply do not manage to achieve market entry as new businesses, however worthwhile the projects they come up with, simply because they do not have access to the necessary capital.

Consumers, for their part, can only access the market if they can afford to. We know that an increasing number of people on the planet cannot afford to buy the foodstuffs essential to their survival. They are excluded from the market altogether. We can, of course, be pleased that the number of people living on less than $1.90 a day has fallen considerably and is now "only" 736 million, which is about 10% of the world population or eleven times the total population of France. But if we take a threshold of $5.50 a day, which is still in the category of extreme poverty, we end up with 3.4 billion people, in other words, almost half of the world's population, more than in the early 1980s.[119]

Market access is thus controlled at all levels. In such a system of hierarchical powers, no player can be its own first point of reference in its actions. It is always defined in relation to someone else, and if it moves up the hierarchy, this will always be to the detriment of someone else. As we will explain further below, such an economy must be qualified as *exogenous*, because each of its echelons will always be at the mercy of the higher echelons, which have greater control over all resources and also greater means to monopolize them. Thus, in such a system, one is forever waiting for the exterior intervention of the more powerful who will come to "develop us," should they so desire and on their terms, hence the power wielded by the threat of non-intervention described by Beck.

This being so, public authorities consider that it is their role to regulate such an economy to compensate for the social aberrations it produces. The function of the public sector would thus consist of redistributing the wealth produced by the private sector in such a way as to limit the damage. Damage control is about the maximum that the public sector can do in our societies, although it can do it less and less, because, as we have seen, the private sector is ever more encroaching on the power of public authorities, the latter being subjected to its logic. We see that this damage-control type of economy is not up to the task and that it constitutes an unstable equilibrium process.

---

119. The World Bank (2018a), *Poverty and Shared Prosperity 2018*. http://www.worldbank.org/en/publication/poverty-and-shared-prosperity. Retrieved June 25, 2020.

Towards a Self-Referent Society

In order to move towards an economy whose main dynamism emerges from within and which is controlled by the community, the social sector must acquire all the characteristics of an authentic sector, embedding itself in the heart of the private and public economy and creating an *operational closure* within which an *endogenous* economy can develop.

The boundary within which operations are carried out is, of course, not physical but consists of a set of rules that define what is internal to the system and what is external. What is external cannot follow internal rules, and conversely, what is internal must follow internal rules.

Such a social economy can only develop in conjunction with public and private economies while remaining autonomous in its operation and faithful to its own logic of cooperation, solidarity, and mutual aid. Though in fact compatible with the rules of the ambient economy, it adds new community rules, thus making the economy a properly human project and radically altering the self-destructive path of current economic development.

The same is true of the social dimension. Placed at the center of each micro-society, the social sector will be able to extend its logic to this entire unit and generate the internal resources to ensure the control and orientation of social and economic development. These units, formed in a network that is operationally closed but open to all, can spread throughout society within a given state. The network can then support the government in its social and sovereignty policies, thus rendering the state more autonomous relative to global neoliberal powers. Moreover, as we will illustrate below, we will see that this network of communities, not being strictly speaking "public," that is, institutionally integrated as an agent of the public sector, can spread beyond the borders of the state and continue to operate according to its own logic. Several states, supported in this way by such a network, will then be able to cooperate to promote in the transnational space this logic of endogenous development originating in the social sector.

Such networks of micro-societies will then develop a *culture of openness* to all and will encourage everyone to *commit* themselves to human development, starting with their own (stage 1). They will promote the culture of *savoir-faire* and inventiveness by transforming the logic of competition specific to the private sector into a logic of emulation which ensures that the success of one facilitates the success of the other rather than being to the detriment of the latter.[120] The *competences* thus developed in an endogenous context (stage 2) will be able to support the efforts developed by the public sector in the field of education and health. In addition, these networks will facilitate the original expression of each micro-society in its specific way of being and expressing itself. The social sector would then become the reference in the community's *expression of identity* and, thus, the guardian of its culture (stage 3).[121]

One then sees the importance of putting in place the missing piece – a strong and autonomous social sector – one capable of interacting with the public and private sectors in full compliance with the rules specific to these two sectors. The role of the social sector is not to replace the strengths of the public and private sectors, but to channel them and integrate them into a potentially self-referential process. Thus, setting up in the current social space *communities that are **in** development* does not suffice. In a circular process characteristic of operationally closed systems, the functioning of each community must also generate the tools of its own development to become a *community **of** development*, that is a *development community*, which obtains its coherence from its own operation and not from the effects coming from the environment. A *development community* is then characterized by endogenous development.

---

120. In his lectures and reflections on education, Albert Jacquard uses the term *emulation* in the sense that is evoked here, but also in another sense, which seems to me incompatible with it, which consists in presenting emulation as competition with oneself. According to the model presented in this book, this is an unfortunate shift of meaning, because if a process shows a limit or constitutes a problem at a given level, nothing is achieved by bringing it back into a lower-level entity. On the contrary, one only pushes the problem at a deeper level. If I establish a relationship with myself that is essentially a competitive one, I am in the same position in relation to myself as the other person I am competing against. I will forever be a loser, constantly trying to outdo past performances, and thus simply recreating the same problem over and over again. Establishing a systematic relationship of competition is as unhealthy at the intra-individual level as it is at the intra-group or intra-society level.

121. See Table 6, Chapter 3.

Emergence of the Social Sector in the Space Constituting the State

It should be pointed out at the outset that one cannot operate directly at the global level of the state. Instead, one must first develop a cell that meets the criteria of a self-referent entity, then multiply such interconnected cells until one encompasses society as a whole. Such cells are microsocieties whose size may correspond to boroughs in a large city or to units such as Regional County Municipalities (RCMs) in Québec. These RCMs are local municipalities grouped around a chief town in supra-local communities on a territory known as a county.

The first operation, therefore, consists of identifying the local community – for example, a city of about 100 000 inhabitants – where the system will be implemented. The second operation is to set up an organization capable of rallying and bringing people together, one whose characteristics will be specified in the following paragraph. This organization will have to set up a social and economic operation characterized by circularity, i.e., that generates products that will be necessary for the maintenance and development of the processes at the origin of these products.

- *Rallying Organization*

The organization to be set up will have to be from the social sector, that is, it must belong to its members. It must take a legal form that is compatible with the laws in force in the state and with the objectives and operations specific to the requirements of the model. For example, the organization should have legal status, be open to all, ensure freedom of membership, not specialize in a particular development sector and not be under the responsibility of the public sector or a private company. For example, in Québec, the legal structure of the *Solidarity Cooperative* meets these criteria by adding certain provisions to internal regulations.

This organization will have to intervene in a structuring manner in the community. From a theoretical point of view, this intervention, as we have said, is called to be that of the *paradoxical agent* in society. However, if we consider the system itself as a whole, we will find as sub-elements the primitive constants of the model, that is, the *active, receptive, identity*, and *paradoxical* dimensions. Thus, within the chosen micro-society, this concrete version of the new social sector will give rise to the differentiation of an internal *agent* of the highest level, in this case the rallying organization, which, as a reference agent within this unit, will take responsibility for the whole while exercising a second-degree structuring power. Such a power will, however, be adapted from the outset and oriented towards the exercise of a third-degree power: one will therefore find at the heart of the unit an authority playing the role of a *paradoxical agent*, mediatizing the functional operations that will be exercised within this unit.

- *Powers Within Rallying Organization*

Let us look at how the various degrees of power are exercised in the organization that constitutes the governing agency within this embryonic micro-society. Let's start with first-degree power.

First-degree power is that of individual members and groups who, beyond their current functioning, seek to self-develop through activities linked to the expression of their own identity, or linked to the implementation of projects offering goods and services in the social space, or linked to the implementation of unifying projects structuring the community. At the outset, the mere fact of belonging to the organization does not change anything in the ability to access these development processes. We will have to show how the circular process can be set up within the organization, whereby the current exercise of first-degree power generates the processes that will, in turn, ensure the exercise and development of this same power. In other words, how the current functioning becomes a tool of self-development.

Second-degree power is exercised within the organization through the application of its internal rules of procedure. These rules must contain provisions that make it possible to go beyond typical democratic functioning in which decisions are taken by majority vote. This dictatorship of the majority cannot suit the objectives of the social sector. All decisions, be it for elections or policy decisions, will then have to be taken by *consent* according to a mode of operation to which Endenburg[122] gave the name of sociocracy, that is, government by the "socius," by those having meaningful relationships with each other and whose Greek counterpart is "oikeios" (οικειος), which means *close, from home.* "Socius" is opposed to "demos" (δεμος), the people, the latter referring to the mass of individuals who do not have personal relationships with each other, but who share a common way of life and common values under the same governing authority. At present, the sociocratic mode of governance appears to be the one that best meets the requirements of the present model concerning the functioning of the rallying organization. The description that follows is limited to a basic presentation. A more detailed discussion of this practice will be more appropriate in a book devoted exclusively to the pragmatic dimension of the model.

The intention behind governance by consent is to allow an organization to behave like a living organism, that is, as a self-referential *whole.* There is then no part of that organism that is the locus of the *totality*, that is the foundation, that has all the information, to which the totality could be reduced. Thus, decision-making and orientation procedures must give rise to emergences that symbolize the *totality* rather than the domination of one of the parties over the others. The principle, peculiar to *democracy*, of decisions based on the addition of individual votes forming a majority is replaced by the *socio*cratic principle according to which each person indicates for himself or herself the absence of a justifiable objection. Thus, no decision will be taken if one of the members has reasonable objections.

Such procedures for achieving consent have been tried in various countries and have produced satisfactory results in the organizations where they have been applied. "Formal evaluations have shown that these organizations report increased innovation, productivity increases of up to 40%,

---

122. The summary description given here is based on the offprint of John A. Buck and Gerard Endenburg, *La sociocratie. Les forces créatives de l'auto-organization* revised in 2004 and translated by Gilles Charest, available on the Internet: http://www.cqib.org/doc/ activit%_C3%A9s/Pr%C3%A9sentation_3%20Sociogest.pdf. Retrieved August 11, 2008. Also see Gilles Charest, *La démocratie se meurt, vive la sociocratie,* Reggio Emilia, Esserci, 2007.

reduction in the number of meetings, decreases in sick leave, and higher staff commitment to the organization." (Buck and Edenburg, 2012.)

Without going into operational details, it is important to give some details on the operational structure of this organization, which, it should be recalled, is the *highest-level agent* of the initial cell called to become a *development community*. The intention here is to see how third-degree power is embryonically inserted at the very heart of the functioning of the agent exercising second-degree power within this community. The notion of representation by a *double link* proposed by sociocracy will be of help here.

First, in terms of carrying out operations, the hierarchical power structure[123] is similar to the traditional structure found in most organizations. However, at the level of policy decisions, that is, in terms of the content of what is to be executed, the "zero objection" rule comes into play. A structure of circles within which decisions are made by consent is superimposed on the execution structure, according to the methodology peculiar to the sociocratic model.

To be more precise: the hierarchical structure for the execution of operations in the organization is relatively simple: it is composed of a board of directors, an executive, and committees responsible for the main development issues, such as animation and training, project management, financial analysis, etc. The organization's operational structure is also relatively simple. The structure of the sociocratic circles is superimposed on this executive structure in the following way: the basic circles are made up of the various committees. The general circle is composed of the director, a person in charge of each committee and another person elected by consent in each committee and who will be called the *double-link*. This double-link emerges from the group to which he or she belongs in the manner of a paradoxical agent. He is not the leader of the group, but he is the one who best represents the spirit of the group outside the operational framework of execution. Since he must link up with the agent constituting the higher-level circle, he plays the

---

123. Let us recall that the notion of *hierarchy of power* is radically distinct from the notion of *hierarchy of levels* discussed in the second chapter.

latter's role within his own group from the receptive angle: he simulates, as it were, its role of ideal welcoming and listening. It is as if he were telling his group, "I, playing the role of the higher-level circle, am listening to you from your own perspective and decisions". Placed in the higher-level circle, however, he switches to active presentation mode, and now solicits the receptive listening of this circle, the exercise he simulated in his group earlier. Thus, consensus decision-making, conveyed from the lowest to the highest levels, with the presence at each level of *double-links* constituting as many paradoxical agents, presides over the *hierarchical reversal* necessary for the advent of governance based on the totality.

The organization, which is the governing entity within the development community, therefore has at the heart of its functioning the key element of hierarchical reversal: the paradoxical agent. But this organization includes user members who are not part of the operational execution structure, except in a representative capacity on the Board of Directors. Several of these users are grouped in circles, but this time they are self-help and training circles whose objective is to promote the self-development of their members (first-degree power). The user members are thus initially in a receptive position with respect to the function exercised by the governing organization.

In order to ensure the reversal of hierarchies not only within the governance agency, but within the development community as a whole, some members will be trained as *development facilitators* mediating the relationships between the governance entity and the members that take place in development interventions. These facilitators will thus exercise in the community the role theoretically defined as that of a *paradoxical agent*. In terms of member development, the hierarchical reversal consists in ensuring that a development intervention for a member leads the latter to take the initiative of his or her own development and to become autonomous in carrying out the process initiated, extending, but also going beyond the framework of the initial intervention. We recognize here the contours of the educational function at the heart of this development community, which is gradually assuming the status of a learning society, or more precisely, of a self-educating society. Let us now explore the economic dimension of the functioning of this micro-society.

- *The Economy in the Development Community* [124]

We have provided a basic picture of the alienation of local, regional, and even national economies resulting from the systemic leakage of the resources they produce, a leakage that facilitates external control over these resources and generalizes the practices of "exogenous development," synonymous in fact with underdevelopment. The solution, already partly described in the preceding paragraphs, consists, first of all, in bringing people together in an operationally closed but open-to-all space, which leads this micro-society to become a development community, that is, a community capable of creating, and constantly recreating, the tools enabling it to counter the dynamics of impoverishment within its borders and to lay the foundations for its endogenous development. Now let us see how such a construction can be triggered.[125]

The first tool, easily applicable in democratic regimes, concerns the repatriation to the community of market access costs for businesses. We have seen the immense power wielded by a simple customer loyalty system, with the example of the Air Miles program. The strategy now is to offer businesses the opportunity to transform the costs of such a service into a profitable investment for their development and that of their community. More specifically, the idea is to create a fund belonging to the community and entirely dedicated to the development of its members. We will see that this fund has no equivalent in today's economy, since it is a fund that does not come from the collection of savings from third parties, but rather from remuneration for a service rendered by the community to

---

[124]. This section is the result of the integration into the present model of an economic mechanism developed by Bernard Estérez, a first sketch of which appears in his book *Pourquoi pas la vie* published in Montreal by Leméac in 1972. More recent information on this economic mechanism originates from the author's personal communications with Estérez

[125]. We will have to enter into a description whose details would appear superfluous if they did not provide concrete support for the developments expected as a result of the application of the proposed method. We will also note that the figures resulting from the calculations carried out are limited to providing orders of magnitude, the purpose of which is to justify the general conclusions drawn from them.

its members who provide goods and services, thus a fund that constitutes new savings that are legally owned by the community itself. As for the user members, they will benefit from various free or low-cost services related to their development.

More concretely, this is how these operations would be carried out. Members would use an ID giving access to various services, such as a multi-service smart card, for example (or any other identifier such as code cards or biometric sensors, etc.). Suppose it is a smart card. This card would allow you to pay for purchases at member businesses or simply to identify yourself, as with the Air Miles card. This card would then become a customer loyalty tool but of the community type. Each purchase made with this card would contribute to a *Community Development Fund*, in the sense that a premium, the percentage of which depends on the merchant's sector of activity, would be paid to the community on behalf of the customer rather than being remitted directly to the customer. The sums thus accumulated in the customer's name would be returned to the customer when he or she retires. But there is more: as we will indicate later, the fund's importance would be such that it would allow user members to benefit from access to various services: educational services, guarantees for development loans, subsidized loans, zero real rate loans in the case of student loans, the possibility of purchasing community-owned property, a complementary retirement pension. And to all these services may also be added specific local incentives. The fund would also be used by businesses to transform their market access costs into productive investments. A concrete example will allow us to illustrate the expected benefits of such a mechanism.

Suppose that a development community has settled in three contiguous boroughs of the city of Montreal, namely Plateau-Mont-Royal, Rosemont, and Hochelaga-Maisonneuve, and that the project has achieved operational autonomy in the fourth year and that the results of the sixth year are simulated. The three boroughs then have a population of approximately 400,000 inhabitants, which corresponds to about 206,500 households.[126]

---

126. Statistics are from Statistics Canada's 2016 Census. This data can be found on the City of Montreal website at:
http://ville.montreal.qc.ca/portal/page?_pageid=6897,68087646&_dad=portal &_schema=PORTAL _Retrieved June 30, 2020.The simulation starts from an

On average, annual household current consumption expenditures are estimated to be $45,000.[127]

Suppose that 10% of the population – therefore of households – are members of the development community and that they manage to spend 35% of their current expenses at member enterprises, which, for their part, contribute on average to the *Community Development Fund* 2.7% of the amount of purchases as a premium (existing loyalty systems have been known to pay 2.8%). The Community Fund then grows by about $8,500,000 that year, not counting the savings already accumulated, which then amount to about $15,500,000 if we refer to a simulation in which investment risk rates are calculated at 7%. If one assumes that membership in the development community reaches 20% of the population and not just 10%, the amount generated that year alone would then be $50,000,000.

This fund, which is essentially a guarantee fund, is primarily used as a lever to enable the reintroduction of new investments into the economy for development projects. The leverage effect of such a fund, it must be recognized, can be very significant. For example, the Réseau d'investissement social du Québec (RISQ)[128] can have a leverage effect of up to 13; in other words, every one dollar of authorized funding results in investments of 13 dollars. If, for the *Community Development Fund*, we assume a leverage effect of 5, the funds for the current year would make it possible to foster investments five times that amount. This means, for that year alone, investments of $42,000,000 assuming a

---

assumption of implementation in 2018. Here we have the 2023 data obtained by linear extrapolation based on population growth between 2011 and 2016, the year of the last census.

127. Current consumption expenditure excludes personal taxes, individual insurance payments, pension contributions, cash donations and charitable contributions. Amounts are in Canadian dollars.

128. The Réseau d'investissement social du Québec (RISQ) provides loans especially tailored for social economy enterprises that provide financially viable and socially profitable goods and services. In existence since 1997, this venture capital fund set itself the mission of providing enterprises in diverse sectors that are structured as NPOs or cooperatives with access to financing adapted to their realities. RISQ supports the emergence, development, growth, and consolidation of social economy enterprises by assisting innovative projects that generate social action and development for their communities throughout Québec." LE RÉSEAU D'INVESTISSEMENT SOCIAL DU QUÉBEC, https://fonds-risq.qc.ca/?lang=en. Retrieved July 10, 2020.

membership of 10% of the population and of $250,000,000 assuming a membership of 20%.

However, one of the operating rules which is essential to the system is that any contribution from the Community fund to investments is granted on condition that all money spent as a result of these investments be spent in businesses that are members of this same Community fund. This means that when a member business pays for a loyalty service, it is actually making a productive investment. In the above example, under the conservative assumption of a leverage effect of 5, member businesses would collectively receive five times more than they invested in the economy of their community, in addition to benefiting from a loyalty system supported by the major players in this same community. And of course, this community economy is open to new businesses that will, in turn, contribute to the fund on becoming members.

This point warrants further reflection. This is one of the keys of the above system's operational closure. Any investment operation must return to the system circuit, including the external contributions linked to this operation. In this way, the first level operators – customers and suppliers – generate by their joint operation a tool of which, in a second stage, they become beneficiaries. Thus, a hierarchical reversal also takes place economically speaking, one in which, to use general terms, the operators generate processes of which they finally become the operands.

This is made possible by the fact that the organization constitutes a totality that has its own meaning. One of the symbols of this reality lies in the fund, which can rightly be described as a properly communitarian one. Let us insist on the fact that this fund goes beyond the idea of a collective fund, i.e., a fund that collects existing savings from third parties: the community, through its solidary functioning, generates new savings that belong to it as a unit, rather than belonging to third parties, shareholders or investors. These savings, therefore, have no cost. On the contrary, they are profitable savings, as they will be invested in a financial institution. The community is therefore not accountable to third parties and can develop according to its own identity.

Moreover, like social funds, this fund has no pre-set standards. It adjusts to the concrete situation of people who want to develop projects. This fund does not replace other funds, but it can support them by taking the initiative for projects in which it assumes part of the risk by providing guarantees. It mainly reduces risk by accompanying those to whom it makes loans, a most effective method if one takes the example of the Grameen Bank, whose risk rates are below 2%.[129] Also, the fund is fed by constant flows and not according to the performance of development projects.[130] This funding does not depend on the will of third parties. The fund thus becomes a lever to make possible local investments capable of compensating for the flight of savings and of stopping commercial leakage in the medium term.

Of course, commercial leaks will not be stopped overnight. Here is how the proposed mechanism will provide a remedy of increasing effectiveness as it develops into an integrated network of communities. The consumer's card (or ID) is assigned to his or her local community. If he or she goes to buy in another locality or a larger center but takes the trouble to buy from a business that is member of the network, the entire premium goes back to the local fund managed by the consumer's community. In today's economy, commercial leakage is a dead loss for the local community. In the proposed system, the leakage is compensated by a return on savings that serves as leverage for proportionally much more significant local investments. Gradually, the local economy can then develop and become as attractive as the surrounding economies.

---

129. The risk rate is defined here as the proportion of bad debts to total investments.
130. An interesting phenomenon here is that if risk rates as low as those of the Grameen Bank can be achieved and the rate of premiums paid by companies is 2.7% as in the previous assumption, the fund would be growing continuously. Indeed, assume investments of 100 and a risk rate of 2%. The fund that guarantees 100 then loses 2. But since these investments of 100 have been spent on member companies and the member companies pay a premium of 2.7, we have a net gain of 0.7. The fund then becomes increasingly self-sustaining through its simple operation despite losses due to bad debts.

- *Generalization of the System: A Strategic Utopia*[131]

The previous description would already suffice to warrant the implementation of the proposed system, but it should be emphasized that this system itself has properties of "endogenous development" that operate according to four factors: 1) a very high probability of growth in premium rates paid by merchants; 2) an increase in the number of members in the community; 3) a high probability of increasing the percentage of the household budget spent on the system; 4) the inclusion of business-to-business trade.

1) Likely Growth in Premium Rates

As far as premium rates are concerned, a member business must pay a previously defined basic rate according to the sector of economic activity to which it belongs. But it can pay more if it wishes. Let us look at the situation as a whole. The value of other loyalty systems is measured in terms of the extra market share it allows a business to have at the expense of its competitors. It thus has motivational, not economic value, since what one gains in an existing market is what another loses. Conversely, the proposed system creates new markets that would not have otherwise existed, a market openly accessible to member businesses only.

The size of this market is commensurate with the development needs that are not being met, and that could be met using the proposed mechanisms. A simple example, which could be multiplied by hundreds of thousands, to illustrate this point: the real case, observed in the field, of a very high-level cabinetmaker whose products are in demand.[132] He would need a new set of tools that would allow him to work on short-term orders without having to uninstall the tooling dedicated to long-term work. Various factors make him ineligible for regular development programs: a past bankruptcy, poor management, inability to calculate cost price, etc. And he also does not meet

---

131. Following Beck, we distinguish strategic utopia from one that would remain merely utopian. In the 1950s, going to the moon was a utopia. The application of adequate strategies allowed this utopia dream to be fulfilled, hence the expression "strategic utopia."
132. Case presented to the author by the Corporation de développement de l'est de Montréal (CDEST).

the criteria set by public development services, so he is unable to find funding. As a consumer, he thus has no access to the market for tools that could meet his needs. A *development community* would first provide him with local support to help him get out of the impasse and then enable him to acquire the management skills necessary to keep his business going. Let's imagine the situation. A *development facilitator* puts this person in contact with project development specialists working for the community. The community agrees to support the project. The applicant will need to take out a $75,000 loan to purchase new equipment. The community gives its guarantee to a financial institution, and the cabinetmaker can carry out the project.

If we go back to the point that prompted this example, we first note that the $75,000 will be spent at a business that is already a member, or that agrees to become a member at the time of purchase. Thanks to the *development community*, the company selling the tools has access to the new market of previously unfulfilled needs, in this case the cabinetmaker, who, for his part, accesses this same market, on the one hand, as a client capable of investing in his business, and, on the other, as a producer capable of continuing to offer his products on the market. It should be noted in passing that if the premium paid by the company supplying the tools is 3%, the purchases related to this project will generate $2,250, which will go into the fund.

Let's continue the reasoning. This access to a new market makes it highly probable that member businesses would accept to increase the average premium base rate of 2.7% they are paying to those currently being paid in the world to access new markets. In order to obtain these new markets, there is no reason why member businesses would not put in sums equivalent to those they put to access or increase their market share in existing markets. These sums in today's world are considerable. They provide most of the funding for sports activities, the press, television, advertising in general, and sponsorship. In such a situation, the opening of a new market leads companies to invest large sums of money to gain access to it, as has been the case for the past decade for the Chinese market. It is conservatively estimated that companies – with considerable differences between categories of companies – spend an average of 5% of their total revenues to this end.

2) Likely Growth in Membership

With the increase in the average rate of premiums, the probability increases that the number of members of the community will grow in geometric progression and that soon, since nothing is asked of the members, the entire population of a given milieu will join the development community. No access fees, no dues are charged to offer each member the possibility of saving by normally spending for their current consumption, thus allowing the poorest to become savers themselves and thus obtain important benefits that are currently inaccessible to them. This system thus allows everyone to significantly improve their economic situation. Let us assume that 80% of the population joins the community. Such an increase in the number of members of the community, all potential buyers, has as a corollary a parallel increase in the number of member businesses and consequently in the number of goods and services offered.

3) Probable Increase in the Percentage of Spending in the System

The above two factors make a parallel increase in the percentage of current expenditure in the system probable. A noteworthy comment here about rental fees and, more generally, housing costs because of their importance in the budget of most households. It may seem that whenever housing is scarce and expensive, landlords have no interest in entering into an economy based on solidarity. However, several landlords may find it to be in their best interest to join such an economy and to accept to grant a premium on the rent of members if this, because of the guarantees granted by the Community fund, assures them of timely rent payments; and if membership also gives them access to credits at a subsidized rate or even at a zero real rate for certain investments (hygiene conditions, thermal and sound insulation for example). Including rents and housing costs in the total expenditures of members radically alters the percentage spent by households in the system. A first approximation would suggest a rise from 35% to 50%.

4) Business-to-Business Exchanges

A final observation. The fourth factor of growing importance should be added to the final consumption mentioned so far: business-to-business trade. Obviously, businesses have a system of exchanges between themselves that they will not seek to modify from the outset. But the mechanism put in place opens a breach in this system. Indeed, the new member businesses benefiting from the guarantee of the Community fund will necessarily have to encourage their suppliers to become members, which is an essential condition for obtaining credits. Thus, increasingly large sums will be paid into the fund from business-to-business trade. Furthermore, since businesses do not have the same characteristics as individuals (for example, they do not retire, etc.), it will thus be possible to allocate the sums paid into the fund thanks to business-to-business trading to the development of member businesses and their network of interaction. The advantages thus created will probably lead to other businesses joining the network, whether retailers, wholesalers, or producers.

Taking these four factors into account invites us to evaluate their consequences for the *development community* formed, in the above-mentioned example, by the three Montreal boroughs. Let us first recall the new parameter values: the average premium rate paid by businesses has increased to 5%. The member population has reached 80% of the total population of the three boroughs, and the share of current household expenditures has risen to 50%. Under these conditions, the gross amount paid into the fund for a single year from members' current expenditure would be approximately $100,000,000. If we take into account business-to-business trade, the simulations allow us to estimate the total amount at $135,000,000. It can be estimated that after plus or minus ten years, the accumulated amounts could reach plus or minus $1,000,000,000 (in other words, $1 billion).

The proposed mechanism leads to a very likely and very significant acceleration of development. Using the example of the three Montreal boroughs, we will try to show how such a mechanism can be used to address the general problem of underdevelopment presented above. It should be remembered that underdevelopment basically stems from the cascading dispossession of the world's economies that are losing a large part of their savings, the latter feeding speculative circuits for lack of sufficient guarantees in national and local economies. Thus, the savings generated in poor countries are being used to develop rich countries, and within rich countries, the poorest sectors are financing the richest sectors.

It should be noted that the primary function of all the data that will be presented here is to support the structure of the reasoning that will follow. They are, therefore, estimates whose accuracy could be questioned. However, these estimates are within a range considered plausible, particularly in the context of our strategic utopia. Changing the value of any of these parameters, in any case, allows one to maintain the same basic reasoning, *mutatis mutandis*.

Let us assume a set of projects worth $400,000,000 that would have been impossible without the fund. These amounts, which are used for community development, would have otherwise been used for other purposes outside the community. The fund consequently avoided a capital flight of this amount.

Now assume that the proven risk rate of these projects is 4%. The fund, therefore, loses $16,000,000. One must bear in mind, however, that the $400 million was invested in development loans in the community. And that these amounts had to be used in purchases from member businesses, which, in the present hypothesis, offer an average 5% premium on all member purchases. So, the latter premium on $400 million generates $20 million, which goes into the fund. Thus, the loss of $16 million in bad debts is immediately written off, and the fund then increases by $4 million.

Now, to be faithful to our utopia, let us imagine that we apply the same parameters to the whole of Québec. The total number of households projected for 2021 is 3 773 386, according to the Institut de la statistique du Québec. We would then have an annual inflow of $1,775,000,000 ($1.7 billion) or $10,775,000,000 ($10.7 billion) after 10 years.

- *Towards a Community-based Economy*

From the perspective of such a constantly growing fund, it would be incongruous to use these sums using a capitalist economy mindset and to allocate them only to investments outside the community. We then have the opportunity to build a truly solidarity-based economy. It will be possible to grant zero-interest-rate loans for projects aimed at protecting the environment or for any other project decided by the community.

It is clear that it will be impossible to invest in the Community, through development projects, the full amount that can be guaranteed by the fund annually. From this point of view, it is worthwhile underlining once again that the method proposed inaugurates a mode of operation exactly opposite to that of banks which manage sums deposited by their clients, sums which do not belong to them. In contrast, the community is called upon to manage sums that belong to it.

This characteristic leads to a new concept, that of *community ownership* of movable or immovable goods which are and remain the property of the community, but which can be used by the members precisely as if they were owners, administering their patrimony with care and responsibility, that is to say, providing for the maintenance and depreciation costs of these goods, which they thus manage on behalf of the community. Moreover, this management can be transferred at any time to another member through an internal community operation.

Let us give two examples where members have access to goods without having to pay interest. A member needs for his work computer equipment costing $4800. The community buys the equipment in cash, and the member, who is entrusted by the community with its stewardship, amortizes it over five years with monthly payments of $80. In the real estate field, following the same principle of prior purchase by the community, a 25-year amortization allows a family to find a place to live for the monthly payment of $800 for a $240,000 house. A 50-year amortization period – as already proposed by some financial institutions – would lower the monthly payments to $400. There is no reason why a basic good such as housing should bear interest and necessarily be subject to the imperative of private profit.

As the system develops ever more, certain imperatives, characteristic of the dominant private sector logic, are gradually removed from the social fabric, for example, the idea that credit, as well as the satisfaction of basic needs, must necessarily bear interest and be the object of profit.

We will see that the interface between the *development community* and the surrounding environment must ensure the compatibility of the coexistence of the two distinct logics, which implies that priority must be given to preserving the operational closure of the system, which may occasionally lead to the strategic adaptation of the unit to certain requirements of the environment, which is the case for all living beings in relation to their environment.

- *Development Community's Culture*

The transition represented by the advent of *development communities* at the heart of the social sector could be understood as the transition from a culture of *doing*, in which human beings have placed themselves at the center in order to collectively control their environment, to a culture of *being*, in which their fulfillment as human beings now becomes the main object of their concerns. In this context, investing in people no longer appears to be a burden, but a real creation of wealth within an economy that is truly at the service of mankind. Our civilization is ready to enter its *identity stage.* Just as historically we have passed from peasant societies centered on the activities of the primary sector, to industrial societies centered on the activities of the secondary and tertiary sectors, so today's society is called to make the transition towards a society of self-development, centered on the activities of the quaternary sector which are education, research, health, creation and individual and collective expression.

Neo-Keynesianism or Post-Capitalism?

One of the first reactions one may have to the model proposed in this book is to ask whether it should be called neo-Keynesian or post-capitalist. Let us first briefly identify these two points of view.

The basic idea of Keynesianism, as summed up in one sentence by F. Houtart (2001),[133] is "... the acceptance of market

---

133. The abbreviated description of the two points of view presented here is taken from François Houtard's intervention, *Des alternatives crédibles au capitalisme*

logic as the driving force of the economy, but only on the condition that the system is regulated, that its perverse effects are limited and that it does not lead to abuses". Within this framework, the state intervenes and acts as a guarantor of the distribution of wealth. This model was applied in various countries after World War II. It should be noted here that the so-called "market logic" – the capitalist market – is dominated by competing private interests and driven by profit maximization, which creates inequalities.

As we have seen, this private sector dominated market economy – capitalism – has since spread beyond the borders of states and led to the kind of globalization we are now witnessing. Neo-Keynesians are attempting to implement the Keynesian model at a worldwide level, by regulating the current market economy and restoring the conditions of competition, while respecting the environment and reducing social injustices. This model presents itself with many variants on a continuum ranging from a George Soros who is trying to save capitalism from running to its ruin, to social democrats whose objective is to safeguard the rights of workers and the sovereignty of states while respecting the ecology. However, we note that these variants all have in common that they do not question the logic of the capitalist system. They operate within the dynamics of this system, merely trying to correct its abuses.

Post-capitalism, on the other hand, challenges the very logic of capitalism, that of an egocentric economy based on competition and aimed at maximizing profits. In post-capitalism, the economy is seen as an activity whose primary goal is to ensure the physical and cultural well-being of all. Here again, the range of variants runs along a continuum from the revolutionary left, which believes that radical and rapid change requires taking power, to "the majority of others who accept the idea that the transition to an alternative model of economy is a long-term process" *(Ibid.)*.

It is clear that the present approach is in line with post-capitalism as a long-term process. However, it is important to clarify this statement. It should be noted at the outset that an

---

mondialisé, at the 2001 World Social Forum. It is accessible on the Internet: https://base.socioeco.org/docs/doc-93_fr.pdf. Retrieved February 18, 2020.

outside observer who would limit himself to a superficial examination would never find the first steps in the implementation of our model very convincing. Analogously, one can carry out a superficial observation of a fertilized human egg and that of a chimpanzee and see similar external characteristics without realizing that the internal coherence of these two living beings generates two radically different identities.

What would then be the criteria that would allow us to distinguish between the two orientations? Firstly, whatever solution is proposed, it cannot escape the fact that it is part of the current situation and will necessarily have to start from there in order to unfold. At first glance, one is led to believe that any force openly critical of the capitalist system and fiercely struggling to dismantle its strategies in the hope of changing its profound identity would be a force more radical than the others and would thus be of a post-capitalist nature. Yet this is an illusion whose longevity is perhaps due to the naivety of a utopia of a merely "utopian" rather than "strategic" nature, to use Beck's terms. Of course, there are necessary, even essential struggles, whose most important function is perhaps to slow down the progression of unfettered capitalism and give more time for the implementation of effective solutions. The demonstrations in Seattle and the impressive mobilization against the Multilateral Agreement on Investment (MAI) are victories that can only be positive. Yet relying on such methods to move society to a post-capitalist mode of operation is not at all promising.

Paradoxically, the least radical and least promising approach is that of the revolutionary left, which wants to take power to overthrow the system. Events unfold as if one cannot learn from the collapse of the various types of communism. In terms of the self-referential model we are proposing, the revolutionary left's approach attempts to establish a second-degree power that must develop at the heart of existing powers, but which is of the same nature and thus merely adds to their numbers. But the objective is to overthrow these same powers to the point of changing the nature of the global system of which all these powers are a part. A radical leftist strategy can only leave us in a struggle of second-degree powers. The energy spent fighting the antagonistic powers then leaves little room for building a system based on another type of power.

What is forgotten here is the fact that at the outset of any self-referential situation, no agent finds himself or herself outside the overall system that he or she claims to be either maintaining or fighting to replace. No agent can take the whole system as an external object and must, therefore, interact with other agents from within that totality. We have seen that altering a totality is a self-referential process that cannot be achieved through one agent dominating the others.

Truly radical strategies are rather those allowing all of the energy to be devoted to building a system based on another type of power. From this point of view, neo-Keynesian solutions are also doomed to an at best relative failure. The argument is the same as that used to criticize the micro-credit experiments that are taking place in our current capitalist system. These experiments are either perverted or recuperated and sometimes even serve to legitimize the logic of the existing system.

It is indeed utopian to believe that one can keep as the engine of development a system whose logic of operation leads to the opposite of what is intended, hoping to correct efficiently afterward the perverse effects it will have generated. It should be noted in passing that this strategy has the same structure as the attempt, on the cognitive level, to explain a paradigm using a core idea incompatible with this paradigm, leading to the need for permanent correction. We have already shown the inconsistency resulting from such an amalgam.

What, then, is the characteristic of the self-referential model that would make it a truly post-capitalist solution? First of all, it acknowledges that one must start in the heart of the ambient system. But it creates in this capitalist system an operationally closed entity whose functioning responds to its own set of rules, so that the simple internal functioning of the units creates the tools by which these units can, in turn, maintain and develop in the sense of their own identity, reinforcing at the same time the identity of the entity itself. These conditions make possible an interaction of the entity with its environment that is such that it not only does not lose its identity but, on the contrary, reinforces it by assimilating and submitting the contributions of the environment to its internal coherence. Subsequently, the entity in question is called upon to differentiate itself and to create a network of entities having essentially the same operational closure characteristics.

Let's use once again a little metaphorical tale. Suppose a gallinaceous animal has spread throughout the city and is roaming free, as occurs in Key West, Florida, where hens and roosters are accountable to no one. In our story, it is the *Gallus Domesticus Capitalistus*. This gallinaceous animal has the unfortunate habit of scraping the ground with its feet to find its food, which compromises the aesthetics of human lawns. Moreover, it reproduces, and all its descendants develop the same annoying habit.

In one part of the city, a highly reputable Neo-Keynesi School ethologist practicing animal psychology is consulted. He proposes to educate the gallus by conditioning it so that it finds its food in ways other than scraping the soil of lawns, in the hope that it will pass on its knowledge to the next generation. The results on a few gallinaceous species are interesting, but limited in time, as the animal eventually spontaneously returns to its usual behavior. Transformation thus did take place but rapidly deviated and was absorbed by the ambient system.

Another scholar is brought in, this time from the Revolutionary School. According to him, one should try modifying the very nature of the *gallus* itself by provoking a genetic mutation, the idea being that when it would fight against unmutated *gallus* it would genetically transmit the characteristics of *Gallus Novus*. The energy expended in struggling against the gallus capitalistus fails, not giving rise to the advent of the Great Evening of Gallus Novus.

Finally, a cunning experimenter of the Autopoetic School decides to put the reproductive power of the *gallus capitalistus* itself, coupled with its limited intelligence, at the service of his project. Into the many *gallus* nests he manages to find, he introduces duck eggs reputed for their fertility. The *gallus* has no objection to incubating these eggs, to which it transmits all the calorific energy necessary for their development. The duck embryo, on the other hand, develops according to its own duck coherence because of the operational closure of its egg, which does not prevent it from withdrawing the maximum amount of energy from the *gallus*. Any input from the *gallus* is recycled into duck production logic. The many eggs hatch, the ducks multiply and supplant the *gallus* because of their high fertility.

One can draw a few essential elements from the above humorous example. First of all, it is possible to develop one's own logic within an organic entity, even in an environment responding to a different logic than that of this entity. All the energy must be used for the development of one's own logic, which implies a certain number of internal rules defining the operational closure of a process entirely dedicated to the identity of the entity in question. This excludes that the strategy is first based on the fight against external forces. Rather than trying to change external rules, new internal rules are adopted, which can be deployed according to their own coherence and harmoniously integrate the external elements by gradually assimilating them to these rules and becoming the dominant mode of operation.

In other words, a market initially dominated by private interests can imperceptibly move towards a community market and finally realize, in the double meaning of the latter word – *to become aware of* and *to make real* –, this five-century-old statement of Jean Bodin: "There is neither wealth nor strength other than people.

Some Perspectives

Let us imagine that this network of *development communities* has spread within a state and that it has flourished to the point of reaching a good cruising speed. It can then support the state in the provision of services related to education, health, and culture. But it can also help the state resist the ongoing wave of globalization that is undermining governments. The power of the autonomous social sector, which, as we have seen, can become considerable, has the potential to relieve the state of its vulnerability. Massive support from an organized population gives a government legitimacy that external intervention can hardly overwhelm.

But there is more: with a growing and ever-stronger network, the power dynamic is reversed. The faceless *global client* and *identityless civil society* to which Beck refers are now taking the form of an organized *development community* whose autonomy now allows it to become a key player in the setting of rules defining the conditions for local and national investments. And the potential for such a network to expand beyond the borders of the state means that other states, as already mentioned, can cooperate in achieving common goals that are not dictated by the logic of global capital, be they political freedoms, strong social programs, or the preservation of the environment.

In terms of the self-referential model, it is the passage from an era in which governance is exercised around second-degree power to an era centered on third-degree power, giving rise to the deployment of the identity dimension through which the human being reveals himself to himself, then justified to claim his title of *self-referent animal.*

Conclusion

Before considering the production of works that would constitute the second step in this journey, let us pause and ask ourselves what has become of our "construction," of our model, this cognitive artifact that has ventured unrestrainedly into the field of all levels of human reality. One will have understood that the fragmented aspect of this "construction" is part of the method and constitutes in a way a requirement of the data and of our situation with regard to this data. The self-referential nature of the approach makes it impossible to look for a system of axioms from which one could derive theorems whose truth could be demonstrated by a step-by-step sequential approach, and which could then authoritatively dictate human conduct.

Instead, we had to use another method, which looks more like a bricolage, which seeks to adjust the intellectual approach to this aspect of human reality according to which it invents itself, akin to the here-and-now process of life which invents itself with the material it finds in its path. But this methodological *bricolage* has been developed on the cognitive axis and is distinct from the existential process it evokes. Indeed, this adjustment of the approach only aims to better assimilate this "object" which, in the end, remains outside the observing "subject," as is the case with any cognitive operation. In short, it was a question of exploring how cognitive activity could adapt itself to this process of human self-construction, without cutting itself off from that which constitutes its essence.

One such essential element, which in many approaches is the first to disappear, is the *totality*. This is so because the latter is inaccessible as a direct object of knowledge on the part of the actors who are an integral part of it. As explained in chapter one, theorists' resignation to operate without the totality leads to inconsistencies. Though prioritizing the totality, our approach nevertheless acknowledges the fact that, for an observer forming part of it, the totality is cognitively empty, this being the condition of all human observers in relation to themselves and humanity. The totality is then the locus of a process, which is distinct from cognitive activity, through which the latter arises and maintains itself in existence, the interaction of the internal actors being the engine room of such a process.

For the totality, in other words, the heart of the matter is *being*. So, the first distinction is the one made from within the totality when it relates to itself and thus becomes an entity with its own identity. The second distinction occurs in that this totality relates to what is not itself, that is to say, to its environment, through a process of adaptation that articulates the distance between what then becomes a *subject* and an *object*. This is how the universe of *knowledge* is born. The complexity of the implications of this problem would justify that we make another brief incursion into metacognitive space

Brief Metacognitive Feedback on the Model

One sometimes sees, as an attempt to make the first distinction, *thought*, which is in the realm of *knowing*, and *action*, which is in that of *doing*, realms that need to be articulated between them. Perhaps such a distinction may be productive in specific contexts, but from the perspective of the self-referential model, it obscures the complexity of the process, for thinking is, in fact, only an internalized action. Without further specification, the two poles are likely to belong to the same cognitive universe, thus keeping us in the comfort of the Western paradigm.

In the model set forth in this analysis, the founding cleavage is that which distinguishes *being* and *knowing*. *Being* is not in the realm of action, even if it can only be realized by giving rise to a specific action, articulating, at the lower level, the interaction of the constituent agents. It is then that action at this level differentiates itself, resulting in *action-constitutive-of-being* and *action-adaptive-to-what-is-not-self*, primacy being given to the first over the second. It is here that a clarification is necessary about what has been called the first distinction: though fundamentally implicit, this distinction also has its explicit side. The implicit aspect is that which distinguishes the *totality* as such from its differentiated state. The explicit aspect is that which distinguishes the *agent* from its *receptive* in the differentiated state. We have chosen to consider these two aspects, implicit and explicit, as two sides of the same distinction, the first distinction, locus of the existential relationship that manifests itself in the deployment of the communicational process. One finds the same pattern at the cognitive level, where the implicit corresponds to the *paradigm* and the explicit to the development of the *core idea*.

On the explicit level, therefore, we find ourselves with two radically distinct forms of *action* that manifest themselves in two different processes: *communication*, in its horizontal or interactional aspect, and *knowledge*, which puts the entity in an adaptive relationship with its environment.

These processes of communication and cognition thus pave the way for the development of two domains, the first being the pragmatics of human self-development, and the other the methodical knowledge of this same development. These two domains are rooted in the same locus, below the domain of object, in a precognitive universe, therefore cognitively empty. On the pragmatic level, this universe is that of the self-referent concrete totality, and on the cognitive level, that of the self-referent paradigm.

Let us return to the cognitive strategy used to exploit this paradoxical situation. We can go back to the beginning of the second chapter to see how the abstract cognitive schema is modeled on the one used to describe self-referential concrete realities. In summary, the *self-referential paradigm* corresponds to *totality*. The *core idea of self-reference* corresponds to the *differentiated agent*. This agent differs from and is complementary to that which it is not. And what is complementary and distinct from self-reference is heteroreference, which then constitutes the *receptive* agency. Thus, *hetero-reference* becomes an obligatory ingredient of the self-reference paradigm.

The hetero-referential field facing this self-referential structuring agent will then be brought to situate itself in relation to this agent and to develop according to its own coherence under the influence of this agent. This initially hetero-referential field gradually takes the contours of the self-referential process and makes the *paradoxical agent* emerge, which will come to enrich the initial agent with its own specificities. Thus, the hetero-referential ingredient, initially foreign to self-referencing, becomes an integral part of it.

Let us recall how this process was applied throughout the book. For example, to address the question of time, we used Erikson's theory. We searched for the internal coherence of this theory and, using the self-referential matrix, confronted it with itself and thus ended up with a self-referential version of human development. By further integrating itself in the self-referential domain, this theory emerged with more internal coherence, a relative one of course, given that it represents but a first approximate reformulation. At the same time, the self-referential matrix gained a system of nested ternary cycles whose heuristic value is greater than the initial matrix.

This was also the case with communication, for which we provided a first approximate self-referential version applicable to all levels of human reality. In chapter 5, we developed this same model at the societal level. Once again, the current functioning of society was confronted with itself in the light of the self-referential matrix, which led to generating the design of a pragmatic artifact of human self-construction, involving the creation of autonomous units endowed with operational closure. New ways of looking at the notions of power and sector, for example, enriched the initial matrix.

Let us summarize as follows: we have, on the explicit cognitive level, two domains, that of the core idea represented by the self-referential matrix, and that of the various fields of observation of human reality, which, in relation to this matrix, constitutes a hetero-referential field. The self-referential matrix then becomes the structuring *agent* that promotes the internal coherence of this field of observation, creating, in a *bootstrap* fashion, small islands of coherence that gradually integrate themselves into the field of self-reference. At the end of the process, therefore, self-reference and hetero-reference reintegrate the world of the implicit and resolve themselves in the paradigm of self-reference, always imperfectly deployed, imperfectly manifested, imperfectly symbolized, never reached except by successive approximations. At the beginning of the next cycle, the self-referential matrix is itself richer, more complete, more coherent. It, therefore, had to be confronted with a world that was initially alien to it to become more precisely what it is, integrating this world into the process that defines it, but being thereby transformed by it.

Pragmatic Research and Development Perspectives

When making first approximate formulations of the various problematics, we indicated a few avenues of research on the cognitive level that we will not repeat here. But on this same level, the field is open to many other avenues. For example, it would be interesting to examine how the present model could be an interpretation of Varela's (1975) Extended Calculus of Indications. This calculus, which is an extension of Spencer Brown's (1972) Calculus of Indication, is based on a boundary operator, which, by its presence, indicates a state that distinguishes itself from the rest. This could correspond to our notion of *differentiation* by which an agent distinguishes itself from that which it is not. Varela introduces another operator, which is precisely the self-referential operator that defines a new state, the autonomous state, which is the fact of a self-indication. It behaves differently from the previous one. Indeed, according to axiom 2, first found in Spencer Brown, if from within the marked state, one crosses the boundary again, one returns to the unmarked state. In other words, crossing the border again is like not crossing a border. But if, according to axiom 3 of the extended calculus, from the differentiated state you pass to the autonomous state by self-indication, the outcome is the autonomous state. It would be interesting to see the correspondences that could be established between the various elements of the model and those of the extended calculus of indications, for example, between the *paradoxical agent* and the *self-referent* operator of the calculus.

Let us nevertheless note that we have so far remained in the realm of cognition as it relates to itself. For its part, chapter 5 announces another level of operation. Though the same strategy is applied here, this time, it is in the pragmatic realm of self-construction. No longer is the objective of building a cognitive artifact and seeing how it behaves in various cognitive contexts, but rather building a concrete human artifact in which humans construct their own reality. Once this ethical and political construction project has begun, the cognitive operation will operate in the same way as it does now, i.e., it will play the role of placing human entities, at whatever level, in front of themselves and the development of their own identity, in the light of a self-referential matrix. But the human artifact will have its own coherence, which will not derive from cognitive activity. On the other hand, this cognitive activity will be able to play a mediating role between the unity created and itself, while enriching itself with new perspectives.

It is important to note that cognitive activity has adapted to the self-referential problematic so that the cognitive tool tends to manifest as much as possible a structure that is isomorphic to the process of self-development in concrete units. The same concepts can be applied to both the cognitive and pragmatic realms. For example, the *paradoxical agent* concept applies here in the cognitive realm to the agent originating from the *receptive* which comes to encompass the initial agent in its own action, but in the pragmatic realm, it applies to concrete actors, as is the case of the *social sector* in society, or the group of *development facilitators* within the development community and the *double link* in the structure of the governing body of this community. Each general concept of the basic schema is enriched through its contact with diverse realities, both theoretical and practical, giving rise to a progression towards an overall coherence that can cover increasingly encompassing and complex realities. The contours of the pragmatic societal artifact, that of a network of *development communities* endowed with an operational closure, have been evoked with enough precision to show that the setting up of such a project can realistically be operationalized and that it can be coherently accompanied by a cognitive operation adapted to this type of object.

Of course, what we set forth in this book represents but a first approximation, but the field of research is open, and hopefully, with enough coherence to foster a meaningful endeavor. We can imagine, at other levels, some pragmatic artifacts that could be subjected to the self-referential matrix. At first glance, we could classify these methodological artifacts into two categories: methodologies directly focused on the invisible foundation of communication involving the vertical link to the totality, methodologies that are more related to the *identity* component. To simplify, we will refer to these as *vertical methodologies*. The second category consists of methodologies focusing on the horizontal interaction of the actors comprising a totality, an interaction highlighting more the *active* and *receptive* components, and which we will refer to as *horizontal methodologies*, all of which can be applied to various levels of human reality, from the individual to the entire species. We will only mention a few examples here.

- *Vertical Methodologies*

Let's take the case of two vertical methodologies, one applied at the level of the person and his/her inner universe, and the other at the psychosocial level, which concerns the inner universe of a small group. The example involving the individual person will be drawn from the various oriental meditation techniques, and that involving a small group will refer to Scott Peck's Community Building Workshop (1994) (CBW). By briefly presenting these two cases, we want to illustrate that comparing two approaches at different levels can help us to understand both better.

Before applying the methodological artifacts, let us first identify the units involved in these two situations. The *totality*, at the individual level, is the person, and at the psychosocial level, the group itself, considered as a unit. The *interveners* at the intrapersonal level are the various mental productions that become explicit through the semiotic function, or, if you like, through the system of representation. These productions are, in fact, messages that define the *totality* at that precise moment. These messages constitute *interventions* within this universe. For example, an idea suddenly comes up in *me*, whatever its form (sensation, perception, image, concept); this is the differentiation of a *communicational* or *intervening agent*: "*I*" have an idea. The idea modifies *me*, informs *me*. Generally, such an intervention gives rise to a reaction, an immediate response, which can be, for example, a commitment to follow up on this idea or to oppose it. Thus, an inner dialogue is engaged in an idiosyncratic language that only partially uses interpersonal language. We can do the same analysis at the group level. When a person *intervenes*, this changes the state of the group and leads to a *response* from one of the participants, and so on. A dialogue takes place in the group.

In the previous description, one will notice the absence of the *paradoxical agent*. It is, of course, present, though only implicitly, given that all the actors are simultaneous witnesses of what is happening. But this function is diluted in the flow of the dialogue and can be contaminated on the side of the active function of intervention or on the side of the receiving function. Thus, ideas are linked to each other within the person, as are interventions within the group. This phenomenon evokes a notion developed in the East, that of karma, which is often misinterpreted in the West.

Let's open a short parenthesis on this subject. An intervention has an effect. If the intervention is perfect in a perfect environment, it generates a process whose outcome is limited to the desired effect, which places the totality in a distinct state from which another intervention can occur freely. But interventions and settings are rarely perfect. Thus, interventions most often have side effects that become direct causes of other interventions that themselves have side effects, etc. It is this linking of causes and effects that constitutes karma. Thus, the action, which should have disappeared after taking place, survives in a chain of side effects to which the intervener remains linked.[134] The ideas jostling inside a person, as well as spontaneous group discussions, are most often of this type: an intervention provokes an effect which is the direct cause of an immediate reaction, in a more or less confused and chaotic sequence.

If we look for manifestations of karma at other levels, we find that our social functioning, for example, is very karmic. For instance, we cut down trees to build our houses, which is a desirable effect. But we do so by destroying ecosystems, which is an undesirable side effect. This destruction becomes a cause of the increase in greenhouse gases. This increase, in turn, leads to global warming, etc. So, there is a chain of causes and effects. We could very well have built our wooden houses without destroying our ecosystems. Another example: we create wealth through our collective activity, which is a desirable effect. But the way we do it enriches some at the expense of others who become poorer. This side effect creates underdevelopment, which reduces people to powerlessness. Powerlessness leads to a reaction of violence, and so on. We could multiply the examples in this way.

Let's come back to our point about mental dialogue and intra-group dialogue. In light of the model we are proposing, the methodological artifacts mentioned above (meditation and Community Building Workshops) share the following common features. First, the intention of the strategy, interpreted within the framework of our model, is to restore the *paradoxical agent*'s

---

[134]. In itself, this notion in no way implies acceptance of the interpretation of the Hindu religion according to which a life full of karma leads to a reincarnation that purifies actions in another life.

Conclusion

autonomy so that there is always a witness to what is happening, one who does not get carried away in the karmic flow of mental productions triggered in individual persons and interpersonal group dialogues. The paradoxical agent makes it possible to remain present no matter what happens, and it guarantees the resolution of the interventions in the totality. Thus, it ensures that any intervention arises from *emptiness*, in other words, from the cognitive emptiness constituting the totality. It is thus by listening to the silence that an intervention will arise.

This is where the vertical and horizontal methodologies differ. With respect to an intervention, a horizontal methodology would first favor a receptive listening, then a response of a certain type within this receptive framework to finally bring about the integration of the intervention and the response in a new coherence. Vertical methodology is more radical. It eliminates the *response* altogether. The paradoxical agent simply makes sure that any intervention emerges from the totality, perceived as a cognitive emptiness, and that this intervention has total right to exist, whatever it is. Silence between two interventions ensures that the next intervention is not an automatic or pre-programmed response to the previous one. Even if it has been activated by the previous intervention, it develops its own content from emptiness and not in response to the previous intervention. This practice reinforces the function of the paradoxical agent that guarantees the advent of the totality by ensuring an empathic receptive presence to everything that happens without intervening in any of the content.

In the group, the paradoxical agent is initially represented by facilitators who ensure that the function is performed as described. Their action fades as the group spontaneously performs the function. In meditation, the function can also be assigned to an internal agent that specializes in paying attention to a mantra. The mantra is a more or less elaborate sound that is repeated and may have a general meaning but has no particular content in relation to the internal interventions that may occur, the attention to the mantra thus merely exerting an attentive presence without favoring the sequencing of ideas. The presence of the mantra becomes ever more subtle and gradually fades away as the function is spontaneously exercised with regard to internal interventions.

The purpose of this too brief evocation is to show, first of all, that the same methodology can be applied at different levels: here, everything happens as if the group as a unit were in a state of meditation as is the person, or conversely that the person is a unit formed by a community of agents. We also want to show that the practice of a methodology at one level can shed light on its practice at another level. For example, one of the typical common-sense beliefs is that meditation consists of trying to empty one's mind, thus "creating emptiness." Such an interpretation is erroneous. Emptiness is not something one makes happen or tries to make happen. It is simply there at the very outset. It is possible, however, that interventions are made from this emptiness, that is, they do not derive from patterns that are already formed and immediately available.

Living a group experience makes one understand that the emptiness referred to here is not nothingness. There are indeed group silences that are felt by participants as dead silences, while others are felt as full of empathic presence. The emptiness we are talking about is such only cognitively, but existentially it is the source of the very identity of a group or person. It is the "language" of totality.

The main thing, therefore, is not remaining silent but rather developing an empathic presence to all manifestations arising from the emptiness of totality. Thus, in meditation, the presence of ideas is not something that one needs to combat while waiting for complete silence to occur. The idea is rather to welcome and accept these ideas with warmth and empathy, for they manifest the state of totality at that very instant. What is to be avoided is the karmic sequencing of ideas that leaves the meditator on the surface.

So it is with a group. If it were merely a matter of achieving silence, one would merely have to instruct the members of the group not to intervene. Such a practice, however, would be futile. Instead, one must listen to what a group is trying to say at a particular instant and welcome it with compassion and empathy without intervening or responding.

Furthermore, masters claim that the most important thing is developing "compassion." The latter may calm the chaotic

CONCLUSION

turmoil and allow the group to experience this empathic warmth in greater silence. The life filling that silence is what then matters.

From these few examples, then, one can see that what is experienced at one level can help one understand and guide what is experienced at another level. Obviously, the elaboration of a human development pragmatics will have to be based on a better foundation than that of the present digression, which only allows us to imagine that the reformulation of various approaches through the present paradigm can lead to a greater unity of vision from which each of the approaches could benefit. For the case under discussion here, for example, it will be necessary to review and reformulate the theoretical and pragmatic description that Peck proposes in his model, which can best be described as empirical-intuitive. Meditation practices will also need to be presented more fully before being reinterpreted in this model.

- *Horizontal Methodologies*

Besides, a presentation of *horizontal methodologies* based on the interaction of actors should be developed to allow for a reinterpretation that tends towards greater overall coherence. Various methodologies should be presented at various levels: first, intra-individual methodologies where characters representing internal agents interact with each other; second, methodologies involving work in dyads in which one of the individuals has developed a particular skill. This is the case of the various individual therapies or communication exercises developed in organizations or in various institutions. Group methodologies should also be discussed, some of which would apply to the functioning of an organization. This is the case, for example, of the above-mentioned sociocracy.

An inventory of these various types of methodological artifacts at multiple levels would make it possible to see how the model presented in this book can schematize some of them and sometimes bring more unity, sometimes more coherence and sometimes more efficiency, always with the idea of reinforcing the paradoxical agent function in the communicational mechanism as well as the time tracking in development.

In short, so many methodological artifacts to be explored, classified, linked, improved, invented... And besides, once the societal methodology presented in the fifth chapter is operationalized, would it not be possible to set up such a research program that would then constitute one of the self-educational activities of this new community in self-construction

In Summary...

The theoretical introduction set forth in this book constitutes a cognitive process whose paradoxical objective is to give primacy to another process preceding and encompassing it, a process in which humanity is engaged even before deciding to do so, and even before becoming aware of it: *the process of its very existence*, through which it discovers itself as having to be its own project, as having to be *its own work of art*, according to the expression of Vico. The *cognitive artifact* is but methodological and in a way provisional, as is the scaffolding around and inside a cathedral, scaffolding that is not part of the cathedral, but without which it cannot be built. Here the cathedral represents the *pragmatic artifact* of human self-construction, and it is the latter, not its scaffolding – the *cognitive artifact* – that has primacy. It is, moreover, to this *primordial endeavor* that Seneca[135] invited us when he asserts:

"While we are among human beings, let us practice humanity."

---

135. On Anger III, 43.

REFERENCES

Acton, E. (1907), *Historical Essays and Studies*. London, N. Figgis and R.V. Laurence.

Bateson, G. (1980), *Steps to an Ecology of Mind: Collected Essays in Anthropology, Psychiatry, Evolution, and Epistemology*. Chicago, University of Chicago Press.

Beck, U. (2001), *La société du risque. Sur la voie d'une autre modernité*. Paris, Flammarion.

Beck, U. (2003), *Pouvoir et contre-pouvoir à l'heure de la mondialisation*. Paris, Flammarion.

Berne, E. (1971), *Transactional Analysis in Psychotherapy*. New York, Grove Press.

Bertalanffy, L. von, (1968), *General System Theory*. New York, George Braziller.

Beth, W. E., Mays, W., Piaget, J. (1957), Étude d'épistémologie génétique. *I. Épistémologie génétique et recherche psychologique*. Paris, Presses Universitaires de France.

Bion, W. (1965), *Experiences in Groups*, London, Tavistock.

Brewer, J. The Perturbation Paradigm Stumbles. *High Energy Physics*, http://musr.physics.ubc.ca/~jess/p200/hep/node5.html (Retrieved on December 30, 2005).

Bronowski, J. (1965), *The Identity of Man*, New York, The Natural History Press.

Bronowski, J. (1966), The Logic of the Mind. *Amer. Scientist*, 54, 1.

Bruck, C. (2006). Millions for Millions. *The New Yorker*. New York, 30 octobre.

Buck, J. A., Endenburg, G. (2004), *La sociocratie. Les forces créatives de l'auto-organisation*. http://www.cqib.org/doc/activit%C3%A9s/Pr%C3%A9sentation_3%20Sociogest.pdf (Retrieved on August 11 2008).

Capra, F. (1985), Bootstrap Physics : a Conversation with Geoffrey Chew. in DeTar, C., Finkelstein, J., Tan, C-I., (eds.), *A Passion for Physics. Essais in Honor of Geoffrey Chew*. Singapore, World scientific publishing, p. 249

Charest, G. (2007), *La démocratie se meurt, vive la sociocratie*. Reggio Emilia, Esserci.

Chew, G.F. (1968), « Bootstrap » : a Scientific Idea? *Science*, vol. 161, p. 762.

Chew, G.F. (1970), Hadron Bootstrap : Triumph or Frustration? *Physics today*, octobre.

Cockburn, A. (2006), A Nobel Prize for Neoliberalism? The Myth of Microloans. *Conterpunch*, Oct. 20/22, Weekend Edition.

De Béchillon, D. (1997), Éditorial, *Transdisciplines*. Paris, L'Harmattan.

Deleuze, G. (1981), « Image mouvement, image temps ». Cours Vincennes-St-Denis : Bergson, *Matière et mémoire* – 05/01/1981. In *Les cours de Gilles Deleuze*. [En ligne] http://www.webdeleuze.com (Retrieved January 3, 2006).

De Libera, A. (2014), *L'archéologie du sujet*. Paris, Vrin.

Dionne, B., Guay, M. (1993), *Histoire et civilisation de l'Occident*. Laval, Études vivantes.

Dumont, F. (1968), *Le Lieu de l'homme – la culture comme distance et mémoire*. Montréal, Hurtubise.

Dumouchel, P., Dupuy, J.-P. (1983), *L'auto-organisation. De la physique au politique*. Paris, Seuil.

Dupuy, J.-P. (1982), *Ordres et désordres. Enquête sur un nouveau paradigme*. Paris, Seuil.

Dupuy, J.-P. (1992), *Introduction aux sciences sociales*. Paris, Édition Marketing.

Erikson, E. (1950). *Childhood and Society*. New York, Norton.

Erikson, E. (1982), *The Life Cycle Completed*. New York, Norton.

Erikson E., Erikson J., Kivnick, H. Q. (1986), *Vital Involvement in Old Age*. New York, Norton.

Estérez, B. (1972) *Pourquoi pas la vie* Montréal, Leméac.

Fichte, J. G. (1982), *The Science of Knowledge*. Cambridge University Press.

Gandré, P. (2012). Le microcredit: fausse ou vraie solution à la pauvreté? Réseau Canopé | « Idées économiques et sociales » 2012/2 N° 168 | pages 22 à 31.

Gendlin, E. T. (1962), *Experiencing and the Creation of Meaning: A Philosophical and Psychological Approach to the Subjective.* New York, Free Press of Glencoe.

Gilligan, C. (1982), *In a Different Voice: Psychological Theory and Women's Development.* Cambridge, Harvard University Press.

Glasersfeld, E. von (1988), Introduction à un constructivisme radical, in Watzlawick, P. *L'invention de la réalité.* Paris, Seuil.

Gormly, A., Brodzinski, D. (1993), *Lifespan Human Development.* New York, Holt Rinehart & Winston.

Harris, T. (2004), *I'm OK, You're OK.* New York, Harper.

Heath, P., Lachs, J. (1982), Preface in Fichte, J. G. *The Science of Knowledge.* Cambridge University Press, p. vii.

Hofstadter, D.R. (1980), *Gödel, Escher, Bach: an Eternal Golden Braid.* New York, Vintage Books.

Houde, R. (1991), *Les temps de la vie.* Boucherville, Gaëtan Morin.

Houtard, F. (2002), *Des alternatives crédibles au capitalisme mondialisé.* http://www.forumsocialmundial.org.br/dinamic/fr/houtartfra.php (Retrieved on September 14, 2008).

Howe, R. H., Von Foerster, H. (1975), Introductory Comments to Francisco Varela's Calculus for Self-Reference. *Int. J. of General Systems,* Vol. 2, p. 1-3.

Husserl, E., (1996), *Leçons pour une phénoménologie de la conscience intime du temps,* Paris, Presses Universitaires de France.

Institut de la statistique du Québec, (2019).
https://www.stat.gouv.qc.ca/salle-presse/communique/communique-presse-2019/fevrier/fev1920.html

Jacquard, A., (1984) *Inventer l'homme,* Bruxelles, Éditions Complexe.

Jacquier, C., Drapel, K. (2005), *Le nombre d'or: réalité ou interprétation douteuse?* http://ic.epfl.ch/webdav/site/ic/shared/article_drapel_jaquier.pdf (Retrieved on February 20, 2008).

Julia, D. (1999), Préface du traducteur in Fichte, J. G. *La théorie de la science. Exposé de 1804.* Paris, Aubier Montaigne, p. 13.

Kuhn, T. S. (1962). *The Structure of Scientific Revolutions* (1st ed.). Chicago, University of Chicago Press.

Lamia, K. (2008), Demystifying Micro-Credit. The Grameen Bank, NGO's, and Neoliberalism in Bangladesh. *Cultural Dynamics,* Vol 20, no 1, 5-29.

Le Moigne, J.-L. (1995), *Les épistémologies constructivistes*. Paris, Presses Universitaires de France.

Le Moigne, J.-L. (2001), *Le constructivisme. Tome I : Les enracinements*. Paris, L'Harmattan.

Le Moigne, J.-L. (2002), *Le constructivisme. Tome II : Épistémologie de l'interdisciplinarité*. Paris, L'Harmattan.

Le Moigne J.-L. (2003), *Le constructivisme. Tome III : Modéliser pour comprendre*. Paris, L'Harmattan.

Luhmann, N. (1990), *Essays on Self-Reference*. New York, Columbia University Press.

Luhmann, N. (1995), *Social Systems*. California, Stanford University Press.

Luhmann, N. (2002), *Theories of Distinction. Redescribing the Description of Modernity*. Stanford, Stanford University Press.

Mahler, M., Pine, F., Bergmann, A. (1980), *La naissance psychologique de l'être humain*. Paris, Payot.

Merleau-Ponty, M. (1961), *Le visible et l'invisible*. Paris, Gallimard.

Merleau-Ponty, M. (2003) *L'institution La passivité. Notes de cours au Collège de France (1954-1955)*, Paris, Belin.

Michelet, J., (1848) *Cours professé au collège de France, 1847-1848*, Paris, Chamerot.

Minsky, M. (1986). *The Society of Mind*. New York: Simon & Schuster.

Morin, E. (1973), *Le paradigme perdu : la nature humaine*. Paris, Seuil.

Morin, E. (1977), *La méthode I. La nature de la nature*. Paris, Seuil.

Morin, E. (1991), *La méthode IV. Les idées*. Paris, Seuil.

Morin, E. (2004), *La méthode VI. Éthique*. Paris, Seuil

Morin, E. (2008), *La méthode*. Paris, Seuil.

Morin, E., Naïr, S. (1997), *Une politique de civilisation*. Paris, Arléa.

Peck, S. (1993), *A World Waiting to be Born*. New York, Bantam.

Perlas, N. (2003), *La société civile : 3ᵉ pouvoir. Changer la face de la mondialisation*. Barret-sur-Méouge, Éditions Yves Michel.

Petrella, R. (2007), *Pour une nouvelle narration du monde*. Montréal, Écosociété.

Piaget, J. (dir.) (1967), *Logique et connaissance scientifique*. Paris, Gallimard. Encyclopédie de la Pléiade.

Piaget, J. (1972), *L'épistémologie génétique*. Paris, Presses Universitaires de France. Coll. « Que sais-je » 1399.

Piaget, J. (1974), *Adaptation vitale et psychologie de l'intelligence. Sélection organique et phénocopie.* Paris, Herman.

Rahman, A. (1999), *Women and Microcredit in Rural Bangladesh: Anthropological Study of the Rhetoric and Realities of Grameen Bank Lending.* Boulder, Westview Press.

Rash, W. (2002), Introduction in Luhmann, N. *Theories of Distinction. Redescribing the Descriptions of Modernity.* Standford University Press, p. 4-7.

Ricoeur, P., (1990), *Soi-même comme un autre*, Paris, Seuil.

Rogers, C., Kinget, M., (1959) A Theory of Therapy, Personality, and Interpersonal Relationship, as Developed in the Client-Centered Framework, *in* Sigmund Kosh, *Psychology: A Study of a Science. Study 1, Vol.3: Formulations of the Person and the Social Context*, p.184-256.Sartre, J. P. (1960), *Critique de la raison dialectique.* Paris, Gallimard.

Sartre, J.-P. (1970), *L'existentialisme est un humanisme.* Paris, Nagel.

Seife, C. (2004), *Zéro. La biographie d'une idée dangereuse.* Paris : Hachette.

Simon, H. A. 1969, *The Sciences of the Artificial.* Cambridge, MIT Press.

Sorokin, P. (1941), *The Crisis of Our Age.* New York, Dutton.

Spencer Brown, G. (1969), *Laws of Form.* London, Allen & Unwin.

Spitz, R. A. (1945), Hospitalism: An Inquiry into the Genesis of Psychiatric Conditions in Early Childhood. *Psychoa. S. of the Child*, New York, Int. Univ. Press.

Statistique Canada. Tableau 11-10-0222-01 Dépenses des ménages, Canada, régions et provinces

Thomas-Fogiel, I. (2000), Les principales caractéristiques de la doctrine de la science in Fichte, J.G. *Doctrine de la science nova methodo.* Paris, Librairie Générale Française.

Vachon, B. (1993), *Le développement local, théorie et pratique.* Boucherville, Gaëtan Morin.

Vandendorpe, C. (1990), Paradigme et syntagme. De quelques idées vertes qui ont dormi furieusement. *Revue québécoise de linguistique théorique et appliquée*, 9, 3, p. 169-193.

Varela, F. (1975), A Calculus for Self-Reference. *Int. J. General Systems*, Vol. 2. p. 5-24.

Varela, F. (1989), *Autonomie et connaissance. Essai sur le vivant.* Paris, Seuil.

Varela, F. (1979), *Principles of Biological Autonomy.* New York, Elsevier North Holland.

Varela, F., Thomson, E., Rosh, E. (1993), *L'inscription corporelle de l'esprit.* Paris, Seuil.

Varela, F. 1999) *Ethical know-how. Action, wisdom, and cognition.* Stanford University Press.

Ville de Montréal (2020). *Montréal en statistiques.* http://ville.montreal.qc.ca/portal/page?_pageid=6897,68087646&_dad=portal&_schema=PORTAL

Watzlawick, P., Weakland, J., Fish, R., Helmick-Beavin, J., Jackson, D. D. (1967), *Pragmatics of Human Communication.* New York, Norton.

Whitehead, A. N., Russell, B. (1910-1913), *Principia Mathematica.* Three vols., Cambridge, Cambridge University Press.

World Bank Group. (2018), *Poverty and Shared Prosperity 2018.* http://www.worldbank.org/en/publication/poverty-and-shared-prosperity

INDEX

A

Adaptive relationship · 79, 80, 82, 141, 269
agent · 15, 27, 28, 30, 32, 35, 62, 72, 83, 88, 89, 91, 92, 94, 95, 96, 97, 99, 100, 102, 104, 105, 106, 107, 109, 123, 124, 125, 126, 137, 138, 142, 145, 147, 148, 149, 159, 181, 191, 193, 194, 195, 196, 197, 199, 200, 201, 202, 203, 204, 205, 206, 208, 212, 213, 215, 216, 219, 220, 221, 222, 224, 227, 240, 242, 244, 247, 248, 263, 268, 269, 270, 271, 272, 273, 274, 275, 277
    paradoxical agent · 35, 89, 90, 93, 96, 97, 99, 106, 110, 145, 148, 149, 191, 200, 201, 204, 206, 208, 221, 222, 245, 269, 271, 274, 275
anti-reductionism · 112, 114, 135
artifact · 130, 131, 132, 133, 139, 211, 267, 271, 272, 278
autonomy · 16, 38, 39, 41, 50, 58, 62, 68, 88, 97, 143, 151, 152, 157, 164, 167, 177, 221, 224, 231, 250, 265, 274
auto-organisation · 279, 280

Autopoiesis · 32, 42, 43, 107

B

Behavior · 23, 164
bootstrap · 58, 59, 60, 66, 270

C

Calculus of Indications · 271
Civil society · 225
cognition · 57, 82, 138, 269, 271, 284
cognitive · 13, 18, 24, 35, 50, 51, 56, 67, 80, 81, 82, 85, 91, 107, 114, 128, 129, 131, 132, 134, 136, 138, 139, 140, 141, 142, 145, 263, 267, 268, 269, 270, 271, 272, 275, 278
coherence · 12, 17, 31, 39, 44, 46, 50, 56, 57, 58, 60, 61, 65, 67, 68, 76, 85, 87, 103, 110, 122, 126, 134, 136, 138, 145, 150, 154, 156, 161, 167, 168, 169, 177, 185, 208, 221, 224, 231, 243, 262, 263, 264, 265, 269, 270, 272, 275, 277
Common sense · 57, 67, 189
communication · 11, 15, 39, 58, 60, 69, 80, 81, 82, 138, 141,

186, 187, 189, 190, 191, 192, 193, 195, 197, 199, 200, 201, 206, 209, 237, 269, 270, 272, 277
Community fund · 251
competence · 163, 166, 167, 173, 177, 179, 183, 213, 214, 216, 217, 221, 223
connaissance · 282
Consent · 245, 246, 247
Construction · 11, 12, 13, 14, 17, 18, 33, 46, 51, 61, 63, 68, 71, 82, 110, 111, 112, 113, 118, 121, 128, 129, 130, 131, 132, 133, 134, 136, 141, 144, 150, 152, 154, 155, 156, 157, 169, 177, 183, 191, 205, 207, 211, 249, 267, 271
Constructivism · 114, 116, 117, 119, 122, 123, 128, 134, 135
constructivisme · 281, 282
control · 38, 39, 83, 103, 142, 159, 161, 166, 178, 180, 183, 212, 216, 233, 239, 240, 241, 242, 249, 260
Conventionalism · 114
Core idea · 109, 263, 269, 270

D

Democracy · 219, 246
démocratie · 280
development community · 243, 247, 248, 249, 250, 251, 255, 256, 257, 260, 265, 272
Dialectic · 113, 116
Differentiation · 56, 78, 82, 83, 89, 93, 94, 95, 96, 123, 125, 126, 127, 145, 159, 181, 200, 202, 208, 209, 216, 226, 245, 271, 273

Dimensions · 12, 31, 65, 85, 93, 103, 117, 156, 158, 160, 162, 164, 165, 177, 209, 212, 245
 active · 156
 identity · 26, 153, 155, 156, 163, 199, 203
 paradoxical · 156
 receptive · 156
Disengagement · 162
Dispersion · 163, 164, 182
Distinction · 38, 52, 53, 54, 55, 56, 74, 78, 79, 80, 82, 89, 94, 111, 123, 126, 131, 138, 165, 268
 explicit distinction · 53
 first distinction · 78
 implicit distinction · 53
 second distinction · 79

E

Ego · 90, 94, 99, 100, 101, 104, 105, 123, 124, 153
Egocentricity · 100, 101
Empirical-intuitive · 67, 68, 156
Empiricism · 63, 114, 117, 137
Emptiness · 77, 78, 85, 92, 184, 275, 276
Enaction · 118, 119, 121
Engagement · 162, 164, 168, 177, 179, 216
épistémologie · 279, 282
Epistemologies · 112, 116, 122, 129
 derived · 112, 113
 internal · 111, 112, 114
Epistemology · 25
Ethics · 15, 22, 111, 133
Existential relationship · 80, 81, 82, 141, 187, 268
Experiencing · 27, 28, 54, 66, 123, 160, 161, 165, 184, 201, 202

Expressive behavior · 141, 167

F

Felt meaning · 28, 160
foundation · 13, 24, 41, 42, 47, 71, 73, 82, 110, 119, 123, 124, 125, 126, 127, 128, 133, 246, 272, 277
Fractals · 63
Freedom of action · 85, 213, 214, 216, 217, 218, 221, 222

G

Genesis · 11, 15, 71, 112, 113, 114, 121, 135, 138, 186
Governance · 11, 103, 180, 181, 212, 226, 246, 248, 265

H

Hetero-reference · 110, 269, 270
Heuristic · 69, 132, 169, 171, 172, 174, 175, 177, 178, 180, 184, 270
Hierarchical reversal · 89, 92, 95, 126, 136, 137, 138, 148, 159, 200, 206, 208, 221, 232, 248, 252
Hierarchy · 40, 53, 63, 89, 137, 142, 143, 144, 150, 195, 211, 241, 247
Holographic metaphor · 61, 65

I

idealism · 116, 117, 119, 123
Identity · 14, 17, 20, 33, 36, 38, 39, 41, 42, 44, 45, 46, 58, 62, 75, 79, 80, 84, 86, 87, 116, 126, 136, 139, 145, 149, 150, 151, 153, 154, 155, 156, 158, 159, 160, 161, 162, 163, 164, 165, 167, 168, 171, 173, 174, 176, 177, 178, 182, 184, 185, 186, 190, 191, 192, 193, 194, 195, 196, 197, 200, 202, 203, 204, 205, 207, 208, 209, 211, 212, 213, 222, 224, 239, 243, 244, 245, 252, 260, 262, 263, 264, 266, 268, 271, 272, 276
Idiocentric · 62, 102
Incompetence · 163, 218
Inertia · 163
Inhibition · 164
Initiative · 151, 152, 154, 157, 163, 165, 168, 177, 179, 181, 207, 213, 223, 248, 253
Integration · 14, 78, 85, 89, 93, 126, 145, 148, 151, 160, 164, 203, 209, 219, 228, 232, 249, 275
Integrity · 151, 152, 154, 163, 164, 168, 202
Interaction · 12, 16, 39, 41, 42, 43, 48, 75, 80, 103, 109, 113, 114, 116, 117, 120, 122, 126, 131, 135, 137, 143, 160, 162, 163, 175, 189, 190, 191, 193, 194, 195, 196, 197, 199, 200, 201, 202, 203, 204, 205, 207, 208, 209, 216, 221, 222, 257, 263, 268, 272, 277
Intervener · 193, 196, 205, 206, 274
Intervention · 106, 114, 116, 132, 137, 139, 159, 161, 163, 176, 192, 194, 195, 196, 197, 200, 201, 202, 203, 205, 206, 208,

213, 216, 221, 222, 223, 233, 240, 241, 244, 248, 260, 265, 273, 274, 275

vertical · 275
Mistrust · 150, 151, 152, 161, 162

K

Karma · 274
Knowledge · 11, 14, 21, 25, 27, 39, 41, 42, 52, 71, 110, 111, 112, 113, 114, 116, 117, 128, 129, 130, 131, 132, 133, 134, 139, 140, 183, 185, 264, 267, 268, 269

N

Narrative · 202, 203, 234
Neo-Keynesianism · 260
Nested ternary cycles · 169, 176, 177, 270

L

Levels · 11, 12, 15, 18, 35, 38, 45, 46, 61, 62, 63, 64, 77, 93, 101, 103, 104, 107, 125, 135, 138, 142, 143, 144, 145, 157, 160, 165, 172, 177, 204, 209, 211, 212, 236, 240, 241, 247, 248, 267, 270, 272, 273, 274, 275, 277

O

Object · 15, 19, 20, 22, 23, 24, 35, 36, 37, 41, 52, 58, 64, 65, 72, 74, 76, 77, 81, 82, 83, 84, 85, 87, 88, 89, 90, 92, 95, 97, 102, 104, 112, 113, 114, 116, 117, 118, 120, 121, 123, 125, 128, 129, 131, 136, 137, 139, 148, 175, 185, 195, 216, 222, 223, 259, 260, 263, 267, 268, 269, 272
Openness · 42, 43, 44, 45, 161, 162, 168, 177, 179, 194, 216, 222, 234, 242
operational closure · 40, 41, 42, 43, 44, 45, 145, 178, 212, 242, 252, 260, 264, 270, 272

M

Mediation · 106, 221
Message · 122, 195, 196, 197, 199, 200, 201, 202, 203, 205
Method · 12, 37, 46, 60, 64, 71, 129, 149, 150, 154, 184, 206, 249, 253, 259, 267
méthode · 282
Methodological individualism · 62, 101
Methodology · 25, 57, 61, 97, 101, 139, 247, 275, 276, 277
horizontal · 275

P

Paradigm · 13, 18, 32, 36, 37, 38, 39, 47, 49, 50, 51, 52, 53, 54, 55, 56, 57, 58, 59, 60, 65, 70, 75, 78, 109, 110, 119, 124, 127, 128, 131, 138, 139, 140, 142, 149, 155, 189, 190, 202, 206, 214, 218, 219, 232, 263, 268, 269, 270, 277

paradigme · 280, 282
Paradox · 13, 25, 26, 27, 29, 31, 32, 36, 39, 55, 72, 73, 75, 76, 77, 83, 125, 128
Person · 14, 24, 29, 38, 45, 50, 51, 73, 75, 82, 83, 84, 85, 86, 87, 88, 91, 93, 94, 102, 103, 104, 109, 123, 124, 125, 134, 140, 149, 150, 157, 160, 164, 165, 167, 168, 169, 177, 179, 189, 191, 192, 193, 194, 197, 202, 203, 205, 206, 207, 214, 216, 231, 243, 246, 247, 255, 273, 274, 276
perturbation · 279
phénocopie · 283
Phenocopy · 218, 219
phénoménologie · 281
Phenomenology · 54, 114
Platonism · 114
Politics · 15, 133, 233, 234
politique · 280, 282
Position
  center · 196
  high · 196, 199, 202, 203, 205, 220
  low · 196, 199, 202, 203, 220
Post-capitalism · 260, 261
Power · 212
  first-degree · 213, 245
  second-degree · 215, 245
  third-degree · 221
Pragmatics · 13, 16, 129, 134, 269, 277

Q

Quasi-decomposability · 143, 144

R

Realism · 116, 117, 119, 121, 123
Receptive · 30, 31, 89, 92, 95, 96, 97, 99, 100, 105, 106, 109, 110, 125, 145, 148, 150, 158, 159, 160, 161, 171, 178, 181, 191, 192, 194, 200, 204, 205, 206, 207, 208, 212, 221, 222, 223, 230, 244, 248, 268, 269, 272, 275
Receptivity · 14, 148, 160, 177
Reductionism · 48, 49, 64, 114, 135, 138
Referent · 84
Response · 23, 66, 76, 156, 197, 201, 202, 273, 275

S

Savings · 214, 235, 236, 237, 238, 239, 249, 250, 251, 252, 253, 257
Sector · 225
  private · 105, 225, 226, 227, 229, 230, 232, 235, 240, 241, 243, 259, 261
  public · 105, 225, 226, 227, 228, 229, 230, 241, 242, 243, 244
  social · 106, 107, 225, 226, 227, 228, 229, 231, 242, 243, 244, 245, 260, 265, 272
self-construction · 45, 118, 132, 134, 135, 140, 142, 267, 270, 271, 277, 278
self-development · 14, 83, 235, 245, 248, 260, 269, 272
self-organization · 43, 124

Self-reference · 11, 15, 17, 18, 19, 22, 26, 27, 30, 31, 32, 34, 35, 36, 37, 38, 42, 43, 45, 46, 47, 52, 57, 58, 61, 62, 63, 64, 68, 70, 76, 78, 83, 84, 85, 86, 87, 94, 100, 101, 103, 104, 109, 119, 127, 128, 132, 144, 148, 189, 190, 211, 218, 269, 270
Self-referent animal · 11, 17, 266
Self-referential matrix · 12, 16, 37, 58, 61, 70, 109, 144, 150, 222, 270, 271, 272
Sociocracy · 246, 247, 277
sociocratie · 279, 280
State · 224, 225, 227, 230, 233, 242, 244, 261, 265
Structure · 14, 26, 45, 50, 63, 64, 71, 73, 85, 101, 112, 113, 114, 117, 121, 135, 142, 145, 152, 156, 157, 169, 171, 176, 177, 195, 201, 202, 204, 205, 206, 217, 235, 239, 244, 247, 248, 258, 263, 272
Subject · 102, 104, 113

T

Totality · 13, 14, 15, 21, 49, 53, 55, 59, 61, 62, 63, 65, 73, 74, 75, 76, 77, 78, 79, 82, 83, 85, 88, 89, 90, 91, 92, 93, 94, 95, 96, 97, 99, 100, 101, 102, 103, 104, 105, 109, 110, 122, 123, 124, 125, 126, 127, 135, 136, 137, 142, 143, 145, 147, 148, 149, 158, 159, 190, 191, 192, 193, 197, 200, 201, 202, 207, 208, 209, 212, 213, 215, 218, 220, 221, 222, 224, 225, 226, 228, 232, 246, 248, 252, 263, 267, 268, 269, 272, 273, 274, 275, 276
Totalization · 21, 113, 135, 136, 137
Transcendental · 77, 79, 113, 114, 117, 137, 138, 175
Transcendentalism · 77, 114, 135, 136
Trust · 150, 151, 152, 154, 157, 161, 162, 168, 177, 179, 216

U

Underdevelopment · 214, 235, 249, 257, 274

W

Witness · 99, 106, 274